Acclaim for

ERIK LARSON'S

LETHAL PASSAGE

"Larson creates one of the most readable anti-gun treatises in years."

—*Washington Post Book World*

"Shocking . . . compelling . . . *Lethal Passage* is a perfect blend of reporting and storytelling."

—*Detroit Free Press*

"Larson touches on all aspects of the gun issue in this country. . . . There is a feeling in America that perhaps enough lives finally have been terminated or forever changed by the pull of a trigger. That something real must be done. Erik Larson gives great voice to that feeling."

—*San Diego Union-Tribune*

"By tracing the path of a firearm that is worthless for hunting or target practice, we see how our nation's laws have fallen out of sync with modern life. . . . Erik Larson shows us just what fearful legacy our national self-image is leaving our young."

—*Dallas Morning News*

ERIK LARSON

LETHAL PASSAGE

Erik Larson writes for the front page of the *Wall Street Journal*. His articles and essays have appeared in *The Atlantic, Harper's,* and *The New York Times Magazine.* He is also the author of *The Naked Consumer.* He lives with his wife and their two children in Baltimore, Maryland.

LETHAL
PASSAGE

LETHAL PASSAGE

THE STORY OF A GUN

ERIK LARSON

VINTAGE BOOKS

A DIVISION OF RANDOM HOUSE, INC.

NEW YORK

First Vintage Books Edition, January 1995

The Library of Congress has catalogued the Crown edition as follows:
Larson, Erik.
Lethal passage: how the travels of a single handgun expose the
roots of America's gun crisis / by Erik Larson.—1st ed.
p. cm.
Includes bibliographical references and index.
1. Gun control—United States. 2. Firearms—Social aspects—
United States. 3. Murder—Virginia—Virginia Beach—Case studies.
4. Elliot, Nicholas Walden Herman. 5. Murderers—Virginia—Virginia
Beach—Biography. I. Title.
HV7436.L37   1994
364.1′523′9875551—dc20   93-34560   CIP

ISBN 0-517-59677-6
Vintage ISBN: 0-679-75927-1

Design by Jennifer Harper

Manufactured in the United States of America

For all children who have
faced a gun

CONTENTS

The essential American soul is hard, isolate, stoic, and a killer.

—D. H. LAWRENCE

LETHAL PASSAGE

CHAPTER ONE

INTRODUCTION

ON A BITTER, COLD DECEMBER MORNING, a sixteen-year-old boy walked into the Atlantic Shores Christian School in Virginia Beach, Virginia, with a semiautomatic handgun and several hundred rounds of ammunition tucked into his backpack. His name was Nicholas Elliot. By midmorning, a forty-one-year-old teacher had been shot dead, and another teacher, struck by two nine-millimeter bullets fired at point-blank range, was extraordinarily lucky to be alive. Two other teachers narrowly escaped Nicholas's bullets. One found herself running a zigzag pattern through the schoolyard as Nicholas fired round after round at her back. The other, a man who tackled Nicholas and saved the lives of a roomful of crying and praying teenagers, felt a bullet breeze past his head.

In a nation accustomed to murder in large multiples, the shootings received little out-of-state coverage. A single homicide barely rates mention beside the events at Stockton and San Ysidro, two names that ring of casual mass violence the way the names of great battlefields ring of valor. But the story of how that gun wound up in Nicholas's backpack, how the gun came to exist at all, constitutes a cultural detective story that tells a great deal about the roots of America's gun crisis. Nicholas in effect carried with him the good wishes of an industry and a culture whose institutions and mores have

1

helped make the things he did that morning so commonplace in America.

Nicholas carried a gun—the Cobray M-11/9—that by any reasonable standard should never have become a mass-consumer product. He acquired the gun from a federally licensed dealer using a means that puts thousands of guns into the hands of illegal users each year, yet that existing federal gun-trade regulations do much to encourage. This dealer was a "good" dealer, yet sold numerous weapons to traffickers and killers, raising a fundamental question of whether the costs imposed on the rest of us even by supposedly honest dealers are simply too high for society to bear. Moreover, Nicholas carried with him a cultural bloodlust fed by marketers and their close allies in the gun press who routinely play to America's homicide fantasy and stoke our widespread belief in the gun as problem-solver.

None of this, of course, absolves Nicholas of his own responsibility for what occurred at Atlantic Shores, nor does it absolve society at large of its responsibility for the mass disenfranchisement of America's underclass, in particular young black men. Clearly, individual responsibility and socioeconomic tension are the tectonic plates that shape crime. As one gun buff proposed to me, half in jest, the way to reduce crime is to buy back guns not with cash, as many cities have tried, but with jobs.

What follows, however, is not so much the story of Nicholas Elliot, but rather of his gun and its travels. I set out to trace his weapon from the moment its design was conceived to its use at Atlantic Shores as a way to explore how guns migrate from the so-called legitimate gun-distribution network to the hands of killers, robbers, and inner-city gangsters. Every gun used in crime starts out in that network, but somewhere along the way gets diverted. But where and how? These questions get lost amid the daily reports of shootings and the numbing tallies of lives lost each year. Pick up a copy of a major newspaper and you see story after story about gunshot death and injury, but you rarely read where the gun came from or how it was acquired. The absence is understandable. Although television cop shows would have us believe otherwise, it takes a lot of effort for the police and the Bureau of Alcohol, Tobacco and Firearms to trace the origins of a gun, largely because of obstacles deliberately inserted into the process by federal law. When a crime has just occurred— that is, when the news is fresh and most marketable—no one can know for sure exactly how the gun reached the shooter. The shooter himself may not know how many others handled the gun before it came into his possession. Some guns simply cannot be traced. By the time the police do learn where and how a gun originated, the shooting is already old news. Yet by tracing the migration of guns, one comes readily and vividly to understand where the nation's current patchwork of gun controls have gone astray, and how easily they could be fixed to the increased satisfaction of gun owners and gun opponents alike.

I chose a single gun, used in a single homicide—not even a terribly lurid homicide—primarily as a means of cutting through the rhetoric of extremists on both sides of the gun debate. Guns are a subject that too often divides America into warring camps, even though the beliefs of the great, moderate mass of Americans, whom we too readily classify in combat taxonomy as pro-gun and antigun, gun nut and gun hater, simply aren't that deeply opposed. Somewhere along the line, extremists on both sides succeeded in shaping the debate so that no one has a choice but to leap into a trench and start firing away with whatever ammunition has been piled near at hand, be it distorted statistics or empty slogans. (My favorite: "If guns are outlawed, only outlaws will have guns.") The two camps have more in common than not: they both want to make sure that guns only wind up in the hands of stalwart, responsible citizens.

Why, then, is it so easy for the bad guys to get guns?

As I followed Nicholas Elliot's gun, I quickly found that a journey along its path was a journey also through America's larger gun culture. In the course of one year I injected myself as deeply as possible into that culture. I acquired a federal gun-dealer's license, not to buy and sell guns but rather to see how easily the license could be acquired and, as a side benefit, to gain access to places and publications that might otherwise be off-limits. Along the way I learned to appreciate the pure hell-raising fun of shooting, and how the fun can obscure the monumental dangers inherent in possessing a gun of any kind. I learned too that the world of guns is marked by peculiar ironies and juxtapositions, and odd little mysteries: people who aren't quite what they seem, secret agendas, unconscionable gaps in firearms laws. I discovered, for example, a little-known federal program that allows convicted felons, explicitly forbidden by federal law from buying guns, to petition the Bureau of Alcohol, Tobacco and Firearms to win back permission to do so. I learned too that no federal agency is empowered to oversee the design and manufacture of firearms and investigate safety defects. The Consumer Product Safety Commission can order the recall of toy guns, just not real ones.

I visited dozens of gun shows, always a novel experience, given the number of private citizens one encounters walking around with guns slung over their backs and FOR SALE signs stuck in the barrels of weapons they hope to sell. I wanted at first merely to find dealers who were selling the Cobray and its predecessor guns, but I quickly found that gun shows opened a clear window into the gun culture. They demonstrate in a vivid way the sheer volume of guns available for sale in America, and how readily those guns change hands. I interviewed scores of shooting enthusiasts; I spoke too with many individuals who had been shot, either in the course of a crime or by accident. One evening I found myself a guest at a dinner in Smyrna, Georgia, thrown by the state affiliate of the National Rifle Association, where the door prizes were ammo boxes full of .38 Special ammunition and the raffle prizes were guns.

Time and again I encountered a none-of-my-business attitude that permeates the firearms distribution chain from production to end sale, and that allows gunmakers and marketers to promote the killing power of their weapons while disavowing any responsibility for their use in crime.

Mostly, I discovered that the story of Nicholas Elliot's gun was the story also of the forces that infuse the gun culture. It describes a de facto conspiracy of gun dealers, manufacturers, marketers, gun writers, and federal regulators that makes guns—ever more powerful guns, and laser sights, silencer-ready barrels, folding stocks, exploding bullets, and flame-thrower shotgun rounds—all too easy to come by and virtually assures their eventual use in the bedrooms, alleys, and schoolyards of America.

Reach out, the culture cries, and kill someone.

CHAPTER TWO

NICHOLAS

THE NAME VIRGINIA BEACH MAY CONJURE weathered cottages set among rippled dunes, but the city has far more in common with places like Ocean City, Maryland, and Atlantic City, New Jersey. Rental houses, motels, and seasonal apartments jam the Atlantic coastline. Tract developments stretch westward, spaced by mini-malls and shopping plazas of the kind anchored by discount hardware stores. The sprawl of concrete and plywood has erased the city's borders, leaving a tightly entwined ganglion of six cities, the others being Portsmouth, Chesapeake, Norfolk, Newport News, and Hampton. Together they occupy a swath of metropolitan terrain larger in geographic expanse than Richmond, Washington, and Baltimore combined and share many of the same big-city problems, including widespread drug abuse, gang warfare, troubled schools, and the ever-increasing incidence of gunshot injury and death. Virginia Beach alone is home to 428 federally licensed gun dealers, 30 percent more than Baltimore even though Baltimore's population is 60 percent larger.

Mapmakers, loath to tease apart the six cities, identify the area collectively as Hampton Roads, the name of the shipping channel that links the James River with Chesapeake Bay and the ocean beyond. The Roads, as local disc jockeys call the region, no doubt ranked high on the former Soviet Union's list of American targets most worthy of nuclear obliteration. The region in and around Hampton Roads comprises a good chunk of America's military-industrial complex, including Langley Air Force Base, Fort Eustis, the U.S. Naval Station at Norfolk, the Newport News shipyard, and the U.S. Naval Weapons Station on the York River. Virginia Beach, which occupies the eastern rim of Hampton Roads, is itself home to the Army's Fort Story, the Camp Pendleton Naval Amphibious Base, and the Oceana Naval Air Station. Life here is textured by the roar of fighter planes and the thumping applause of giant helicopters. Where there is water, there are fighting ships, pale gray in the noon sun, spiky black in backlit silhouette.

The second most influential force here is the Baptist Church. Branches seem to sprout every few blocks or so in simple frame houses and soaring concrete towers. As in many cities now around the country and particularly in the South, the churches in Hampton Roads provide more than spiritual solace. They offer parents a sheltered alternative to the harsh and at times profoundly dangerous conditions that exist now in so many urban public schools. The Atlantic Shores Baptist Church in the Kempsville Road district of Virginia Beach, a suburban expanse of closely packed tract homes, is one of the largest churches in Hampton Roads, with four thousand official members and seventeen hundred who show up at church each Sunday. By the church's own estimate it has the third-largest congregation in the Roads.

The church itself is a sturdy if austere structure, with a concrete spire that each evening casts a long swordlike shadow deep into the shopping plaza across the street. The church school, the Atlantic Shores Christian School, offers fully accredited elementary, middle, and high-school programs and draws many children of the faculty of Pat Robertson's Christian Broadcasting Network University, located nearby on the Centerville Turnpike. The school consists of permanent and portable classrooms arrayed around a courtyard. As of December 16, 1988, it had five hundred students, of whom only twenty-three were black, and seemed as sheltered a place as one could possibly find. Shakedowns, beatings, gunplay, the stuff of a contemporary urban public-school education—all this occurred elsewhere. "As far as I know, we'd never even had a fistfight before," said George Sweet, senior pastor of the church and president of the school.

Every school, of course, has its tensions and petty rivalries among students. Every school has its loners and outcasts who don't fit the woof and weave of school culture. One such student at Atlantic Shores was Nicholas Elliot—to be exact, Nicholas Walden Herman Elliot—a lean, gangly boy who lived in Norfolk's Campostella neighborhood. Campostella is a black community of neat, tree-lined streets separated from the bulk of Norfolk by the Elizabeth River. He lived with his mother in a small, green frame house in a block of similarly styled houses.

The fact Nicholas was black would by itself have kept him from readily blending in with the other students at Atlantic Shores, although school officials and students insist the school did its best to make its black students feel welcome. In Nicholas's case, his color amplified a gulf that would have existed anyway. He had dyslexia, a learning disability that is difficult to diagnose yet terribly efficient at undermining the self-esteem of children, who must endure its constant interference in such basic functions as reading and writing. A Virginia Beach psychiatrist, Dr. Erwin D. Sax, examined Nicholas on May 5, 1989, and found he possessed "borderline to low-average" intelligence. Another psychiatrist, Dr. Duncan S. Wallace, would later testify that Nicholas had a mental age of twelve or thirteen and exhibited what he called a schizoid personality disorder: "A lack of feeling, a lack of sensitivity to other people. . . . It leads you to a very isolated, shy, withdrawn sort of life situation."

Nicholas had no close friends, just glancing school-hall relationships. Race, according to Nicholas, had indeed proved a powerful dividing line. He told Det. Donald Adams, a Virginia Beach homicide investigator, how the other students would pick on him. "They called me racial names and were like racial to me, and they punched me and hit me."

The detective, a youthful-looking man of middle height with a mustache and an easy manner, tried hard to make Nicholas feel comfortable during his interrogation. He got him a Sprite to drink. He called his mother and had her join them—a mistake, as it happens, for her anger and sorrow would soon distort the interview and make it virtually impossible for the detective to get a clear sense of what had occurred an hour before. It would be the only detailed, publicly available statement Nicholas would make about what he had done.

The worst antagonist, according to Nicholas, was Billy Cutter. The name is my invention, although Billy's true identity would not escape any student at Atlantic Shores. Billy was an abrasive white boy who seemed to vex everyone, not just Nicholas. The two shared many of the same classes. At times they seemed to be friends, at times the worst kind of enemies. "Like fire and ice," as Rev. Mr. Sweet put it.

Billy would call Nicholas a nigger. Nicholas would call Billy a honky or white cracker. Half the time Billy would be the first to start calling names, according to Billy; half the time Nicholas would start. "The whole thing was a joke," Billy testified later. He said Nicholas laughed about it. Billy added, "It was nothing I thought serious."

But the relationship had a profoundly dark edge to it. At six foot one, 170 pounds, Billy was far taller and heavier than Nicholas. From time to time, at odd moments, Billy would shove and strike Nicholas. "There was some slapping," Dr. Wallace testified at Nicholas's sentencing hearing. "There was some sticking him with a probe in biology. . . . There was hitting in the stomach or in the belly area . . . repeated acts of this type."

Dr. Wallace found that Nicholas had suppressed his anger and fear to the point where, that Friday morning, he experienced a "disassociative" episode. "He kept so much within him, like a pressure cooker," Dr. Wallace said. "It built and built and then exploded, and that was the accumulation of all of the repressed and suppressed emotions."

One week before Nicholas decided to go hunting for Billy, he and the other boy got into another war of words, this time during gym class. This time, however, Billy's taunting seemed to wrench something loose inside Nicholas. The taunting and teasing may indeed have been a perverse game indulged in equally by both boys, but suddenly it became something far more sinister. As Nicholas left the class, he shouted to Billy, "I'm going to kill you."

◆ ◆ ◆

"I can't take him picking on me," Nicholas told Adams. He had been afraid, he said, that Billy Cutter "would end up killing me. He always threatened me. . . . Like he would hit me in the back of my neck."

His mother interrupted, "You could have gone to the phone and called me at work."

"If he would have broke my neck," Nicholas said, "my life would have been over. He kicked me. He hit me in the back of the neck."

"Not all people, bullies, can threaten you," his mother said. "That's what I'm telling you."

"But, Mom, he actually hit me and I don't want my neck—if he would have broke my neck—"

"I'm trying to reason with you. You could have gone to the office and asked the people to call your mom. The other kids do. You could have called me."

"You only use that for when you are sick, Mom," Nicholas protested. "You can't use it for being threatened. The teachers are supposed to handle it, but they don't do anything."

Nicholas seemed able to find solace consistently only in his pet birds, and in guns. Everyone at school knew of Nicholas's passion for firearms. It served only to widen the gulf between him and his peers. At lunch while all the other boys were reading skateboard magazines, he'd thumb through *Guns & Ammo*. His locker was papered with glossy ads depicting powerful handguns. In conversation, according to a fellow student, Nicholas loved to discuss "which bullets had more firepower." His classmates worried about Nicholas. One told a Norfolk newspaper, "All the kids said he was going to shoot someone."

Even the guns became fodder for taunts from Billy Cutter, and from other students. "They were always making fun of me," Nicholas told Adams. "They always said stuff: 'You know so much about guns. You never even shot a gun in your life.'"

His mother worried most about her son on Fridays, the day, she believed, when passions kept in check all week were most prone to be released. "Nicholas," she said. "Why would you take a gun today? You said that Billy hadn't hit you since Wednesday, so why would you take a gun on Friday? I told you how Fridays are. You lay low on Friday, because everybody is upset."

When she arrived at headquarters to meet Adams and her son, she was consumed with grief and guilt over Nicholas's attack on the school.

"I will be up praying all night, all day tomorrow," she said, "I'm going to pray."

Nicholas, trying to rein in the day and get things normal again, abruptly shifted the conversation to matters of daily routine.

"Are you going to work?" he asked.

"No. I don't want to go to work."

Genuinely perplexed, Nicholas asked, "Why not?"

"Because that's what got me, trying to work and earn, to try to keep my head above water and losing you."

"You can take my money out of the bank," Nicholas offered.

"Gaining the world," his mother cried, "and losing my soul—"

"It's not losing me," Nicholas pleaded. "It's just people picking on me. That's all it is. If God would have just stopped them—if I was nice enough and He would have made it so they were nice to me and didn't hit me, everything would be fine. That's as simple as it is, or He could have just made them keep their hands to theirselves. That's very simple."

His mother, during a later hearing, described Nicholas as a "very obedient, quiet child." She and Nicholas had moved to Norfolk from California in 1983, so that she could care for her ailing mother. Nicholas's father, Clarence, stayed behind.

Nicholas had always done poorly in school. In California, he failed the first grade. "At that time," Dr. Wallace testified, "he was tested in the California school system and started in learning disability classes, which continued until the time the family left California." By the time Dr. Wallace saw him, in April and May of 1989, Nicholas was sixteen and in the tenth grade. Dr. Wallace's examination, however, found Nicholas lagging far behind his fellow sophomores. "On the wide-range achievement testing, he was reading at about a seventh-grade level," Dr. Wallace testified. "But his spelling I believe was at a second- or third-grade level, and his math about a fourth- or fifth-grade level."

On arriving in Norfolk, Mrs. Elliot enrolled Nicholas in Kempsville Elementary School, a public school, but in September 1987 transferred him from the public system to Atlantic Shores. Even though Atlantic Shores would cost an additional $240 a month—hard to afford on her salary as a public-school nurse in the city of Chesapeake—she felt the school would be well worth the cost. She told the court, "The public schools seem to have a lot of problems, and he was a child who needed special help, and I felt in a Christian environment he would get that help, and I was advised he would."

Atlantic Shores brought no miracles, however. School remained a chore for Nicholas. Once, he overheard a female teacher and a secretary discussing his poor progress. "She said something about getting help in English that I am not good in," he told Detective Adams. "She said, 'I can't believe this. He started off with a third-grade book . . . and he can't even do that.' "

"Did it make you mad?" Adams asked.

"I can't believe she was talking about me. She didn't have to tell the whole world."

Adams asked Nicholas if he had overheard anything else, from other teachers.

"I've heard the secretary say that 'he's just the worst kid in school.' I heard her say that."

Adams then asked Nicholas which teachers in particular seemed to dislike him. He named a few, but the list omitted Karen Farley, a popular teacher who taught typing and other business skills, and whose own two children, Lora and Will, were also enrolled in the school.

When Adams asked Nicholas whether he got along with Mrs. Farley, Nicholas nodded yes.

This was clearly evident in a videotape Mrs. Farley made of her typing class earlier in the school year. The camera captured her voice as she simultaneously filmed the class and reminded her students to type without looking at the keys. At one point, as the typewriters clatter away, she asks the few students present if any other students are likely to show up that morning. She learns that two students, Nicholas and a girl named Shirley, have simply stepped out of the room for a moment, Nicholas for a drink of water. "Oh, that's right," Mrs. Farley says. "I'll have to get Nicholas. He'll just die if I don't get a picture of him."

And soon she does. Nicholas sits facing the camera, a big, endearing smile on his face. He is wearing a white polo shirt, a black jacket, and light pants. He is small boned, lean, well groomed, his hair trimmed close. In this image, in the bright sun that floods the classroom, he is just a boy. Nothing in the smile suggests the stress and anger he is supposed to have felt—although by the time this videotape was made, he had already acquired his gun. The smile is one of brilliant delight.

Nicholas did not hate Karen Farley. It is doubtful anyone could have. She spoke in a soft, measured way, with a Tidewater pace and cadence. She was devoted to the school. The morning of December 16, 1988, she returned a check the school had given her as payment for the extra time she had put into helping produce the school year-book. She told Rev. Mr. Sweet the school needed the money more than she.

She had begun her teaching career in 1970 at Booker T. Washington High School, an all-black school then on the verge of being integrated. The school had decided to integrate the faculty first, then the student body. She stayed for three years until the strains and dangers of teaching there and of trying to motivate a group of disinterested city kids wore her down. She resigned to become a first-grade teacher at the Faith Christian School, operated by Faith Baptist Church in Chesapeake. She left after one semester to have her first baby, Lora. A boy, Will, followed.

Mrs. Farley stayed home with her children until 1978, when she returned to Faith. She continued teaching there until the school closed in 1987, at which point she joined the teaching staff at Atlantic Shores. A colleague from the Faith Christian School, Bonnie Lovelace, recalled a night when she and Mrs. Farley found themselves still at work long after everyone else had gone home.

"Do you think anyone knows we're here?" Mrs. Farley asked.

Probably not, her friend answered.

"Oh, well," Mrs. Farley said. "Someday we'll make headlines."

CHAPTER THREE

THE LETHAL LANDSCAPE

BEFORE ADVANCING ANY FURTHER, I SHOULD first make my bias clear, for bias more than any other force shapes debate about guns in this country. I am not opposed to guns, not even handguns, provided the owners acknowledge the monumental responsibility conferred by ownership; provided too that they invest the time necessary to become safe, proficient users and to store those guns in a cabinet strong enough to hold burglars and toddlers at bay. When I see rural road signs perforated with large-diameter bullet holes, I realize responsibility is not something universally practiced by America's gun owners. I now ask the parents of my daughter's playmates if they own guns and, if so, how they store them. If they store them loaded, even in a locked cabinet, my children do not play at their homes. Period.

I can appreciate the lethal appeal of weapons and the fine craftsmanship evident in such premium handguns as the Colt Python and, yes, the Smith & Wesson Model 29 used by Dirty Harry. When I go to gun shows, as I do now in my capacity as a federally licensed firearms dealer, I am drawn, as are most of the rest of the browsers around me, to pick up the guns spread so invitingly across the exhibitors' tables, especially the notorious weapons, the fully automatic AK-47s and MAC-11s, the Sten guns and pistol-grip

Mossbergs. As a creature of the James Bond era, I am particularly fascinated by the silencers, which can be acquired by anyone with a clean record willing to pay the $200 federal transfer tax covering such devices. At gun shows, the urge to touch is strong and has caused many dealers to spread a soft black mesh over the guns on their tables. I confess to at least thinking the words "Make my day" or "Hasta la vista, baby" on my rounds, although I do not own any guns and, as a parent of two resourceful children age five and three, have no plans to buy any. I am content to let hunters hunt and can certainly appreciate the fun of getting out into the wilderness on a crisp autumn day in the company of one's friends, although I confess the charm of "blooding," or dumping a pail of deer viscera over the head of a novice hunter on the occasion of his very first kill, still eludes me.

Where I run afoul of the tenets of the National Rifle Association is in my belief that people should be allowed to acquire guns only after going through a licensing process *at least* as rigorous as getting a driver's license. As things stand now, a blind man can buy a gun. I hasten to add here that I mean no offense to the sightless. It just seems to me that anyone who buys a firearm ought first to be asked to prove he or she can see well enough to distinguish between a burglar and the paperboy. When I first mentioned this notion in print, I took it to be an unassailable position. I soon heard from two irate souls who accused me of stereotyping the blind. One of my critics wrote: "I know several blind persons (men and women) who have guns—for all the reasons anyone else might own them. These people represent the same cross section of sensitivity to the issue . . . and they demonstrate behavior as responsible as that of anyone else." The author accused me of believing "that blindness should be prima facie disqualification for owning a gun." Such a belief, he wrote, was "totally unsupportable on any basis other than unreasonable discrimination."

Nonetheless, I stand my ground.

Where I further risk abrading the prickly sensibilities of the gun camp is in my belief that a federal firearms dealer's license of the kind I now possess should be the hardest, most expensive professional license to acquire in America, instead of one of the easiest and cheapest. I cross the friend-foe line too in my belief that America is currently in the midst of a gun crisis that can no longer be considered just a manifestation of that good old frontier spirit but instead has become a costly global embarrassment.

That a handgun crisis does exist should be well beyond dispute by now, given the bleak slag heap of statistics on gunshot death and injury now casting its shadow over our society. These statistics could kindle outrage in a stone but have failed, somehow, to shake any tears from America's gun industry and the gun culture that supports it.

Over the last two years firearms killed almost 70,000 Americans, more than the total of U.S. soldiers killed in the entire Vietnam War. Every year handguns alone account for 22,000 deaths. In Los Angeles County, 8,050 people were killed or wounded in 1991, according to a report in *The Los Angeles Times*—thirteen times the number of U.S. forces killed in the Persian Gulf war. Every day, the handguns of America kill sixty-four people: twenty-five of the dead are victims of homicide; most of the rest shoot themselves. Handguns are used to terrorize countless others: over the next twenty-four hours, handgun-wielding assailants will rape 33 women, rob 575 people, and assault another 1,116.

A relatively new phenomenon, originating in the mid-1980s, is the inclusion of young children on the list of urban gunshot homicides. In 1987 a team of researchers from the UCLA Medical Center and King/Drew Medical Center in Los Angeles found that until 1980, King/Drew hadn't admitted a single child for gunshot wounds. From 1980 to 1987 the center admitted thirty-four. The study, published in the *American Journal of Diseases of Children*, included a macabre one-page table that listed the children's injuries, the relationship of the shooter to the victim, and other data that sketched the true horror of gunshot wounds, a horror ordinarily spared us by reporters pressed for time and news space who concentrate on the dead and dismiss any other victims as simply being wounded. The children, ranging in age from one to nine, were shot in the head, neck, chest, leg, and rectum. A five-year-old lost a hand. A three-year-old, shot in the rectum, endured a colostomy. Other children on the list lost fingers, eyes, and brain tissue, with at least one—an eight-year-old girl—consigned to an institution most likely for the rest of her life. They were shot by grandfathers, robbers, cousins, snipers, friends, and in a particularly cruel twist, by gang members seeking to exact revenge on an elder sibling by killing a younger brother or sister.

No one knows how many people in all incur nonfatal gunshot wounds each year. The most common estimate is that there are five nonfatal wounds for every fatality, or more than 150,000 injuries a year. No one knows for sure, however, because no federal entity keeps track. The Consumer Product Safety Commission, responsible for monitoring injuries from virtually every other consumer product, does not tally gunshot injuries because its founding legislation explicitly excluded firearms from its jurisdiction. One might assume this circumstance came to exist after a pitched battle between the Commission's backers and the National Rifle Association. The story is less dramatic, but far more disappointing. The sponsors excluded guns because they *feared* such a battle, and the damage it might do to the rest of the proposed legislation. There was ample reason for this fear, however. The firearms industry and gun lobby have a vested interest in suppressing detailed information on gunshot injuries and accidents, especially when such numbers are linked to specific models of firearms. Accurate statistics would be invaluable to bereaved families seeking to win negligence suits against gun dealers, distributors, and manufacturers. A true tally of nonfatal injuries, moreover, would by itself change the contours of the national debate over guns by providing a more realistic picture of the widespread prevalence of gunshot injury. That Congress should carve an exception for firearms is all the more remarkable given that guns comprise the one class of mass-market product designed from the start to kill.

◆ ◆ ◆

The nation began arming itself in earnest in the roaring sixties amid student protests, Cold War terror, race riots, and assassinations. Over the most tumultuous years, from 1967 to 1968, the number of handguns annually made available for sale to civilians in the U.S. rose by 50 percent—by some 802,000 pistols and revolvers—to 2.4 million, the greatest single annual leap in American history. In 1960, there were 16 million handguns in America; ten years later, the total had risen to more than 27 million. As of 1989, according to a study by the Bureau of Alcohol, Tobacco and Firearms (ATF), there were 66.7 million handguns and 200 million firearms of all kinds in circulation in the United States.

If these guns were controlled by a legion of sober adults, we might have far less to worry about. One study of eleven thousand teenagers in ten states found that 41 percent of the boys and 21 percent of the girls said they could obtain a handgun whenever they wished. A July 1993 poll of students in grades six through twelve conducted by Louis Harris for the Harvard School of Public Health found that 59 percent said they could get a handgun if they wanted one; 21 percent said they could get one within the hour.

Handgun access among children is not strictly an urban problem. The Harris poll found the degree of access to be surprisingly constant between rural, suburban, and urban communities. More than 60 percent of children who lived in cities said they could get a handgun if they wished; 58 percent of suburban kids claimed they could too. A University of North Carolina study of adolescents in suburban and rural communities in the Southeast found that 9 percent of the boys actually *owned* a handgun. Boys typically received their first firearm—usually a shotgun or a rifle but seven percent of the time a handgun—at the age of twelve and a half.

More than a fifth, however, received their first guns at the very responsible age of ten.

Kids have begun using their guns against each other. From 1965 to 1990, according to the Federal Bureau of Investigation, the rate at which children age ten through seventeen were arrested for homicide increased by 332 percent, despite a slight drop in that segment of the population. Anyone inclined to dismiss these figures as reflecting merely the high rate of homicide in the nation's black urban neighborhoods would be profoundly mistaken. The incidence of homicide arrests of white children increased in the same period by 425 percent.

Increasingly, you don't need to own a gun or be the intended target of someone else's gun to get shot. As guns have proliferated, the rate at which bystanders are wounded and killed has soared. In 1985 stray bullets killed four New Yorkers; in 1990 they killed forty.

Gun merchants and hobbyists steadfastly protest that guns aren't the problem and, even if they were, that gun ownership is explicitly endorsed by the Second Amendment of the Constitution—the much misquoted "right to bear arms" clause—and is therefore as much a part of the American way as, say, voting. A comparison of international homicide statistics proves that guns do indeed set America apart from the rest of the developed world.

In 1987, America's civilian guns were used to murder 3,187 young men age fifteen to twenty-four, accounting for three-fourths of the annual homicide rate in this demographic group of 21.9 per 100,000 people.

In Canada only seventeen young men were murdered with firearms, for an overall rate of 2.9 per 100,000.

In Japan, with 0.5 homicides per 100,000 people, eight young men died in gunshot homicides—as many killings as New York police encounter on a single busy weekend.

What accounts for the difference? Incidence of poverty, surely. Racial division. America's frontier history and the myths it conjured. The influence of television and movies.

And the sheer number of guns.

It is easy to challenge any study that purports to show a direct relationship between firearms proliferation and the rate of violent crime. Which came first, the challenge goes, the rise in gun sales or the crime rate? Did the increase in the number of guns encourage more people to commit crime? Or did the increase in crime drive more people to buy guns to defend themselves? The ease of making this challenge and the impossibility of ever fully defending against it have allowed the gun camp to obscure the debate over firearms distribution, when in fact there is an abundance of credible evidence that where there are more guns, there are more deaths from guns. The NRA's sloganeering notwithstanding, the evidence suggests that guns do indeed kill people.

A landmark study in King County, Washington, which includes Seattle, found that a gun kept at home was forty-three times more likely to be used to kill its owner, a family member, or a friend than an intruder. A Pittsburgh psychiatric hospital reported that the mere presence of a gun in the home more than doubles the odds that an adolescent member of the family will commit suicide. In 1987, Dr. Garen Wintemute, a researcher with the University of California at Davis Medical Center, plotted the annual firearm homicide rate per 100,000 people for the years 1946 through 1982. On the same graph, he plotted ATF's estimates of the number of new firearms made available for sale each year. The two lines track each other over the page with the eerie precision of a pair of figure skaters, both peaking around 1974, both dipping in 1976, both rising to another peak, both falling in concert toward 1982. (The rates of both have increased since then.) A 1986 study from the National Institute of Mental Health found similarly striking correlations between the increased proliferation of firearms and the rate of gunshot suicide among people age ten to twenty-four.

One of the foremost researchers in this forbidding territory is Franklin E. Zimring, a law professor at Earl Warren Legal Institute of the University of California, Berkeley, who has studied the issue since the 1960s. He established that although handguns only account for about a third of the guns owned in America, they are used in more than 75 percent of gunshot homicides and 80 percent of firearm-related robberies. "On average," Zimring reported, "rifles and shotguns are seven times less likely than handguns to be used in criminal violence." In one of his early studies he reviewed records of 16,000 violent assaults in Chicago to see whether the attacker's choice of knife or gun influenced the outcome. He found, first, that in seven of ten cases where the victim died, the attacker inflicted only one wound. That is, the attacker did not repeatedly stab or shoot the victim to make sure he was dead. The major difference among these attacks was that "an assault with a gun was five times more likely to result in a fatality than an assault with a knife." Zimring described the heightened danger posed by the attacker's choice of a gun as an "instrumentality effect" attributable to the inherent lethal character of guns.

In one of the most compelling studies of the impact of firearm proliferation, Dr. Arthur Kellermann, an emergency-medicine physician at Emory University, and associates from the Universities of Washington and British Columbia studied the rates of homicide and assault in Seattle and Vancouver from 1980 through 1986. The cities are close to each other. They have similar economies and similar geophysical locations. Their populations have a similar demographic profile. Presumably they watch the same movies and many of the same TV shows. During the study period, they also had similar assault rates. They differed markedly, however, in the degree to which they regulated access to firearms. Vancouver allowed gun sales only to people who could demonstrate a legitimate reason for having a firearm. Seattle had few regulations. The researchers found that attackers in Seattle were almost eight times more likely to use a handgun than those in Vancouver. Seattle's homicide rate, moreover, was five times higher, with handgun-related killings accounting for most of the difference.

The proliferation of guns continues, however. In the 1980s gun manufacturers feared they might have sold so many guns to American consumers that they had sated the market. Indeed, slack demand helped cause the failure of Charter Arms and drove Colt's Manufacturing into bankruptcy. Gunmakers, cheered on by the National Rifle Association, sought to improve their prospects by pitching guns—handguns in particular—as the only sure way to protect ourselves against crime. The Los Angeles riots of 1992 proved a godsend. Millions of TV viewers watched a white truck driver beaten senseless by black marauders. They saw Korean businessmen, the new heroes of American enterprise, brandishing guns to guard their inner-city businesses in scenes that evoked our most favorite Wild West myths: a good man standing alone, gun drawn and squinting into the setting sun, waiting for nightfall and the next attack of the barbaric hordes, be they Indians, cattle rustlers, train robbers, or, in this modern transmogrification, black gang-bangers in the ghetto. The most striking images and the most beneficial to the gun marketers were those scenes played over and over again of a group of L.A.'s Finest retreating posthaste to their police cars and leaving the good settlers of Indian country to their own devices.

The NRA was quick to extract the obvious message of the riots: you better get a gun because no one else is going to protect you. A 1992 recruitment ad for the NRA featured blocks of text against photographs of looting, burning, and destruction. "WHAT WILL IT TAKE?" the ad asked. "Must your glass be shattered? Must your flesh and blood be maimed? Must your livelihood be looted? Must all you've built be torn down? Must your once-proud nation surrender to more gun-control experimentation while its citizens tremble behind deadbolts and barred windows? . . . What will it take before you stand up with the one group that will stand for no more? . . . We warned gun laws would fail, and they have. We said gun control is wrong, and L.A. PROVES IT."

The newest targets for this sales pitch are women, considered especially receptive, the argument goes, because so many now are single heads of households and increasingly hold important jobs that require late hours and lots of travel. Gun magazines, such as the *American Rifleman*, published by the NRA, and *Women and Guns*, published by the Second Amendment Foundation, routinely carry stories about armed women who killed, wounded, or at least scared off their attackers. Such testimonials may require close examination, at least in light of one example printed in a 1989 issue of *American Rifleman*. The story described how a female cabdriver in Phoenix, Arizona, picked up a customer early one morning, only to have him hold a broken bottle to her throat and force her to drive to a deserted area. He took $70, then pushed the woman from the cab. "When her assailant ordered her to crawl in the dirt, [she] responded by emptying her pocket semiauto into him," the magazine reported. "He died later in a hospital."

By emptying her gun the cabdriver did indeed save herself, but not quite in the way this heroic account would have us believe. She later told the *Arizona Republic* how her enraged and wounded attacker then seized her gun, jabbed the barrel into her neck, and pulled the trigger—not once, but several times.

Had she not emptied the gun first, clearly her attacker would have done so.

The *American Rifleman* does not print tales of the risks associated with firearms ownership, such as the story carried by the Associated Press in October 1991 about a woman who shot herself in the face late one night. She blamed the accident, the AP reported, "on sleepy confusion between two objects she keeps under her pillow—her asthma medication dispenser and a .38-caliber revolver." The dispatch then quoted the woman as saying, "I didn't even know I had hold of the gun until it went off." She survived with surprisingly minor injuries.

Gun manufacturers now peddle their weapons to women using advertisements that show guns juxtaposed with photographs of small children and that describe gun ownership as a necessary act of women's liberation. A controversial Colt ad, run in 1992, featured photographs of two Colt pistols under a larger photograph of a mother putting her young daughter and her Raggedy Ann doll to bed. "Self-protection is more than your right," the ad reads, "it's your responsibility." Even Davis Industries of Chino, California, gets into the act. "What with all the crime in the streets these days," the Davis ad says, "a woman needs a bodyguard more than ever"—a rather ironic declaration, given that the company's cheap handguns and those produced by its sister company, Raven Arms, are among the guns most often implicated in urban crime.

A Smith & Wesson ad shows a young woman intently firing the company's LadySmith revolver at a shooting range. This is the newest incarnation of the LadySmith. The company produced its first LadySmith, a small .22 revolver designed for a woman's hand, in 1902 and manufactured it until 1921, when it learned some disturbing news: the revolver had become the weapon of choice among prostitutes. Horrified, the company quickly halted production. The woman in the most recent ad appears under a headline that asks, "What Would Mom Think Now?"—a slogan clearly meant to evoke the famous or perhaps infamous Virginia Slims pitchline, "You've come a long way, baby!"

"We're seeing the same thing we saw with promoting cigarettes," said Dr. Wintemute, the University of California researcher. "An inherently hazardous product is being associated with images of equality for women, of liberation for women, of independence for women, with the added approach of using fear—which you can't use to sell cigarettes but you can certainly use to sell guns."

◆ ◆ ◆

While tracking Nicholas Elliot's gun I became convinced that anyone who wishes truly to understand America's gun crisis and the culture that fuels it, especially anyone who intends to write about the subject, must first learn to appreciate the powerful appeal of firearms— the fun of pulling the trigger, feeling the explosive surge, and watching a portion of a distant target erupt for no visible cause. It is an appeal that crosses lines of class, race, and gender. Joyce Mays-

Rabbit, a money manager in Los Angeles, told me that when she goes hiking and fishing in deep wilderness, she carries a .44, the handgun equivalent of a cannon. "When you start shooting a .44," she said, "it's a real power trip. The flames shoot out of it. It's like playing cowboys and Indians as a kid. It's not that you want to kill anything. It would be very similar to having a really hot car."

I took the first step toward learning to shoot in October 1992 when I took a beginner's course in self-defense shooting from a woman named Paxton Quigley, a near-celebrity among gun owners. Although I took the course when I was already well into my journey through the gun culture, I present it here as a kind of introduction, for it taught me worlds about why the shooting passion burns so bright. It demonstrated how guns can seem such a compelling solution to the helplessness so many Americans now feel in the face of what they perceive to be a wild surge in violent crime.

In the hands of so astute a marketer as Paxton Quigley, the concept of armed self-defense becomes nearly irresistible. She brings to the fray a carefully crafted image, that of a former antigun activist who saw the light after the rape of a close friend. In fact, she was a marginal activist at best—"a glorified gofer," as one contemporary put it. And the rape was nowhere near as influential as Quigley's realization that a book on armed self-defense by a former antigun activist might be a hot seller. E. P. Dutton published the book, *Armed & Female,* in 1989, and soon afterward Quigley began teaching women to shoot. Shooting became a vehicle for feminine empowerment. "By getting over their fear of guns and knowing they can take care of themselves," Quigley told me, "they become more confident human beings."

Although the message may at first seem novel, at its root it is nothing more than a repackaged and redirected version of the message broadcast repeatedly to Americans since the late nineteenth century by presidents, newspaper reporters, Hollywood producers, TV writers, novelists, poets, and painters: just as guns won the West, they will win you peace of mind on the wild and woolly urban frontier. One of Quigley's students, Noelle Stettner, a Libertarian disc jockey from Gainesville, Georgia, synthesized this idea aptly when she told me she saw armed self-defense as "the last frontier of feminism."

◆ ◆ ◆

"Okay," Paxton Quigley bellowed, "on the count of three, everyone say, *'Get the fuck out of here!'* "

Nineteen Georgia women stood in a circle inside the meeting room of the Cherokee Gun Club in Gainesville, Georgia. Inside the circle stood Quigley. As always, she had begun the course with a couple of hours of instruction on basic self-defense techniques and on helping the women to stop thinking like victims.

"I don't want you smiling," Quigley said. For a small woman she had a surprisingly powerful voice. She was petite, blond, and by anyone's standard, drop-dead gorgeous. She wore a snug black blouse, a purplish tweed blazer with a peach kerchief in the pocket, and skin-tight jeans, with a gold chain looped a few times around her tiny waist. She moved within the circle in long concussive strides, the hard heels of her python-skin boots slamming the linoleum. "I want you to be angry, because women are basically fearful," she told the group. "I want you to come from a strong position."

The women screamed again, with considerably more conviction. The room erupted in laughter, war whoops, and scattered shouts of "Aw *right!*"

Although the message was serious, Quigley had designed the exercise to keep the mood light, part of her strategy for helping women shed their fear of guns and get them in the mood to shoot. Typically, most of the women who take Quigley's beginner class have never shot a gun before. Here, however, all had done so except me and three of the women. Several in fact possessed concealed-weapons permits. One was an NRA pistol instructor, although she did not disclose this to her fellow students until the class had ended. When Quigley expressed her surprise at the level of expertise, one woman drawled with mock menace, "You're in Georgia now."

The smiles faded rapidly, however, when Quigley played a tape supplied by the NRA of a 911 emergency call placed by a Kansas City woman as a rapist made his way toward her bedroom.

The operator advised the woman to lock her bedroom door.

"He's here," the victim cried. "He's in the room."

She grew increasingly terrified until at last she screamed, "Who are you? Why are you here? Why are you here? *Why?*"

The line went dead, followed by the ominous flat chord of a dial tone.

The tape had a curious effect. "I was furious," Linda Lovejoy, an Atlanta accountant, told me. "She should have been able to protect herself. The helplessness is what really got to me. She had no means of fighting back." The tape struck Noelle Stettner, the disc jockey, the same way. "You start thinking, 'This stupid bitch'—to be honest."

This is how Quigley wants her students to feel. "Obviously," she told the suddenly subdued class, "if she'd had a gun, that would have helped the situation. She didn't fight. At that point, you don't ask, 'Who are you, why are you here?' She was a victim, a horrible victim. It's awful to show, but you don't want to be a victim."

She then invited the women who'd brought their own guns to pull them from their purses, fanny packs, and locked steel gun boxes. To those who needed guns, she loaned top-quality Smith & Wesson revolvers.

Her choice of brand was no accident. Quigley received a monthly stipend from Smith & Wesson, as well as a supply of guns, in return for giving talks to gun groups, visiting gun dealerships to advise women on the guns they ought to buy, and of course helping to staff the Smith & Wesson booth at the annual SHOT Show, a huge trade show for licensed firearms dealers. She loaned me an expensive Smith & Wesson .357 revolver, black, with an elegant wood grip and red-dot sight. "Of course. What am I going to do, give you a lousy gun?" she told me later. "I want you to do well."

After a series of loading and unloading drills, Quigley sketched the upper torso of a man. She circled the broad area between the sternum and shoulders known to combat shooters as the "center of mass," the area where a bullet is most likely to cause enough destruction of tissue and bone and such catastrophic neural shock as to stop an assailant before he can complete his attack. This is a nice way of telling the women to shoot to kill.

"We're also going to practice some head shots," Quigley said. "It's hard to shoot someone in the face because we think of the face as the person, as the soul—I hate to talk like this, but if you shoot someone in the face, you have a very good chance of stopping him."

She led the class down to one of the Cherokee Gun Club's outdoor ranges. Everyone wore safety glasses. Quigley carried a bullhorn so she would be heard through the earplugs and pistol earmuffs everyone wore as protection against the damaging roar of the guns. "To those of you who've never shot before," Quigley said, a warm smile playing across her face, "welcome. You'll have a wonderful time."

Many of Quigley's former students report that the act of firing a gun for the first time triggered a revolution in their lives. Michelle Sullivan, of South Pasadena, California, took her fifth course from Quigley in January 1993. She took her first early in 1992. "The first time I stood there with a loaded gun, I wanted to cry," she told me. "I thought, is this what my life has come to—I'm standing here holding a loaded gun?"

Sullivan hit the target on her first shot. "It was like I walked up to a psychological barrier, crossed it, and everything was fine. It was a complete turnaround in thinking. Complete."

Each of twenty targets was papered with the black silhouette of a man's upper body. Clear plastic bags draped the silhouettes to protect them from the rain. Half the class stood along the firing line seven feet away.

The distance may seem absurdly close, but armed encounters often occur at that range, according to police firearms experts. Quigley had an additional motive for putting everyone so close, however. She wanted her students to hit the targets as often as possible to bolster morale. Aiming and shooting a handgun is not the easy matter TV cops and robbers make it out to be. Even at seven feet, many of the women taking the course missed the silhouette portion of the target and struck only the background.

After a few basic shooting drills, Quigley moved on to more advanced exercises, including one she called Mozambique—two shots to the body, one to the head.

"It's awfully fun to do this," she said.

She issued the command to begin shooting. There was a wild, prolonged crackle of gunfire. Sharp puffs of air from my neighbor's gun tapped at my temple. Georgia clay erupted from the hillside beyond the targets.

"I hope we all got some good head shots in there," Quigley said heartily, "because that's what's gonna stop him."

She checked the targets to see how well everyone was doing. A few wildly spaced holes led her to suspect some students had been jerking the trigger instead of squeezing it.

"Squeeze smoothly," she told the class, a sly grin again playing across her face as she moved along the firing line. "It's really kind of a sexy move. I always say be sexy about it. Squeeeeeeeze," she murmured, "squeeeeeeeze. Okay? That'll kind of get your mind into it."

We shot our guns one-handed, first with our dominant hands, then our weak hands. We shot while lying on our backs, an exercise intended to simulate firing while still in bed. One woman, supine on a muddy ground cloth, hit the target in the face with the first shot.

"Ooh," another said in admiring disgust. "Right where it counts!"

More exercises followed. Empowerment was in the air.

"Feels good, doesn't it?" Quigley exhorted. "You feel the power!"

When the class at last returned to the meeting room, Quigley asked her students one by one to tell their reactions to the course. The room took on the feel of a revivalist camp meeting. "Lisa," Quigley said to Lisa Hilliard, an Atlanta bank executive who had never shot a gun before. "When you first walked in, I said, 'Oh, God, she's scared.'"

Quigley turned to the other students. "I could see it on her face. She was scared."

Then back to Lisa. "How do you feel now, Lisa?"

Hilliard considered. "Great. I can't believe how much fun it was. I mean, I just wanted to get through it; I didn't expect to enjoy it."

Quigley pointed to another woman. "Ginger?"

She was Ginger Icenhour, manager of a computer store in Tucker, Georgia. She too had never shot before but now professed to be ready to take on an assailant. "If he walks through that door, he'll be surprised because I'm gonna shoot him."

It is a tantalizing fantasy. Who among us hasn't imagined walking down a dark street, being accosted by a bad guy, and reveling in his surprise as we draw our Dirty Harry Model 29s and blow him away? The myth of self-defense depicts the gun as a foolproof talisman capable of warding off trouble and restoring peace of mind.

But armed self-defense is a far more problematic venture than Quigley and the gun culture would have us all believe.

◆ ◆ ◆

The NRA's 911 tape, played by Quigley, was indeed powerful, so compelling the NRA played it at its 1993 annual meeting in Nashville. There is another tape, however, that Quigley could have played just as readily. It is the 911 recording of a ten-year-old Florida boy, Sean Smith, who called the emergency line just after shooting his eight-year-old sister. At first his voice is soft; he pleads for understanding. He could be any little boy trying to explain a breach of household rules.

"I didn't know my dad's gun was loaded," he says.

"Okay," the operator says.

"And I shot her." The boy's voice wavers. "I didn't mean to. She's dead."

Even the dispatcher is startled. He snaps, "She's *dead?*"

The boy loses all composure now. "Yes," he cries, "please, get my mom and dad. Oh my God!"

The act of owning a gun for self-defense forces the gun owner to confront a paradox central to such ownership: to be truly useful for self-defense, a gun must be kept loaded and readily accessible at all times. "In other words," Quigley wrote in her book, "an unloaded gun that is perfectly safe is perfectly useless."

But a gun that is accessible to the parent is, by definition, just as accessible to the parent's children or anyone else who visits the home, be it a jealous boyfriend or drunken spouse. Researchers fear the gun industry's strategy of pitching handguns to women, particularly professional women and single mothers, will only heighten the risk to children. Even Quigley argues that certain households should not have guns, in particular those with a member who is alcoholic, takes antidepression drugs, or is prone to extreme bursts of temper—a sizable portion of the U.S. population. "If you have children at home," she warned the Gainesville class, "really think about whether you should have a gun."

Inherent in this last warning was the notion that women who did not have children should feel free to buy a gun. The warning, however, ignores the potential for collateral disaster that always exists in the presence of a gun. Women who live alone may have nieces, nephews, and grandchildren; their neighbors, friends, and lovers may have kids; the women may teach grade school, operate day-care centers, or baby-sit for friends, sisters, cousins, and colleagues. A study of accidental shooting deaths of children in California highlighted how a momentary lapse of vigilance by gun owners could quickly lead to tragedy, even in households that treated guns with exemplary care. In one case, the study reported, a six-year-old boy shot himself in the head with a handgun he found "in the purse of a houseguest."

It is widely thought that Sarah Brady, chairperson of Handgun Control Inc., began her crusade against guns immediately after her husband, Jim Brady, was permanently injured in John Hinckley's attempt to assassinate Ronald Reagan. In fact, she told a writer for the *New York Times Magazine,* the pivotal moment came later, in 1985, when her five-year-old son found a .22 handgun in a pickup owned by a family friend and pointed it at her. At first Brady thought it was a toy, then saw it was real and loaded.

Parents, however, seem all too willing to ignore the risks and to assume that their own kids are responsible enough to recognize the harm guns can do and to learn to "respect" them. A June 1993 Louis Harris survey, also conducted for the Harvard University School of Public Health, found that only 43 percent of parents who owned guns kept those guns under lock and key. Another study found that 10 percent of America's armed parents openly admitted they kept their guns not only loaded but also unlocked and "within reach of children." The mere fact that a full 10 percent of respondents actually admitted courting tragedy in this way should itself give us pause. It raises the suspicion that many other parents do likewise but are unwilling to confess to a practice many gun owners would find reprehensible.

Debbie Collins, a sixth-grade teacher who took Paxton Quigley's course at the Cherokee Gun Club, has a daughter and a Smith & Wesson revolver (she doesn't know the caliber). When we spoke late in 1992, her daughter was one and a half years old. Collins had been carrying a gun for about five years. During the workweek she locked her revolver in the glove compartment of her car in the school parking lot. While at home, she stored it loaded on top of the refrigerator. Her husband kept a loaded handgun at their bedside during the night.

Keeping her daughter safe from the family's guns, Collins said, "is a real fear for me." But Quigley's course, she added, made her more confident. "I'm more aware now of where [the gun] is all the time. And making sure it's in a safe place all the time."

But would she always know exactly where it was?

"I'm sure gonna try. I can't say that I'll always, but since that course I've been very aware of it. I like to feel like I'll always be aware of it." Once, however, she left the gun in her car, with the car unlocked but in the garage. "That kind of frightened me."

When her daughter is older, Collins said, "we're going to take her out, show her how it works and what it can cause, and that way make her less curious about it—I think that's why a lot of children use them, out of curiosity." She thought she might follow Paxton Quigley's suggestion of bringing along a melon to demonstrate the damage a handgun can do to the human head, an idea that evokes the practice sessions of the would-be assassin in Frederick Forsyth's *Day of the Jackal.* In *Armed & Female* Quigley wrote, "Once a child understands how a gun operates and has heard the sound of a gunshot and witnessed the potential damage, he or she will have a different view of a gun and will gain respect for it."

Dr. Kellermann, the Emory University researcher, called this idea "well-intended but hopelessly naive." Parents overestimate the good sense of their children and their ability to resist outside pressures, he said. "Teaching a child respect for a gun doesn't change the child's willingness to use it if he's depressed, if he just failed a test that he felt the rest of his life depended on, or just broke up with his girlfriend or he's mad at his best friend. Tragedies of this kind are played out in this country on almost a daily basis."

Others, however, including the NRA and Quigley, argue that the low annual death toll from accidental shootings proves how safe gun ownership is in America. A 1991 study by the U.S. General Accounting Office reported that in 1988 there were 1,501 unintentional shooting deaths; 277 of the victims were children fifteen years old or younger. This is tragic, the gun camp concedes, but not a bad showing considering that half of America's households are thought to possess one or more guns.

Proponents of this view neglect to mention the number of nonfatal injuries that occur in accidental shootings. The GAO began studying firearms accidents in order to gauge how many lives could be saved each year if guns were required by law to include loading indicators, magazine safeties, and other safety devices currently not routinely installed on guns. (A loading indicator provides a visual warning that a cartridge is positioned in front of the firing pin and ready to fire. A magazine safety disables an auto-loading pistol the moment you pull the ammunition magazine from the base of the grip. Mechanical logic might lead you to assume that when you remove the magazine from a pistol, you unload the gun and render it safe; in fact, a cartridge may be left in the chamber.) Faced with the dearth of information on nonfatal gunshot injuries, the GAO's investigators did some primary research of their own. They discovered that police typically do not keep such records. Nonetheless, they managed to find ten major police departments that did. Using the records from these departments, the GAO investigators studied 532 accidental shootings that occurred in 1988 and 1989 and found that only five had resulted in death, for an injury-to-death ratio of 105 to 1. The survey sample included records from the Dallas police department, which had recorded only one accidental shooting death but 248 injuries.

The GAO report cautioned that the survey sample, limited by the lack of available injury data, was hardly representative; the 105-to-1 ratio could not be projected to the country as a whole. The report noted, however, that this ratio fell in line with others reported by the National Safety Council. The overall ratio of injuries to deaths for all accidents of all kinds in America was 94 to 1; for household accidents, 151 to 1. If the 105-to-1 ratio were indeed accurate, it would indicate that 157,600 accidental, nonfatal gunshot injuries occur each year. Even if one excludes Dallas as a statistical outlier, the ratio comes out to seventy injuries for every death, or 105,070 nonfatal gunshot injuries each year.

A gun is an ego pump. It can give a fifteen-year-old mugger absolute power over anyone he encounters except perhaps another armed teenager. Likewise, police fear, a gun may impart a false sense of security to anyone who keeps one for self-defense, especially anyone who carries it outside the home. "There's just so many what-ifs," said Officer Joanne Welsh of the San Francisco police. The mother of a four-year-old, she won't bring her service weapon into her house. "A weapon is really only good if that perfect situation you may have envisioned occurs."

Guns certainly don't make police officers feel safe, despite weeks of training and drilling in combat-shooting tactics. They know that just hanging on to a gun in an armed encounter can be difficult. From 1980 through 1989, 735 police officers nationwide were shot dead in the line of duty; 120 were killed with their own guns.

"The typical NRA line is, you can't rape a .38," said Col. Leonard Supenski, a Baltimore County firearms expert, who testified in a landmark civil suit arising from Nicholas Elliot's shooting spree. "Well, that's absolutely false. If the guy's got his gun out first, you're gonna lose. If you've got a .38 in your purse and the guy gets to it first, you're gonna lose. If a guy attacks you from behind in the dark with the element of surprise, you're gonna lose."

Armed encounters involve a daunting array of split-second decisions. The self-defense shooter must first identify the target. Next, he must gauge the degree of threat. Does the intruder or assailant really pose a mortal danger? In broad daylight, these questions may have ready answers. But a self-defense shooting is most likely to take place under less than optimal conditions, with fear complicating the decision process.

Analysis of police shootings shows that a wild surge of adrenaline quickly impairs fine motor control, Supenski said. "You have tunnel vision, your eyes tend to focus on the threat, you see nothing else around you. Your auditory senses are diminished. It's called auditory exclusion. You hear only what's in front of you."

One of the absurd myths of gunplay nurtured by television and Hollywood is the idea that during a gunfight one can actually count the number of bullets the other guy fired and thus know whether or not his gun remained loaded. Police officers involved in shootings often report never hearing the sound of gunfire.

Amid the confusion of sleep and the distortions of fear, an armed homeowner has yet one more crucial question to answer: What's behind the target? A bullet that misses its target, or even one that strikes its target dead on, can continue traveling with enough momentum to pass through interior walls into adjacent bedrooms, even exterior walls into neighboring homes. A miss is likely. In gunfights, Baltimore County police officers miss with seven of ten shots fired, Supenski said. "If the cops miss—and these are the guys who had the training, the retraining, and the recertification—how much more so does somebody who buys a gun and sticks it in the drawer?"

Gun magazines feed America's gun owners a steady diet of advice on how to behave during a gunfight, much of it written by police officers from small-town departments no one has ever heard of and where gun battles are few and far between. Typically, these stories fail to discuss the emotional aftermath of an armed confrontation. Big-city police departments know the psychic toll can be devastating. In Boston, for example, the police department established a "Shoot Team," composed of officers who have survived shoot-outs, which gathers after each new incident to help the officers involved come to grips with the terror they felt during the confrontation and the emotional upheaval they experienced afterward.

One of its members, who asked not to be identified by name, lived through two shoot-outs. In the first, he and his partner—for narrative purposes, I'll call them Nolan and Dougherty—wound up in high-speed pursuit of a stolen Lincoln, chasing it up one-way streets against oncoming traffic. "It was like something out of the movies," Nolan recalled. "I remember my heart was pounding out of my chest."

The fleeing car rounded a corner and stopped. One suspect leaped from the car and ran headfirst into a telephone pole so hard he was knocked to the ground. (When the officers later caught this suspect, they knew immediately they had the right man by the splinters in his face.) The other suspect drove the big Lincoln into a vacant lot where it struck a boulder, briefly went airborne, then came to rest. The officers positioned their car to provide defensive cover. The suspect fired.

"All I remember is hearing the crack of the gun going off," Nolan told me. "The next thing I saw was blue pieces of plastic flying all over the place. My partner went down—I thought he'd been shot."

In fact, Dougherty had ducked for cover as the first bullet struck the blue roof light and shattered it. The suspect was firing a powerful .357 Magnum revolver and carried a speed loader, a device that holds six bullets and allows them to be inserted quickly into the empty chambers.

Nolan fired every shot in his service revolver and reloaded. The suspect took off. Nolan sprinted after him. At one point Nolan told him to halt, then dropped to one knee and aimed at his back. He didn't fire. "If I had shot him in the back, I'd be in state prison right now," he said. He and Dougherty returned to the Lincoln, where they found evidence that allowed them to track the suspect to an address in Boston's Dorchester section. He was hiding inside an oil furnace. "To this day," Nolan said, "I don't know how he got in there."

Until the capture, Nolan had been running on adrenaline. "It happens so quickly," he recalled. "All these little items, like a checklist. Is it a clear shot? Is everybody out of the way? Then boom, boom, boom—all in a split second. I was trained to do this, but I wasn't trained how to deal with it." Afterward, he said, "I came apart at the seams. I just started shaking. I did what I do best. I got absolutely drunk out of my mind."

The incident had a lasting impact. He became an alcoholic. He lost his wife to divorce. Now on the wagon, he tries to help other officers vent the powerful emotional reactions they experience after a shooting. Nolan agrees people who feel moved to buy a gun for self-defense ought to be able to do so, but with a caveat: "You need to get some extensive training. Appreciate what a handgun is and what it can do."

On the whole, he said, society needs to take a longer view and examine why it is that many people feel the criminal justice system has failed them. "I don't want to see any more guns," he said. "Guns kill people. That's what they're for. They kill people. And there's just too many of them out there already."

Such concern, however, has little persuasive power for people who see crime encroaching from all sides. Lisa Hilliard, the banker who took Paxton Quigley's Georgia course, told me she realized how vulnerable she was when she wound up stranded alone on an Atlanta freeway late one night. "I couldn't help but imagine my name on the news, you know, 'Decatur woman, age thirty-three . . .' "

Although she had never shot before, she lived among guns. Her husband owned many and kept one loaded by the bedside. The time had come, she reasoned, to learn how to use those guns and take responsibility for her own safety. "Girls grow up believing that they're going to be taken care of," she said, then added softly, "But it just ain't so."

◆ ◆ ◆

Why do we place so much trust in guns to solve our problems? What accounts for the official deference we as a nation afford guns, despite the growing count of dead and wounded and the fact that polls show most of us favor federal regulation of firearms? The belief in guns as tools for self-defense certainly contributes to this national tolerance. So too, obviously, does America's rural passion for hunting deer and other game. Neither, however, can fully explain how firearms became lodged in the national psyche as objects of almost sacred stature.

A good deal of the answer lies in the frontier West—not the real frontier as experienced by the hundreds of thousands of pioneers and gold-seekers of American history, but the imagined West, conjured over the last century by Hollywood directors, TV producers, nineteenth-century reporters, dime novelists, and the frontier heroes themselves, of a vast plain of violence that only guns could subdue. "What people believe to be true is often as important as reality," wrote historian W. Eugene Hollon, "and generations of Americans have grown up accepting the idea that the frontier during the closing decades of the nineteenth century represented this country at its most adventurous as well as its most violent."

Somehow, we came to believe that guns really did win the West. But how was this notion instilled? Where did we lose the thread of history and pick up instead the silken ribbon of myth?

At times, surely, the early frontier lived up to its wild-and-woolly reputation, as when the Indian wars were in full swing, and when competition over the use of land led to bloody range battles such as the April 1892 Johnson County War in northern Wyoming. For the average resident of the frontier, however, life was more often marked by hard work, loneliness, and stupefying boredom. People rarely locked their doors, or for that matter, even bothered to install locks. Burglary was rare, rape close to nonexistent (although rape has always been, and undoubtedly was then, an underreported crime). Frank Prassel, an Old West historian, examined records of the U.S. District Court in New Mexico Territory dating to the court's opening in 1890 and found that of its first twenty-six cases, twenty-two involved charges of "fornication" and adultery. Prassel observed, "The West's lawless element obviously had something on its mind other than bank robbery and cattle theft."

One of the great entertainments was the rare hanging, which attracted spectators from far off. Hangings were festive events at which the condemned man was expected to offer a remark or two. Moments before Jeremiah Bailey was executed in Abilene, Kansas, on January 5, 1872, he told the crowd below, "I am on the scaffold about to be launched into the other world. What has brought me to this? Let me tell you, and let these words ring forever in your ears. It was whiskey and the carrying of firearms. Whiskey and the bearing of pistols have ruined me."

The proliferation of guns and alcohol throughout the West, with the added incendiary influence of gambling, made for dangerous conditions late on a frontier night, especially in mining towns whose occupants were primarily adventurous young men. According to historian Roger D. McGrath, who studied life in the mining towns of

Bodie, California, and Aurora, Nevada, a chance remark, an old grudge, or an ill-advised challenge to another man's ego could readily ignite an impromptu gun battle. If one of the parties died, his killer would typically be acquitted for having fired in self-defense. Ordinary citizens tolerated such "fair fights" among consenting hard characters. Anyone who stayed out late with armed, drunken men invited trouble.

Nonetheless, the homicide rate in many frontier towns was surprisingly low. Robert Dykstra, a specialist on Kansas cattle towns, found evidence of only forty-five homicides from 1870 to 1885 in the fabled towns of Abilene, Caldwell, Dodge City, Ellsworth, and Wichita. That works out to 0.6 killings per town per year, not quite the frequency Hollywood has led us to expect.

Citizens of the real West seemed far more appalled by the levels of violence back east. On March 19, 1872, the *Missouri Republican* called New York City a "Murderers' Paradise" and reported that "New York . . . has settled down into the usual condition of chronic indifference, and the murdering business is carried on with an impunity which would be really amusing, were the matter less serious. Hardly a day passes that some one does not receive an eternal quietus at the hands of an assassin."

Meanwhile, the novelists, pulp writers, and news reporters who comprised the nation's media were busy confronting a creative challenge: how to rationalize the sheer excitement of the westward expansion, with its attendant gold and land fevers, and the mundane, harsh reality of ordinary frontier life. The answer came readily. Sheriffs became avenging angels, bar fights turned into ritualized duels in the hot noon sun. Dime novelists began transforming frontier characters into heroes even as the real flesh-and-blood figures went about the business of killing, robbing, or peacekeeping. Buffalo Bill Cody was the hero in 557 dime novels. Frank Tousey gave us the James Boys series about Jesse and Frank James even as the pair continued committing crimes. Edward Z. C. Judson, writing as Ned Buntline, turned Wyatt Earp and Wild Bill Hickok into the steely-eyed lawmen of contemporary myth. The first book about Billy the Kid appeared July 15, 1881, the day after Sheriff Pat Garret killed him. The book described Billy as wearing a dragoon jacket "of finest broadcloth" and a hat "covered with gold jewels." Owen Wister's *The Virginian*, published in 1902, became a best-seller and the prototype of the modern western. Wister gave us one of the most-quoted passages of literature when his hero, having been called a son of a bitch, replied, "When you call me that, *smile!*"

The press spared no exaggeration to populate the West with living legends. Between Dodge City and Tombstone, Deadwood and Sacramento, was a vast, bleak terrain whose immensity we can only begin to appreciate today when flying over such still-desolate territories as Nevada and Utah. The robberies, murders, and Indian battles that did occur were big news partly because that immense expanse of desperately lonely acreage generated so little other news.

The press rose to the challenge.

After Jesse James and two accomplices robbed a Kansas fair on September 26, 1872, the *Kansas City Star* applauded the deed: "It was as though three bandits had come to us from storied Odenwald, with the halo of medieval chivalry upon their garments, and shown us how things were done that poets sing of. Nowhere else in the civilized world, probably, could this thing have been done."

Never mind that these chivalrous heroes shot a young girl in the leg.

After Jesse was murdered in 1882, the *Kansas City Journal* wailed, "Goodbye, Jesse!"

The *National Police Gazette* made a goddess of Myra Belle Shirley, known best as Belle Starr and commonly imagined as a beauty. (She was played by Gene Tierney in the 1941 movie *Belle Starr*.) The *Gazette* described her as "the Bandit Queen," and reported: "She was more amorous than Antony's mistress, more relentless than Pharaoh's daughter, and braver than Joan of Arc."

The true West of course was nothing like what readers in the East were instructed to imagine. Belle Starr, for example, was no Gene

Tierney. Belle was a profoundly homely woman with a deeply pocked face who stole cattle and horses, robbed stagecoaches, and had a penchant for sleeping with killers and one of her two illegitimate sons. This boy, Ed Reed, later shot her in the back and, after she had fallen, shot her again for good measure, killing her.

Strip away the legends enshrouding the famous outlaws and what you find are pathological killers. Billy the Kid, far from being the glamorous James Dean–like character of popular imagination, was once described as an "adenoidal moron." In a rare act of clear-eyed journalism, the *Silver City New Southwest and Grant Herald* observed: "Despite the glamour of romance thrown about his dare-devil life by sensational writers, the fact is, he was a low-down vulgar cut-throat, with probably not one redeeming quality."

Clay Allison, one of the most feared outlaws, was by all appearances a psychopath. He was discharged from the Tennessee Light Artillery after being judged "incapable of performing the duties of a soldier because of a blow received many years ago." This head injury apparently caused wild swings in his moods, "from mania to intense despondency." He was alleged to have killed fifteen men in his career as a "shootist," and to have cut the head off one of them and brought it with him to a bar. Fabled gunfighter John Wesley Hardin killed forty-four men, perhaps as many as seventy-seven, yet the power of outlaw myth was such that in 1968 Bob Dylan still felt able to describe him in the title song of his album *John Wesley Hardin* as a Robin Hood–like character who "was always known to lend a helping hand."

The national myth-*werkes* reserved its greatest distortions for the lawmen of the West. Contrary to popular belief, in many frontier counties and towns, sheriffs and marshals often went unarmed. Rather than shooting it out all day with itinerant gunmen, they confronted the mundane duties familiar to any city policeman today. In Leadville, Colorado, in 1880, the twenty-two-man police force made 4,320 arrests, most for intoxication and disturbance of the peace. The real marshal of Dodge City was responsible for street repair and killing stray dogs, but we never heard a word about this on "Gunsmoke." In that mythic realm, Matt Dillon courted Miss Kitty; the real marshal of Dodge had to contend with Big Nose Kate, Noseless Lou, and Squirrel Tooth Alice. Wyatt Earp and his friend Bat Masterson were adept con men and gamblers who also happened to be lawmen. They were known around Dodge as "the Fighting Pimps." Earp abandoned his common-law wife, Mattie, who later committed suicide. In a letter to her surviving family, the attending coroner called Earp "a gambler, blackleg, and coward."

In the mythic West even homicide became a clean, honorable affair that adhered to the Code of the West. In fact, frontier homicide was just as mean and gritty as urban murder is today. Ambush was often the tactic of choice, preferably when the target was stone-cold drunk. Morgan Earp, one of Wyatt's brothers, was assassinated by a rifle fired at him through a window. A thief named Robert Ford murdered Jesse James by shooting him in the back of the head. The police officer who crept up behind John Wesley Hardin in an El Paso bar and shot him dead no doubt believed he was merely being prudent, given Hardin's reputation. In one notorious attack, members of the John Daly gang in Aurora, Nevada, set out to kill William Johnson, the operator of a way station whose employee had killed a horse-thief friend of Daly's. After running an errand in town, Johnson went to a bar where a member of Daly's gang pretended all was forgiven and bought him a few drinks. When the bar closed, they moved to another saloon, where Daly and other members of the gang were waiting. The good fellowship continued until about four-thirty A.M., when Johnson left. Daly and three other gang members, including a man named William Buckley, ambushed him. Buckley knocked Johnson down. Daly shot him through the head. Then Buckley slashed his throat.

The strategy for such attacks may have been dictated partly by the fact—a fact one does not see mentioned very much in contemporary firearms ads that evoke the frontier—that the cowboy's trusty six-shooter wasn't all that trusty. Accidents and malfunctions were common. "Lawmen and outlaws alike knew the dangers and limitations of the revolvers they sometimes carried but rarely displayed," wrote Frank Prassel. "Shooting would be avoided whenever possible, and when demanded it would often be done from cover or concealment."

The Colt Peacemaker, introduced in 1873, is often called "the gun that won the West," but it was so prone to accidental discharge that many U.S. Army officers carried the gun loaded with only five cartridges, with the empty sixth chamber under the hammer. On cross-country wagon journeys, firearms accidents sometimes proved a more serious problem than disease. On one journey, a pioneer mistook his mule for an Indian and shot it twice. Of the four men killed in the famous Johnson County War, two died from accidental gunshot wounds. In Bodie, California, Roger McGrath discovered, one man "accidentally shot himself in the jaw while inspecting a revolver that had misfired." Even the West's celebrities had their accidents. Clay Allison shot himself in the foot and eventually had to walk with a cane. Wild Bill Hickok accidentally killed one of his deputies. On January 9, 1876, Wyatt Earp's revolver fell from his holster as he sat in the back room of the Custom House saloon in Wichita. According to the *Wichita Beacon* of January 12, "the ball passed through his coat, struck the north wall, then glanced off and passed out through the ceiling. It was a narrow escape and the occurrence got up a lively stampede from the room."

Frontier celebrities also did their best to assist in myth manufacturing. They seemed extraordinarily aware of the great significance later historians would assign to their epoch. When Pat Garret published his rather exaggerated account of his pursuit of Billy the Kid, "his name became almost synonymous with western law enforcement," according to Frank Prassel. Jesse James's brother Frank, a member of the James Gang, toured the country with another outlaw, Cole Younger; they billed themselves as the "Cole Younger–Frank James Wild West Show." Frank later opened the family farm to tourists, charging fifty cents a head. Bill Tilghman, a famous Oklahoma lawman, also toured the country and in 1914 made a film called *The Passing of the Oklahoma Outlaws*. A former train robber, Al Jennings, eventually wound up acting in silent-film westerns, a career that lasted from 1908 to 1920.

The frontier figure who most influenced how America now thinks about the Old West, and indeed about guns, was William Frederick Cody—Buffalo Bill—a frontier scout turned master of self-promotion who first achieved fame in 1869 when Ned Buntline featured him in one of his dime novels. Cody's fame was greatly enhanced in 1876 when, while serving as a scout during the Plains Indians wars, he encountered a lone Cheyenne brave. Cody's horse stumbled, causing Cody to fall. As the brave charged, Cody coolly shot him dead, then scalped him and waved the scalp over his head. By winter, he was reenacting the incident over and over in a stage drama called "The Red Hand; or, The First Scalp for Custer," in which he played himself.

In 1882, Cody founded "Buffalo Bill's Wild West," a traveling show consisting of dramatic scenes supposedly meant to capture real life on the frontier. Real life, however, wouldn't have sold many tickets; Cody's version consisted of stagecoach robberies, Indian attacks, buffalo hunts, and stunning feats of marksmanship. Cody was the star of the show. As if to dispel any doubt, one showbill noted: "The central figure in these pictures is that of THE HON. W. F. CODY (Buffalo Bill), to whose sagacity, skill, energy and courage . . . the settlers of the West owe so much for the reclamation of the prairie from the savage Indian and wild animals, who so long opposed the march of civilization."

The scenes presented a grossly distorted view of the West, but to reinforce the illusion of authenticity, Cody included such props as real buffalo and a bona fide stagecoach. He even recruited the help of Indians who had fought in the Plains wars and participated in the slaughter of General Custer and his men. Sitting Bull, the Sioux chief, joined the tour in 1885 for a limited engagement.

The show was immensely popular. In 1885, Cody took his "Wild

West" to forty U.S. cities. In 1886, the show reached New York. Staged in Madison Square Garden, the set included a reproduction of the town of Deadwood doomed to be destroyed in each performance by a mock cyclone. In a single week, the show drew two hundred thousand people. The following year, Cody took the show to London, accompanied by ninety-seven Cheyenne, Kiowa, Pawnee, and Sioux Indians (including the Sioux chief Red Shirt), one hundred eighty horses, eighteen buffalo, ten elk, ten mules, and a dozen or so other animals. He also brought Phoebe Anne Moses, a twenty-seven-year-old woman from Tiffin, Ohio, who had begun shooting when only eight years old to help feed her family. She performed as Annie Oakley. At one point during the "Wild West" 's London engagement, Cody's Deadwood stage careened about the exhibition stadium carrying three crown princes and five kings, including the Prince of Wales. When the Indians attacked the stage, Buffalo Bill himself came riding to its rescue, as always.

Richard Slotkin, author of the 1992 book *Gunfighter Nation: The Myth of the Frontier in Twentieth-Century America,* contends that from 1885 to 1905, Cody's "Wild West" "was the most important commercial vehicle for the fabrication and transmission of the Myth of the Frontier. It reached large audiences in every major city and innumerable smaller ones throughout the United States. The period of its European triumph coincided with the period of massive immigration to America. As many immigrants testified, the 'Wild West' was the source of some of their most vivid images and expectations of the new land."

Undoubtedly, the show also persuaded many Americans and immigrants that the gun was central to the building of America. The proliferation of guns on and among the actors would alone have made the point, but Cody's showbill addressed the matter directly in a discussion titled "The Rifle as an Aid to Civilization." "The bullet," the program declared, "is the pioneer of civilization, for it has gone hand in hand with the axe that cleared the forest, and with the family Bible and school book. Deadly as has been its mission in one sense, it has been merciful in another; for without the rifle ball we of America would not be to-day in the possession of a free and united country, and mighty is our strength."

Buffalo Bill and his contemporaries the dime novelists, pulp writers, and overly enthusiastic reporters also assisted in myth manufacturing in a more indirect, but possibly more significant way. They provided the plots that Hollywood would soon use to relay and reinforce the distortions of myth, among them the notion that when all else fails, a gun can save us. From the earliest days of the film industry, movie directors recognized the lasting appeal of the frontier. In 1903, Edwin S. Porter made *The Great Train Robbery*, considered the first western and an important precursor of modern narrative cinema. It was an immediate success, imitations quickly followed, and within five years the western became an established genre. The real frontier, however, was left further and further behind.

By 1925, William Hart had vividly established the good badman as a film archetype. Next came Tom Mix, who perhaps did the true West the gravest injustice by inventing the fancy cowboy with his tailored clothes, silver-inlaid boots, diamond-studded spurs, and pearl-handled Colt six-guns. No one ever walked into Tombstone, Arizona, in the late nineteenth century wearing such clothes, yet after Mix's death in a car crash in 1940 a plaque was installed at the crash site that read: "In Memory of Tom Mix, Whose Spirit Left His Body on This Spot and Whose Characterizations and Portrayals in Life Served Better to Fix Memories of the Old West in the Minds of Living Man."

The popularity of westerns rose steeply through the 1920s, then alternately rose and fell until the end of World War II when Hollywood revived the genre once again, this time with a vengeance. Fourteen feature-length westerns appeared in 1947; more than twice that number appeared in 1948. Forty-six westerns debuted in 1956 alone. All to some extent reinforced the notion that guns tamed the frontier. Some westerns did so by casting guns as central protagonists, as in *Colt .45, Springfield Rifle, Winchester '73*, and of course, *The Gun That Won the West*.

Others portrayed gun violence as the only effective course of action against evil, as in George Stevens's 1953 blockbuster, *Shane*. In the movie, Alan Ladd plays a gunfighter who rides into the middle of a conflict between homesteaders and the local cattle baron and soon takes the side of the homesteaders. Marian, the lead female character, played by Jean Arthur, loathes violence and guns. But Shane tells her, "A gun is just a tool, Marian. It's as good or as bad as the man that uses it." In Shane's hand, clearly, the gun is a force for good. The underlying message, writes Richard Slotkin, is that "'a good man with a gun' is in every sense the best of men—an armed redeemer who is the sole vindicator of the 'liberties of the people,' the 'indispensable man' in the quest for progress."

The barrage of Hollywood westerns was soon matched, if not exceeded, by television westerns, which conveyed the same message, but now on a weekly basis. In 1959, the networks broadcast twenty-eight different series westerns, or 570 hours of imaginary frontier history, the equivalent of four hundred movies. And we loved them. In 1959, eight of the ten most highly rated shows were westerns.

Many of the TV westerns gave guns star billing, among them "Restless Gun," "The Rifleman," "Yancy Derringer," "Have Gun Will Travel," and "Colt .45," whose theme song week after week reinforced the mythic role firearms played in establishing the nation:

> There was a gun that won the West,
> There was a man among the rest,
> Faster than any gun or man alive,
> A lightnin' bolt when he drew his Colt .45.

One direct impact of all this fabrication was the kindling of a desire among many gun owners to experience the myth in some small way, sometimes with drastic and lethal effect. A growing number of gun owners now strap on low-slung holsters and participate in quick-draw competitions and "Cowboy Shoots." An advertisement in the July 1993 issue of the NRA's *American Rifleman* offered a $169.95 frontier-style holster called The Laredoan. Firearms manufacturers market guns to fill such holsters. In the "Wyatt Earp" TV series, which debuted in 1955, Hugh O'Brian, playing Earp, carried a long-barreled Buntline Colt, named for Ned Buntline, the dime novelist. Colt had halted production of the gun, but demand ignited by the Earp series prompted the company to reintroduce it. In 1982, Colt again merged fact and myth when it produced a "John Wayne–American Legend" commemorative edition of the Colt Peacemaker, complete with a gold-inlaid engraving of the actor's face. In 1992, Colt introduced a new .44-caliber revolver, the Colt Anaconda. The gun embodied a modern design, but Colt nonetheless linked the gun to the company's frontier heritage. The headline read: "The Legend Lives, Larger Than Ever."

The master at marketing guns that evoke the Old West, however, is Sturm, Ruger & Co. of Southport, Connecticut. In 1953 its founder and chief executive, William Ruger, sensing that the advent of Hollywood and TV westerns signaled a marketing opportunity, introduced a line of single-action revolvers intended to resemble the old Colt Peacemaker, which Colt at the time no longer produced. Ruger sold 1.5 million of the guns. But the company had made them too authentic, to the point of retaining the old Colt's propensity to fire when dropped. Sturm, Ruger halted production of the guns in 1973 when it introduced a line of similar revolvers equipped with a safety device to prevent such accidents. By mid-1993, however, the old guns had been linked to accidental firings that had injured more than six hundred men, women, and children, killing at least forty.

One case merged present and past, myth and reality. In the autumn of 1979, a young woman named Kelly Nix set out from Phoenix, Arizona, and headed for Tombstone to take part in the city's annual "Helldorado Days," a celebration of the city's history. She was accompanied by her sister and her sister's boyfriend. They stopped at a motel in Tucson. The boyfriend had brought his Ruger single-action revolver—the early version without the new safety device—and for reasons no one can explain was carrying the gun by the holster belt inside the motel room. The gun fell from its holster just as Nix emerged from the bathroom. The gun fired; the bullet struck her heart and killed her.

Ruger continues to introduce new guns intended for the same Wild West market. In 1993, for example, Ruger introduced the Ruger Vaquero, a single-action revolver resembling the Colt Peacemaker. Its 1993 catalog said the gun was "sure to be a hit with traditionalists and participants in Old West action shoots."

Practicing for these action shoots can be profoundly hazardous. A report in Ruger's product-liability log captures in a few terse words a lethal side effect of frontier mythology. A Canadian man had shot himself to death with a Ruger frontier-style revolver while twirling the gun and practicing quick draw. The log entry reads: "He was found with a western-style quick-draw holster around his waist and a stopwatch in his hand in front of a full-length mirror."

How do we measure the deeper, psychic impact of a century's worth of myth building? "It is quite impossible to conceive the cultural imagery which 'Gunsmoke' and its dozens of imitators have created," wrote historian Frank Prassel. "Impact must be measured in tens of billions of viewer hours on an international scope, for such series are broadcast throughout the world in many languages. Yet it is here rather than in fact that the American derives his typical impression of the West."

Guns and violence were integral components of all film and TV westerns. ". . . Since the western offers itself as a myth of American origins," Richard Slotkin observed, "it implies that its violence is an essential and necessary part of the process through which American society was established and through which its democratic values are defended and enforced."

The seamless barrage of dime novels, movies, and television conflated guns with history. In this milieu, any attempt to regulate the free flow of guns becomes nothing less than an effort to repudiate history. In 1970, historian Richard Hofstadter framed the central enigma of America's enthusiasm for guns: "In some measure our gun culture owes its origins to the needs of an agrarian society and to the dangers and terrors of the frontier, but for us the central question must be why it has survived into an age in which only about 5 percent of the population makes its living from farming and from which the frontier has long since gone. Why did the United States, alone among modern industrial societies, cling to the idea that the widespread substantially unregulated availability of guns among its city populations is an acceptable and a safe thing?"

The best answer is a question: How could we possibly have done otherwise?

◆ ◆ ◆

Gun manufacturers have little interest in saving lives, although they struggle to convey the image that they are the last defenders of hearth and home, that their guns will stand by you long after marauding gangs force the police into retreat. To imagine such beneficial purpose is to confuse corporate image with corporate imperative. The domestic gun industry, despite its privileged status as the least regulated of consumer-product industries, sold so many guns in America that it saturated the market and now must scramble for ways to open new markets. The industry relies on Paxton Quigley, and other outspoken sales promoters, including gun writers and the leadership of the National Rifle Association, to make guns more palatable to a society that reads daily of gunshot death and injury.

There is ample proof of the industry's disregard for the health and safety of its customers. In a time when even children's vitamins have childproof caps and electric drills have safety triggers, gun manufacturers still do not manufacture child-safe guns. Likewise, most manufacturers still fail to equip their handguns with loading indicators and magazine safeties. Sturm, Ruger & Co. has yet to order a formal recall of its original Peacemaker look-alikes, even though some 1.3 million remain in the hands of consumers. Instead of launching a campaign to buy back the guns, or even to publicize their real dangers, Ruger launched an advertising campaign that bemoaned the national decay of gun-handling practices and told customers the right way to handle the guns. An Alaska jury was so incensed by Ruger's apparent disregard for safety, it voted a $2.9 million punitive-damages award against the company. The Alaska Supreme Court later limited the award to $500,000.

There is evidence too that manufacturers don't see crime as being an entirely negative phenomenon. Why else would the now-defunct Charter Arms Co. engrave the barrels of a brace of husband-and-wife revolvers with the names Bonnie and Clyde?

The gun industry has long contended that only a small percentage of guns are used in crime, while at the same time resisting efforts to document the true number and to identify the most popular crime guns by maker, model, and caliber. As of 1989, rather late in the computer revolution, the Bureau of Alcohol, Tobacco and Firearms at last became able to provide some rudimentary statistics on which guns turned up most often in federal traces. Reports from the new database have already battered the NRA's "guns don't kill" stance, proving beyond doubt that certain guns turn up during the commission of crime far more often than others. The company whose handguns were traced most often from January of 1990 to December of 1991, simply because of the sheer magnitude of its production, was giant Smith & Wesson. However, when the frequency of traces is compared with each company's production, S.W. Daniel, the company that made Nicholas Elliot's gun, shows a tracing rate far higher. By 1989 the company had produced some 60,500 handguns and an untold number of accessories, including silencers and machine-gun kits. It fondly advertised Nicholas's gun, the Cobray M-11/9, as "the gun that made the eighties roar."

Condemned by police, ridiculed even by those who sell it, the gun has been inordinately controversial ever since its initial design by Gordon Ingram, a California engineer and gunsmith who sought to make a cheap, reliable submachine gun for close military combat. How that gun went on to become a readily available mass-consumer product—something S.W. Daniel once even gave away free in a monthly contest—provides a clear example of the culture of nonresponsibility at work in America's firearms industry. It is but one example of how this commercial ethos governed the gun's progress from conception to its use as a murder weapon in a Virginia Beach classroom.

"We've got technology running amok," said Col. Leonard Supenski, the Baltimore County firearms expert. "No gun manufacturer ever decided in its R-and-D process that the product it was developing might not have any useful purpose for society and might in fact harm society. When Gordon Ingram began production and eventually tried to get into the commercial market, I'm sure the thought never entered his mind. The people at SWD don't give a damn who gets those guns."

CHAPTER FOUR

NICHOLAS

ON FRIDAY, DECEMBER 16, 1988, NICHOLAS Elliot awoke feeling ill. He had an ear infection and was taking medication for it, but that did not account for his malaise. He had made big plans for the day, and suddenly those plans seemed too big. The anxiety sickened him. "I didn't feel like going to school," he told Detective Adams. "But I knew I would get in trouble if I didn't, so I went. . . . I was just so sick."

He planned to bring his gun to school for the express purpose of scaring Billy Cutter, his tormentor, and at last getting some respect. He had bought the gun two months before, a Cobray M-11/9 semiautomatic pistol capable of firing thirty-two rounds before requiring the shooter to reload. His mother did not know about his acquisition. Nicholas told Adams he had hidden the gun in a bird cage, but Adams believed he probably kept it in his attic.

"I was scared," Nicholas told the detective, "because I didn't know how I would feel with a gun at school."

He packed his backpack and caught his usual bus. He attended the first of his classes. "I was looking for him from the beginning," Nicholas said. "I wasn't angry . . . I wanted to scare him, to make him see how much of a wimp he was in front of everyone."

During Nicholas's ride to school, the knowledge of what he carried in his backpack and what he could do with it deeply frightened him. "I was scared," he said. "I was looking for Billy, but I also was scared."

At one point, he considered abandoning his mission. He could not find the boy and was surprised at the fear he felt walking around school with a gun. "I was kind of thinking about just hiding the gun and getting it later on . . . take it home and just leave it."

"Just forget the whole thing?" Adams prompted.

"Well, sort of, yeah, I mean, I wasn't planning to shoot them."

Briefly he had imagined an alternative means of getting back at Billy Cutter. "I was thinking about having someone do something to him. Well, like, you know, beat him up and teach him not to pick on people. Just do something to him, you know. I wanted to scare him. That's what I really wanted to do."

CHAPTER FIVE

THE GUN

THE BALTIMORE COUNTY POLICE SHOOTING RANGE occupies a wooded area just north of Towson, Maryland, where the broad six-lane strip roads of Baltimore city taper to rolling two-lane highways. I heard the range the moment I stepped from my car, the sound like something you would get if you put a microphone beside a package of microwave popcorn in midpop. The range was a flat plane carved from a hillside so as to leave an earthen cliff at one end, which serves as a backstop to keep stray rounds from bounding north into Baltimore County horse country. Colonel Supenski arrived carrying a gray attaché case and led me onto the range where a group of county corrections officers was undergoing pistol training. He asked their instructor to have the group stand down for a few minutes, even though he and I were headed for the far end of the range roughly one hundred yards away. His caution was a measure of the deep respect police officers have for the quirky dangers of bullets and guns. During my pursuit of Nicholas Elliot's gun, I often observed a subtle dance that law-enforcement people do whenever an amateur in their midst handles a gun, whether the gun is loaded or not. As the gun shifts, they shift, but ever so slightly in an instinctive, drilled-in twitch meant to ensure that if an imaginary line were drawn outward from the muzzle, it would never intersect their bodies.

Supenski occupies an at-times uncomfortable position in the gun debate. On the one hand, he is a big fan of guns. I accompanied him to a gun show in Westminster, Maryland, one Sunday morning. Despite his constant contact with guns he still could not resist handling some of the handguns we encountered, especially the old collector's guns and the "tricked out" competition guns with their scopes, compensators, and hand-checked grips. "I grew up in the era of the B westerns," he told me. "Loved them, still love them. My single most prized possession is an original Colt single-action 'cowboy' gun. Nickel-plated, hand-engraved, ivory stock." But the Colonel, as everybody calls him, also believes in reasonable controls to force a heightened level of responsibility in the sale and use of firearms. This has not won him many friends among the gunslingers of America. He received a lot of sober stares from dealers at the gun show. One pro-gun group twice threatened to kill him, prompting a mischievous female assistant to don a bulletproof vest before joining him for lunch. "If I want to go sit behind the wheel of a fifteen-foot powerboat, I've got to get certified," Supenski said. "I've got to go through a nine-week course, take a take-home exam, and have a natural-resources exam, and go through every conceivable aspect of safe boating—to sit behind the wheel of a boat." He pointed to a handgun. "To buy one of those I don't have to do squat. Now you tell me that's sane."

His is a pragmatic stance. He worries that irresponsible behavior by gun dealers, manufacturers, and the National Rifle Association may soon lead to truly restrictive controls well beyond the simple, yet crucial, regulations sought by moderate gun-control proponents, such as the 1993 Brady law's mandatory waiting period and background checks. "My concern as a person who enjoys the shooting sports is that unless some reason comes in, things will get worse, and when that happens, those three million people in the NRA are going to find out what the *fifteen* million in the AARP [American Association of Retired Persons] are all about. Right now the other side hasn't been mobilized."

He considers the Cobray pistol made by S.W. Daniel Inc., and the means by which Nicholas Elliot came to own it, a study in irresponsibility in the gun marketplace, and he testified to that effect. The gun, he argues, serves no useful purpose—certainly none of the purposes traditionally cited by the gun camp when opposing new controls. It's not useful for hunting, Supenski said. "First of all, you couldn't use it to hunt. Most states have a limit on magazine capacity for hunting, three to five rounds. [The Cobray has a thirty-two-round magazine.] Second, most states have a minimum-caliber rule—clearly nine millimeter is not something you would use. It's too big a cartridge to be used to hunt small game, it's too small to hunt big game."

Nor is the Cobray a target gun. Its two-inch barrel sharply reduces accuracy. It is a clumsy, heavy weapon, prone to rock up and down when fired. "It's almost impossible to shoot one-handed, except at point-blank distances," Supenski said. "It is a *hands* gun, plural, because you need both hands to employ it effectively. About the only thing you can do with it is hold it someplace in front of you, pull the trigger as fast as you can, put as many bullets out as you can, and hope like hell they'll hit something. Now that may be nice on a battlefield. It isn't so nice in an urban environment where that bullet may go through your bedroom into your child's bedroom or into your neighbor's bedroom, or may go outside and kill a passerby."

Supenski opened his attaché case. Inside, against a thick layer of foam, was a Cobray pistol and a magazine packed with gleaming nine-millimeter cartridges. His department had confiscated the gun during an arrest; it was the same gun he had brought with him to Virginia Beach to show the jury in a civil trial against the dealer who sold a Cobray to Nicholas. He passed it to me.

Black, functional, it had none of the gleaming machined beauty of more expensive weapons. It was a brick of black steel with a pistol grip jutting from the center of its bottom face and a tiny barrel protruding from the front. To cock it, you need a good deal of strength. You pull back a black knob on top, which forces the bolt against a spring. When you pull the trigger, the bolt springs forward, stripping a fresh cartridge from the magazine and firing it. The pressure of the gases released from the cartridge forces the bolt backward, ejecting the now-empty cartridge case. An internal mechanism prevents the bolt from automatically coming forward and holds it cocked for the next shot. The gun's ancestor was a submachine pistol, in which the bolt would immediately leap forward after each shot to fire a new round, repeating the process over and over at incredible speeds until the magazine was emptied or the shooter released the trigger.

It was undeniably, if darkly, appealing in its lethality. It was heavy, the weight of a six-pack of beer. Its grip had none of the warm, close-fitting contours of more costly guns, such as the expensive Smith & Wesson nine-millimeter Supenski carried. I held the Cobray out in front of me with one hand and tried to "acquire" the sights—that is, to line up the sight at the rear with the stub of metal at the front. The bolt knob, which protruded from a point midway along the frame, made this virtually impossible. My arm sagged. The gun was cumbersome. As trite as it sounds, however, the gun did look evil. It was a Darth Vader among guns.

Its reputation matched the look. A 1989 study by the Cox Newspapers found that the pistol ranked fourth among assault guns most often traced by the Bureau of Alcohol, Tobacco and Firearms (ATF). A study of all guns confiscated in Detroit from January of 1989 through April of 1990 put the Cobray first among assault guns, fifth among all models—higher in the rankings than guns made by Beretta, whose production dwarfs that of the S.W. Daniel company. The head of ATF's Atlanta office told me early in 1992 that his agents conducted twenty to thirty traces involving S.W. Daniel guns each month.

The Cobray and its ancestors became the favorites of drug rings, street gangs, and assorted killers throughout the 1980s. Shortly after nine P.M. on June 18, 1984, a member of the Neo-Nazi Order used the Cobray's ancestor, an Ingram MAC-10 machine pistol, to assassinate Denver talk-show host Alan Berg as he stepped from his car. Within seconds Berg suffered a devastating array of bullet wounds—thirty-four entry and exit wounds in all from a dozen .45-caliber bullets that crushed one eye, destroyed his brain, and caused massive injuries throughout his upper body. During a sweeping investigation of the Order, federal agents seized eight MACs and MAC successors. Later, on April 15, 1988, another member of the Order allegedly used a nine-millimeter MAC, converted to full auto, to kill a Missouri state trooper.

A note on terminology is in order here. A machine gun fires rifle-caliber bullets; a submachine gun fires pistol calibers. Both are fully automatic or "full-auto" weapons, meaning that they continue to fire for as long as you pull the trigger. The MAC-10, therefore, is a fully automatic submachine gun. The Cobray, which closely mimics the MAC-10 and is often described as a MAC, is a semiautomatic. A semiautomatic fires one round per pull. That the term *automatic* is sometimes applied to a pistol like the Colt Army .45 confuses the issue. When used to describe a pistol, *automatic* is simply the short form of "automatic reloading," which means the gun uses the explosive force of each cartridge to load and cock itself after each shot. Such pistols are in fact semiautomatics.

The popular TV series "Miami Vice" fanned interest in the MAC family of weapons. "It slices, it dices," one character said as he used a MAC to shred two female mannequins that had been chained to a wall. In March 1989, a Colorado man used a MAC-11 (a smaller cousin to the MAC-10) to kill two women and wound two deputies. The same month, Modesto, California, police arrested Albert E. Gulart, Jr., for illegal possession of explosives and found he possessed a semiautomatic variant registered to his half brother, Patrick Purdy. Two months earlier, Purdy had killed five children and wounded thirty others when he sprayed a Stockton schoolyard with an AKS rifle, a semiautomatic version of the AK-47. While investigating Purdy's background, Stockton detectives paid Gulart a call in Modesto. The investigators said Gulart told them that before the schoolyard shootings he and Purdy had planned to kill at random a member of the Modesto police force. Gulart, according to the police account, also made a chillingly cryptic remark: "Patrick was successful in what he did, and I have a hard time driving by any school." Although unsure just exactly what Gulart meant, Modesto police began round-the-clock surveillance, which led to the explosives arrest.

Six months later, Joseph T. Wesbecker packed himself a small arsenal, including two Cobray pistols, and marched into a Louisville, Kentucky, printing plant where he killed eight people and wounded twelve. Wesbecker never used the Cobrays, according to the Louisville homicide detective in charge of the case; he carried them in a gym bag, which he tucked under a stairway apparently because the bag interfered with his ability to handle the AK-47 he used in the shootings.

In February 1990 the Cobray came up for review by Maryland's Handgun Roster Board, which had been created by legislation designed to restrict the sale of Saturday night specials. The S.W. Daniel handgun passed muster, but only because of the law's strict limits on what characteristics can allow the board to ban a gun. Cornelius J. Behan, then chief of the Baltimore County police and a member of the board, found himself forced to vote for the gun. "It's a terrible killing instrument that has no business meeting quality standards. But our law . . . doesn't cover that weapon." The day before, Behan had appeared in a full-page ad in the Sunday New York Times paid for by Handgun Control Inc. holding the gun under a bold headline that asked, "Who Goes Hunting With a MAC-11?" The third speaker, Elmer H. Tippet, also a board member and at the time head of the Maryland State Police, said he "echoed" Behan's assessment. "I certainly question the legitimacy of a weapon like that for sporting or self-defense or anything else, but as the law is written I have no alternative other than to vote what the law says I must do, and that's what I will do." The gun joined the twelve hundred other handguns on the roster.

The list of killings involving MACs and Cobrays continued to grow; the crimes often achieved national notoriety.

At about midnight, September 27, 1990, an Iranian immigrant named Mehrdad Dashti fired into a popular bar in Berkeley, California, with a Cobray and two other weapons. He killed a university senior, then began a seven-hour standoff during which he wounded four other students. He was shot dead by a police SWAT team. California had outlawed the Cobray in 1989.

In May 1990 police in Vancouver, British Columbia, became profoundly alarmed after discovering three MAC submachine guns in six weeks. One officer predicted that soon a police officer or bystander would be injured or killed by such weapons. "They're a recipe for disaster," he told the Vancouver Sun.

His remarks were prophetic. On October 20, 1991, a Chinese immigrant, Chin Wa Chung, humiliated by the failure of a restaurant he had opened with his partner, Sheng Cheung, went to Cheung's Vancouver house early one morning and used a Cobray M-11/9 to kill Cheung, Cheung's wife, their seven-year-old son, and their fourteen-month-old baby before at last killing himself.

The same month a disgruntled ex–postal worker named Joseph M. Harris walked into the Ridgewood, New Jersey, post office clad in battle fatigues, a bulletproof vest, and a black silk face mask and shot and killed two of his former colleagues. Earlier he had stabbed his former supervisor to death at her home after first killing the woman's boyfriend with a single gunshot to the head as the man sat watching television comfortably nestled under a blanket. Harris carried two fully automatic weapons: an Uzi and a MAC-10.

The Cobray was involved in an odd lot of other incidents. In 1991, New York City police were astonished to find that the sniper who had just barely missed hitting a clerical worker in a Bronx office building was a nine-year-old boy wielding a Cobray. Asked how he learned to operate the gun, the boy answered, "I watch a lot of TV." The following year, in Denver, a sixteen-year-old boy used a Cobray M-11/9 to kill a fifteen-year-old with whom he had argued a few moments earlier. His mother, involved in a live-in relationship with a Denver police officer, had bought the boy the gun. "She's certainly guilty of not having good sense," a Denver police spokesman told the *Denver Post,* "but that's not a criminal act."

The Cobray and its MAC progenitors became icons of America's inner-city gun culture. A Baltimore rapper called himself MAC-10, although when his group posed fully armed for a photograph, he held a .45 semiautomatic pistol with a laser sight. He was later shot and seriously wounded. Another member of his group was arrested for allegedly ordering the murder of a teenager; a third member was shot dead at a phone booth. At least two gangs, one each in Las Vegas and Jacksonville, Arkansas, also took the name MAC-10. Detailed renderings of the weapon periodically turn up in gang graffiti in Baton Rouge, Louisiana. In 1992, police in Indianapolis, as a warning to the city's officers, posted rap lyrics written by a local group:

Let me get my toys and play
Sit down mother fucker, and watch the MAC-10 spray
Better close up shop
Cause we teaching Indy how to kill a cop.

The best evidence of the admiration accorded the killing power of these guns by would-be felons came late in 1992 when Drug Enforcement Administration (DEA) agents in Boston videotaped a conversation between Edward Gaeta, a Massachusetts man suspected of conspiring to deal narcotics, and a DEA agent posing as a Colombian drug trafficker. Gaeta had previously arranged the sale of two MAC-10 submachine guns complete with silencers to a DEA informant and hinted that he could get more.

"I'll make it up like a story," he told the agent. "Once upon a time, one week ago . . . I saw some MAC-10s go by with silencers on them. . . . That's a nice, that's an interesting weapon."

"Very!" the agent said.

"With subsonic bullets. It sounds like a cat pissing."

The dream guns "were beautiful," Gaeta said. "You'll go through your whole clip in, ah, one and a half seconds. Thirty-two rounds. And I'll tell you what, I could kill thirteen people in the bathroom and you wouldn't even know I had it."

In Towson, Maryland, Supenski hefted the Cobray he had brought in his briefcase. "When you look at the utility or purpose for those weapons as balanced against the potential harm they can do to society, to the police who have to protect society and to the public themselves," Supenski said, "the risks far outweigh the benefits. If there was a gun industry with a conscience—if there was a gun industry out there that would understand that even though they have a right to make these things and put them into the commercial mainstream, it may not be the right thing to do—we wouldn't be here talking about this issue, and gun dealers wouldn't be selling these things legally or illegally."

Where did the Cobray come from? How did this weapon, designed for use in close combat by commandos, paratroopers, tankers, and, yes, Latin American guerrillas on a tight budget, become a mass consumer product?

◆ ◆ ◆

The gun's direct lineage begins in the stormy 1960s when Gordon Ingram, an engineer with Police Ordnance Co. of Los Angeles, paid a visit to an illegal machine-gun company operated by a friend and former colleague named Juan Erquiaga Azicorbe, a former officer of the Peruvian Army who had emigrated to America. Erquiaga was struggling to fill an order for five hundred machine guns of his own design and five hundred silencers for anti-Castro exiles training in Costa Rica. During this visit, according to Thomas Nelson, an authority on the history of machine pistols (ATF technicians often consult his dictionary-size volumes), Erquiaga explained the qualities his rebel customers demanded of a gun. According to Nelson these qualities included "small size, to facilitate concealment; sound suppression, to deter detection; and low cost."

Ingram saw a way to improve on Erquiaga's gun and built the first prototype, the M10, which looked very much the way the Cobray M-11/9 looks today. About this time, according to Thomas, Erquiaga hired Ingram to be his chief engineer and to help speed production of the Cuban order.

The United States had given Erquiaga's effort tacit approval, granting him the necessary tax stamp to make machine guns despite the fact that until that point he had been making machine guns illegally and, on a previous occasion, had fled the country just ahead of a federal raid on a machine-gun factory he ran in his garage. The political winds shifted again, however, and in 1965 federal agents swept down on Erquiaga and confiscated all the weapons he had produced for the Cubans. Erquiaga, however, managed to escape to South America.

Ingram continued refining his ideas and developed several more prototypes, all having essentially the same look. The Army bought one and tested it at the Frankford Arsenal in Philadelphia. Soon afterward, the gun caught the eye of an Atlanta soldier of fortune, Mitchell L. WerBell III, founder of the Sionics Co., which made "counterinsurgency" equipment and an efficient silencer. WerBell, who wore a uniform of his own design and called himself an "international general," bought a nine-millimeter prototype of Ingram's machine gun and took it with him on a sales trip to Southeast Asia. In 1969 Ingram left his job as an engineer for Fairchild Hiller to become chief engineer at Sionics, which was by then based in Powder Springs, Georgia, just outside Atlanta, where WerBell established a paramilitary training camp. To best capitalize on Ingram's designs, WerBell and Ingram decided to produce two weapons: an open-bolt fully automatic machine pistol for military markets, restricted for sale to civilians since the National Firearms Act of 1934, and an unrestricted semiautomatic version for civilian buyers—the first glimmer of the weapon's emergence as a mass-consumer product.

From 1969 through 1970, WerBell and Ingram took the military version of their machine pistol on the road, demonstrating it to U.S. authorities at Forts Benning, Gordon, and Belvoi and at the Quantico Marine Base. (Historian Nelson notes that military policemen at Fort Gordon even fired Ingram's pistol on full-auto underwater in the base swimming pool.)

The gun attracted enough interest to convince a group of New York investors that it might replace the standard .45 pistol as the military sidearm of choice. The investors, acting as Quantum Corp., renamed the company Military Armament Corp. from which the acronym MAC derives. It was not a match made in heaven. Within a year Quantum had ousted WerBell and Ingram from their jobs as manager and chief engineer. Conflict between the investors and the founders grew; the company suffered production delays and had difficulty raising money.

About the only good news was a welcome burst of free publicity from none other than John Wayne himself, in his starring role as Lon McQ in *McQ*, a 1974 movie about a tough Seattle police detective who sets out to solve the murder of a colleague, only to discover the colleague was involved with a notorious drug ring. It was *McQ*, according to ATF officials, that put the Ingram in the public eye and made it the gun most favored by America's drug gangs—although ironically the bad guys in the movie used only revolvers and shotguns, mere toys compared to the arsenals deployed by today's drug cartels.

The company could not have hoped for a better advertisement. At one point big Lon McQ visits the shop of a gun dealer he knows. The screenwriter wasted little energy on subtlety in introducing the weapon.

"Hey, Lon," the dealer says, "what are you doing?"

McQ offers a wry grin. "Buyin' a gun."

"Got a minute? I got somethin' I want to show you out back."

McQ lumbers after him into the back room of the gun shop

where a small shooting range is conveniently equipped with a water-filled garbage can raised on two sawhorses.

"Lon," the dealer says, "I have a little equalizer here. We're going to try to sell it to the department." He holds up the gun. With an unmistakable touch of reverence, he says, "The Ingram."

"The Ingram, huh?"

"Nine millimeter," adds a gunsmith seated nearby. For some reason the gunsmith is wearing a white lab coat, about as alien to most gun shops as an autographed photo of James Brady.

McQ hefts the gun. "Six or seven pounds?"

"Six point two five," the gunsmith says. He screws on a silencer. "Silencer makes a good handle."

"Lon," the dealer says, "this can here is filled with water. Go on. Squeeze off a burst."

"Why not?" McQ says.

McQ blasts away, filling the can full of holes as water spurts from all sides. The camera cuts to McQ's face and an expression that comes as close to awe as John Wayne could muster.

McQ looks down at the gun. He looks back at the pail.

"How about that?" the dealer says. "Those thirty-two slugs came out in a second and a half."

Ruggedly, slowly, McQ says, "Yeah."

"You ever see anything like it?" the dealer asks.

McQ, who by now has quit the police force in order to work the case more efficiently, walks off with the gun without paying a penny or signing a single document. (Doing so anywhere but in a movie would constitute an immediate felony.) He uses it later to mow down a band of dope dealers and grind their car to steel mulch. Afterward, of course, he gets his badge back from a grateful department. True to the traditions of cinematic gunplay, no one asks about the gun or the corpses strewn over a Pacific beach.

Just in case anyone in the audience had any doubt about where to buy this wondrous weapon, Warner Brothers provided a full-screen credit that read, "Special Weapon: Military Armament Corp."

This enthusiastic bit of advertising wasn't enough to save the company, however. Military Armament Corp. filed for Chapter 11 protection under federal bankruptcy laws in mid-1975, without ever having produced a semiautomatic Ingram for the general consumer. The remains of the company, including ten thousand submachine guns and two thousand silencers, were sold at auction, most to a group of investors who had formed another Atlanta company called RPB Industries Inc. They too planned to bring Ingram's weapons to full-scale commercial production, but in 1978 sold out to yet another group of investors, this one headed by Wayne Daniel, the son of a Georgia minister.

◆ ◆ ◆

Under Wayne Daniel, RPB had more success selling the Ingram line and by mid-1979 had made sales of varying amounts to some twenty countries, including seven Latin American nations, the United Kingdom, Saudia Arabia, and Israel. An operating manual for the RPB version of the Ingram M10 came in a camouflage cover and, on its first page, noted how "the compact size of the M10 makes it especially suitable for tank crews, gun and mortar crews, etc." The manual also displayed a range of available accessories, including the RPB "Operational Briefcase," an attaché case packed with a silenced M10 that could be fired with the gun still in the case. A business card inserted in a card holder on the side of the case obscured the muzzle.

"Looks like an ordinary briefcase with your calling card in front," the manual reads. "However, this case contains the world's deadliest submachine gun, ready for action." The blurb noted that anyone who bought the briefcase would have to register it with ATF, which had classed it as an "assassination device."

Under Wayne Daniel and his partners, the new RPB faced an array of business obstacles not typically included in the syllabi at Harvard Business School. One partner was convicted of bribing a prosecutor to drop a client's drug charge. Two others, Robert Morgan and John "Jack" Leibolt, got involved in the narcotics smuggling operations of Pablo Escobar-Gaviria and the Medellín Cartel. Morgan was convicted in 1979 for smuggling two tons of marijuana into Florida and was sentenced to thirty years in prison. Leibolt, according to a sweeping 1989 indictment of the Medellín Cartel, once piloted a plane for the cartel and, in September 1979, supplied the group with six silencer-equipped machine guns. (He pleaded guilty in August of 1990 to conspiracy to import cocaine.)

Despite all this, RPB succeeded in at last transforming the Ingram from a limited-circulation military weapon into a semiautomatic handgun for general use. Previously, the company had been restricted to selling its full-auto Ingram variations only through dealers specially licensed to sell machine guns, who in turn—if they followed the law—sold them only to buyers who had undergone an ATF background investigation and paid $200 for the necessary tax stamp. Now, however, any adult with a clean record could buy an Ingram look-alike, even a mock silencer to go with it. "It became available everywhere," said Earl Taylor, a twenty-one-year ATF veteran who retired to become a vice president with Norred & Associates, an Atlanta security concern that as of 1992 counted among its varied assignments the protection of Kroger supermarkets and ex-colonel Oliver North. "All gun shops everywhere were selling it. Everywhere. The distribution of it became widespread."

Taylor is a tall, lean man whose courtly manner and slow, easy way of speaking suggest quiet authority. Over the years he came to know RPB and its successor, S.W. Daniel, intimately, first as resident agent-in-charge of ATF's Rome, Georgia, office, later as supervisor of criminal investigation in the agency's Atlanta office. He deployed undercover agents to order the guns from illegal suppliers. Demand was so high, they had to wait for delivery, Taylor recalled. "It was a hot item."

What made the gun particularly popular was its internal design, a delight to anyone interested in skirting federal restrictions on ownership of machine guns. "ATF was concerned because those damn weapons were so easily converted to full-automatic fire," Taylor said.

"An individual could convert one in a minute or two, or maybe even less time than that." ("In seconds," said another retired ATF agent familiar with the guns.)

All a buyer had to do was file down a small metal catch—the "trip"—that caught the bolt after each shot, thereby leaving the bolt free to spring forward and fire machine-gun style. Demand for the guns soared nationwide, and black markets formed as middlemen, including one Georgia policeman, bought large quantities, converted the guns, and resold them to the drug underworld. These weapons triggered the arms race that today confronts law-enforcement officers across the nation.

In October 1981, Wayne Daniel married a striking Alabama woman named Sylvia Williams. In November, Sylvia, and Wayne's son from a previous marriage, Wayne "Buddy" Daniel, became members of RPB's board of directors. Sylvia would soon prove a feisty, outspoken opponent of ATF, bent on pushing the limits of the law in the name of the Second Amendment and free enterprise, at no small cost to society at large. She and Wayne made no secret of their loyalties. At one point, they produced little plastic badges that read BATF SUCKS.

◆ ◆ ◆

By the autumn of 1981, Wayne Daniel found himself struggling against increasing pressure from the FBI, ATF, and the Georgia Bureau of Investigation, as all three agencies investigated the activities of John Leibolt, by now one of RPB's three shareholders. (The other two shareholders were Wayne Daniel and Leibolt's son.) ATF threatened to pull the federal license that allowed RPB to make and sell guns—its Federal Firearms License—because of Leibolt's suspected criminal activities. Minutes of RPB's board meetings show that Leibolt's legal troubles had made it difficult for RPB to secure credit and, moreover, had left the company exposed to the threat of criminal charges.

In a special board meeting held December 14, 1981, Wayne, according to the minutes, denounced "the general irrepute that the association of Mr. Leibolt" had brought to the company. Because of John Leibolt's dabbling in the narcotics trade, Wayne said, he "personally did not want to be in business with either one of the Leibolts."

Two weeks later the board met again and resolved to buy back Leibolt's stock and thus sever his ties to the company. Leibolt, however, had fled Georgia. The minutes of RPB's January 20, 1982, board meeting noted that Leibolt "refuses to come to Atlanta and has stated he will not step foot in the State of Georgia due to fear of being arrested." The board resolved to liquidate the company.

ATF, meanwhile, classified RPB's semiautomatic Ingram as a machine gun, arguing it was so easy to convert that even in semiautomatic form it should fall under the far stricter regulations that governed the sale of automatic weapons. The ATF technical branch in Washington made a videotape to show just how easily a buyer could convert the gun.

RPB challenged the ATF decision. A federal judge backed the agency, but to reduce the fiscal hardship imposed on RPB by the ruling allowed the company time to continue manufacturing the weapon and selling off existing stocks. Any gun assembled before June 21, 1982, would be classed as a semiautomatic; the same gun made one day later would be a machine gun subject to federal restrictions.

This delay, a surprise bonus for RPB, provided another example of the willingness within our culture to overlook the inherent deadliness of guns. The threat of a ban boosted demand for the gun, and according to Earl Taylor, RPB accelerated production and sales. "They knew that weapon was going to be outlawed, they knew it was going to be worth a hell of a lot more money once you couldn't produce it anymore, so I guess it made sense to go for it."

June proved a profitable month for RPB. Gun consumers—far from being put off by the gun's lethal reputation and the ATF ruling—rushed to buy the last of the weapons before the deadline. The company's final after-tax profit doubled over that of May, for a profit margin—net income as a percentage of gross sales—of 37 percent.

The next month, with the ruling in effect, the company's net income plummeted to just one-sixteenth of the June total.

In September, the RPB board approved a final plan for liquidating the company; in October, an auction house sold its assets for half a million dollars.

A reasonable man might expect that at this point the gun, this weapon built to kill soldiers in close combat and adopted by dope peddlers and urban gangs, would be allowed to disappear from America's arsenal and consigned to Thomas Nelson's history books. But RPB Industries rose quickly from the tomb, this time as S.W. Daniel Inc., named for Sylvia Williams Daniel. After ATF's ruling the Daniels set out in earnest to develop a weapon that could be sold readily to the public. They succeeded—introducing by 1983 the Cobray M-11/9—but nonetheless continued sending prototype after prototype to the ATF technical branch in Washington, as if probing for holes in the law. Once, for example, they sent a prototype of what they claimed was a single-shot weapon. It was the same weapon that previously had been ruled a machine gun, but with a plate over the bottom of the grip where the magazine would otherwise be inserted. ATF, however, found that the plate could be removed and classified this weapon too as a machine gun.

The company also sold machine-gun "flats," stamped and notched pieces of steel that could be bent to form the frame, or "lower receiver," of a machine gun. Under federal law, a machine-gun receiver is treated as if it were a complete firearm. The flats, however, were legal, provided they were left unbent and certain holes were left undrilled. All a consumer had to do to commit an instant felony was to drill out a single hole—but that was the consumer's problem.

The Daniels knew their market well, said Earl Taylor. "I've always had a hunch that Wayne and Sylvia were not so much believers in all the pro-gun propaganda that goes on and that they so freely talk about, but that they were more interested in making money than anything else." Of Wayne, he said, "He's got a reputation for testing the waters, so to speak. He'll come close to the edge of the envelope—maybe not blatantly doing something illegal, but he's very anxious to test and see how far he can go in the weapons field."

Wayne's attitude, according to Taylor, made his products all the more attractive to gun buyers. "He can kind of feel the pulse of this gun culture out there and kind of say things and do things and market things that appeal to those people."

Indeed, far from embarking on a PR campaign to sweeten the gun's reputation, Sylvia and Wayne played up its bloody history, marketing the Cobray as "The Gun That Made the Eighties Roar."

The company's marketing ideology soon led it to begin a business venture that provides a case study in how powerless our society is to control the easy traffic in the tools of murder. This new venture would trigger a nationwide ATF investigation that exposed widespread illegal sales of weapons to neo-Nazis, the IRA, and assorted felons; exposed the illegal practices of federally licensed gun dealers; and resulted in the arrests of hundreds of the company's customers—yet left Sylvia, Wayne, and their corporation virtually unscathed.

◆ ◆ ◆

Wayne Daniel may have felt it a personal affront to work alongside John Leibolt, but he felt no such moral reluctance when in January 1983 he and Sylvia invited two men, Joseph Ledbetter and Travis Motes, to their home to make the men a proposition.

Ledbetter and Motes had installed air-conditioning in the RPB offices and had wired S.W. Daniel's corporate headquarters. The Daniels suggested that their two visitors diversify into the business of making the outer tubes for silencers. S.W. Daniel would make the interior parts. The two companies would advertise in the same gun publications and travel to the same gun shows. By selling only parts, both would stay on the right side of federal laws requiring registration of completed silencers. Indeed, no law barred the sale of silencer parts. In the eyes of the law, however, any consumer who accepted delivery of both internal parts and tubes would automatically possess a completed silencer—regardless of whether he put them together to produce a working silencer or not. If the consumer had not first acquired the ATF approval and tax stamp necessary to own a silencer, he would be guilty of a felony. But again, as far as S.W. Daniel was concerned, that was the consumer's worry.

Wayne Daniel went so far as to give Ledbetter and Motes a measuring gauge to guide them in fashioning the tubes, according to government affidavits. He also allowed them to use S.W. Daniel's slogan, "Silence is golden," which the Daniels had used to sell a line of completed silencers through *Shotgun News,* a thick tabloid containing only firearms advertising. Ledbetter and Motes founded L&M Guns and likewise began selling their tubes through *Shotgun News* and at gun shows around the country. The Daniels, meanwhile, began advertising their internal-parts kits and displaying them at the same gun shows. On at least one occasion, according to a statement by Ledbetter, the two companies found themselves facing each other across an aisle.

Details of this arrangement emerged in February 1984, when ATF agents received a tip from the sheriff's department in Mono County, California, that its officers had discovered silencers while searching the home of a Bridgeport, California, man named Frank Wedertz. Wedertz, who had not registered his silencers, told ATF he had bought them from a licensed gun dealer in Tehachapi, California. ATF agents then searched the dealer's home and found records indicating he had bought the components from L&M Guns and S.W. Daniel, had assembled the silencers, and then sold them. The dealer said he had seen ads for the parts in *Shotgun News* and had been able to assemble the completed silencers in minutes.

The investigation began gaining momentum. On April 27, 1984, ATF special agent Peter Urrea, posing as the president of the Widow Makers Motorcycle Club, telephoned L&M Guns. He first told the company's order taker that he had received kits containing the internal parts for a silencer from S.W. Daniel, then asked whether or not the parts would fit the L&M tubes. The operator assured him the S.W. Daniel parts would indeed fit. Urrea ordered three tubes. He also ordered machine-gun flats from S.W. Daniel and L&M.

On April 30, Agent Urrea called S.W. Daniel and ordered three sets of internal parts for silencers, one kit containing the operating mechanisms of an S.W. Daniel nine-millimeter machine gun, and one the frame flat. He expressed concern about the kinds of records S.W. Daniel kept, explaining that he was concerned because he had a criminal record. The company assured him it only kept shipping invoices.

Urrea also ordered a machine-gun flat from L&M Guns and persuaded Travis Motes to bend the frame for him. Motes mailed the shaped frame to Urrea. In the process, according to ATF documents, Motes violated provisions of the Gun Control Act of 1968 prohibiting any company from manufacturing a lower receiver without an ATF license. ATF charged, moreover, that by mailing the frame to California, moreover, Motes violated the act's provisions against shipping firearms across state lines directly to consumers. (Companies can sell guns to out-of-state residents by mail but must ship them first to a licensed dealer in the buyer's home state.) Urrea also asked Motes whether he could provide twenty-five more machine-gun kits with already-shaped flats so that he could make twenty-five machine guns and sell them to friends in South America. Motes said he might be able to accommodate him.

Urrea continued buying silencer parts and machine-gun kits from S.W. Daniel, L&M, and a third company, La Vista Armaments of Louisville, Kentucky, gradually building enough evidence to convince a federal judge to grant search warrants to allow ATF agents to search the companies. On July 19, 1984, ATF agents raided L&M and S.W. Daniel, seizing firearms, firearm parts, and, most important, customer lists and shipping records. Urrea and a colleague spent a month examining these records and found that in California alone some twenty-four consumers had received all the components necessary to build a silencer—and thus possessed the equivalent of completed silencers—but none had bothered to register the device.

The bureau used the seized records to launch some four hundred individual criminal investigations relating to arms trafficking and illegal possession of restricted weapons. In June 1985, ATF agents arrested Sylvia and Wayne and, using an experimental tactic, charged them with conspiracy to sell illegal silencers. (By now Sylvia and Wayne had divorced but continued a close working relationship.) In formal court arguments, they claimed they were simply trying to fill a valid need for replacement parts for silencers owned by legitimate users.

The ATF investigators found a rather different story.

All in all from November 1983 to July 1984, the government charged, S.W. Daniel had mailed six thousand silencer kits and machine-gun kits. Only four buyers had bothered to register the devices. When ATF checked the customer lists through the FBI's National Crime Information Center, it found that more than fifty customers had prior criminal records or were believed to be involved in drug peddling and other forms of organized crime. Posing as IRA gunrunners, Mexican narcotics smugglers, and assorted ne'er-do-wells, undercover ATF agents were welcomed by international arms traffickers, narcotics smugglers, and assorted ne'er-do-wells.

An ATF agent posing as a member of the Irish Republican Army ordered $15.6 million of silencer-equipped machine guns, hand grenades, and rocket-propelled grenades from a group of New York arms traffickers who, according to Treasury documents, illegally manufactured and sold firearms and explosives to countries forbidden by U.S. law from receiving domestically produced weapons. A Treasury case report noted that the leaders of the group "were dealing directly with Sylvia and Wayne Daniel . . . for the purchase of the machine guns and silencer kits, which were then sold to the ATF undercover agent." The leaders were convicted of violating federal firearms laws.

Agents also arrested an Oregon man who sold machine-gun lower receivers to the Neo-Nazi Order, the group whose members assassinated Alan Berg in Denver and allegedly murdered a Missouri state trooper. After his initial arrest, the man bragged to friends that ATF had failed to find his real stash of weapons hidden underneath his water bed. A tipster leaked the secret to ATF. Agents returned to the man's house, drained the bed, and found two S.W. Daniel machine guns and five silencers, all made from kits.

Another investigation captured a Texas man after he sold seven S.W. Daniel machine guns, with silencers, to an ATF undercover agent who had posed as a Houston narcotics dealer. The suspect had received forty-four silencer kits from S.W. Daniel and twenty-five tubes from L&M Guns.

In Ohio, agents arrested a convicted felon named Joe Canatelli, who had also sold machine guns and silencers to an ATF undercover agent. Canatelli had purchased silencer tubes and internal components directly from L&M and S.W. Daniel, and from a federally licensed firearms dealer in Youngstown, Ohio, who had agreed to order the silencer kits and machine-gun kits for Canatelli. The dealer, in a formal affidavit, stated that Canatelli "had previously told me that you can make a buck by putting the kits together, and that he knew some guys that wanted to buy some M11s with silencers for the mob. He further explained that they 'would be used only once for hits.'" Agents seized three machine guns made from "flats," and three silencers. Canatelli and an associate were convicted and sentenced to prison.

The growing list of arrested S.W. Daniel customers included a San Jose man who made machine guns and silencers and distributed them in Mexico; an Aurora, Illinois, man found during a search to possess an arsenal of more than thirty weapons and a large supply of cocaine, marijuana, and amphetamines; two Tucson narcotics dealers who had sold two machine guns and three silencers to an ATF agent posing as a Mexican narcotics smuggler;

and a federally licensed firearms dealer in Florida found during a search to possess one and a half pounds of uncut cocaine and ninety-four blank Granadian passports. The dealer told the ATF agents a child had found the passports "in the road." When the agents asked the dealer to open a safe in his closet, he hesitated and asked, "What if there's something in here other than guns that I don't want you to find?"

Agents found the cocaine.

"There are literally thousands of persons now in the United States and probably outside the United States who have a fully operable silencer which is not registered to them and which is possessed unlawfully," wrote Brian C. Leighton, the assistant U.S. attorney assigned to prosecute the Daniels, in a pretrial statement. "It was incredibly easy for these people to receive the silencer; they merely had to order the internal-parts kit from SWD and order a tube from one of the many tube distributors—all of whom advertised in *Shotgun News*." These were "assassin-type weapons," he said, and posed "a definite danger to the community."

As the case approached the trial phase, however, the government found itself compelled to abandon its conspiracy strategy and admit that no law forbade the sale of silencer components or the machine-gun parts as sold by S.W. Daniel. Indeed, federal law expressly excluded silencer parts from ATF regulation. The Daniels pleaded guilty to a misdemeanor for failing to pay taxes in the sale of two firearms. They were sentenced to six months' probation and forced to pay $900 in taxes and fines, but because they had escaped felony charges, they were allowed to retain their Federal Firearms License.

The investigation had not cowed the Daniels. On May 1, 1985, *Shotgun News* ran an ad placed by Wayne Daniel titled, "Now It's Happening in AMERICA," and featuring a large photograph of Hitler and Mussolini. The ad recounted the ATF raid on S.W. Daniel and listed the names and home cities of the agents involved. Wayne referred to them as the "Gestapo" and likened their search to a Nazi search for Polish gun owners in 1939. "The uniforms of this new 'Gestapo' may not be taylored [sic] and bear the eagle and swastika on the sleeve, rather they choose to wear a business suit or sport jacket and slacks from the racks of a cut-rate department store—but their purpose is the same, they want total control and YOU, as an American citizen, DISARMED!"

The agents named in the ad, among them Earl Taylor, demanded that Daniel retract the advertisement. He refused.

In a handwritten letter he replied: "I am at a complete loss of words perhaps from bending over laughing. No malice was intended by the ad. . . . It is my opinion that nothing in the ad is anything but the truth, as you know nothing is libelous or slanderous if the truth is published with no malice."

The agents filed a private libel suit against Wayne Daniel and Snell Publishing, the publisher of *Shotgun News*. "It wasn't the fact that he was attacking ATF, because ATF was accustomed to being attacked," Taylor told me. "It was the fact that he mentioned the ATF agents by name. I was offended by it and so were most of the other agents."

None of the agents hoped to get rich from the suit, Taylor said. They knew that at the time Wayne Daniel had few personal assets. "It was, by God, to let them know that they couldn't do that to law-enforcement officers who were doing their mandated duty."

The court ruled in the agents' favor and ordered Wayne Daniel to pay each agent $1,000 in damages, a symbolic victory. The court found Snell not liable.

Undaunted, the Daniels branched out into other firearms. They introduced a pistol-grip shotgun with a high-capacity drum magazine and a forward grip and called it the Street-Sweeper, best described as resembling a shotgun version of a tommy gun. "Delivers Twelve Rounds In Less Than Three Seconds!!!!" one ad proclaimed in *Shotgun News*. "Time for spring cleaning," the ad continued. "Why try clean-ups with inadequate equipment?? Buy the machine designed to clean thoroughly on the first pass."

The company's latest innovation is the Ladies' Home Companion, apparently intended for use by women to protect themselves and their homes. A variation on the Street-Sweeper, it is just under two feet long, has a twelve-shot revolving drum, and fires a heavy rifle-caliber .45-70 "government" cartridge that causes explosive recoil—yet the gun has only a rear pistol grip and no other handle. A gun dealer submitted the weapon to the Maryland Handgun Roster Board for consideration as a "revolver." The trigger requires thirty to forty pounds of pressure, according to tests by Don Flohr, a Maryland State Police firearms expert who tests weapons for the board. S.W. Daniel advertised the gun as being "ideal for use in confined spaces," yet Flohr refused to test-fire it for fear of damaging the backstop to the state's indoor pistol range. With the degree of understatement common to forensic investigators, Flohr noted that anyone shooting this gun "may be somewhat disturbed by the force of escaping gases, noise, and recoil experienced."

The board ruled the gun had no valid use, thus making it one of the precious few handguns awful enough to be banned for sale in Maryland. An official with the Maryland board described the gun as "a sick joke."

I would have liked to ask Sylvia and Wayne why they seemed hell-bent on skirting firearms laws, but neither returned the many calls I made—and the faxes and overnight letters I mailed—to their Atlanta headquarters. I asked Earl Taylor whether the Daniels were driven in their corporate antics by some kind of Second Amendment fundamentalism.

"Shit no," he said. "I think Wayne's strictly in it for the money. That doesn't make him a bad guy—he's a sharp businessman. And Sylvia's a sharp businesslady."

Sylvia in particular makes an appealing character for America's gun lovers—"those assholes" in the NRA, as Taylor put it. "Here's a woman who's a manufacturer of a submachine gun. She brings law-suits against the government all the time for mistreating us gun own-ers. She's just a person they can identify with."

◆ ◆ ◆

In Towson, Colonel Supenski had me slip on pistol earmuffs and safety glasses, then handed back the Cobray, now fully loaded with a thirty-two-round clip. He invited me to fire away.

I fired slowly at first, trying to accustom myself to the trigger action and the roll of the weapon. The trigger action was uneven, but quick. I fired with abandon, trying to aim at a series of steel man-shaped targets named Pepper Poppers after their inventor. The tar-gets are designed to fall backward when struck by a bullet. The cliff came alive as if a tribe of beetles had suddenly decided to decamp. I downed all four targets and then turned the gun on a loose piece of wood embedded in the earth behind them. Shards blew off in all directions. Shell casings rocketed past me, one striking the rim of my safety glasses and bouncing off my eyebrow. In a matter of seconds I'd used up all thirty-two rounds.

Watching the dirt fly, one can be lulled into believing this is, after all, just fun and games. I wanted to fire off another clip; hell, I wanted to "rock and roll," the gun culture's euphemism for firing a machine gun in full auto. This was fun. Remote destruction is a dy-namite rush.

As I drove home, however, I was struck by the dissonance be-tween the innocent clink of the Pepper Poppers and the deadly power of each bullet. What cost, this fun and games? Any one of those bits of lead invisibly traversing the space between me and the target would have been enough to blow a man's brains out.

"You put a gun like this in the hands of a juvenile," Supenski testified at the civil trial that examined how Nicholas Elliot acquired his gun, "and you've got death waiting to happen."

The judge struck this and most of Supenski's testimony from the record as prejudicial and inflammatory.

"Well, I should say so," Supenski told me, nodding fiercely. "Damn right! It should have been inflammatory. A whole lot of people should have heard it and they should have been inflamed."

At his office, Supenski placed two weapons on a conference table, one the Cobray M-11/9, the other the new Smith & Wesson nine-millimeter he carries each day, a beautifully machined weapon with a wood grip and three different safety mechanisms designed to prevent accidental shootings. "The gun industry, unlike any other, is allowed to run amok," he said. "If you had industry regulations, or if you had safety regulations or product-liability regulations, you better believe they'd see the light, you'd see a lot more of those"—he pointed to the Smith & Wesson pistol—"and none of those. And you wouldn't need the California assault-weapon ban, you wouldn't need a New Jersey ban, a Maryland Saturday-night-special law. You wouldn't need them because that kind of garbage would never be released into the mainstream.

"Could Nicholas Elliot have killed people with this?" Supenski said, touching his own pistol. "Yeah, he could have. That's true. But he wasn't drawn to that one. He was drawn to this one." The Cobray lay on the table, dull and black. The only gleam came from the holes left where the previous owner had drilled out the serial numbers. "The sad part of it is, you look at what happened and you ask, is that something that with a little bit of foresight and a little less greed or maybe stupidity, or whatever the hell it was—is that something that could have been prevented? The answer, quite simply, is yes."

He pushed his glasses higher on his nose. "You know the part of that case that really bothered me—the clerk who sold the kid that goddamn gun. He was an ex-cop."

CHAPTER SIX

NICHOLAS

NICHOLAS DID COME ACROSS BILLY CUTTER on Friday morning, and true to form Cutter again called him a name. Nicholas went into a bathroom and took his Cobray from his backpack. He left both there, however, and exited the room. What he did next is not entirely clear. According to his own statement, made to Det. Donald Adams, the lead homicide investigator, he wandered into the band room and, at one point, helped a man with the very apt name of Mike Lucky.

At some point between ten-twenty and ten twenty-two that morning, Nicholas walked into one of the trailers—the relocation modular units—that had been partitioned into classrooms. The room, called T108, was small, one of three classrooms built from a large trailer akin to those that serve as field offices at large construction sites. Each classroom had windows, its own door, and a stairway down to the central courtyard of the school. Other similarly divided trailers were positioned around the courtyard. Room T108 was occupied at that moment by a single individual, Sam Marino, who taught French and English at the school.

Nicholas, who that semester was taking Marino's sixth-period French I class, asked Marino if he could help him practice dialogue. Nicholas offered to go to his locker and bring back a tape recorder he claimed to have brought with him that morning. It might help with the practice, he told Marino. Could he go and get it?

Marino said he would be glad to help, but not right then. He knew Nicholas was scheduled to be in the Bible class just getting under way in the trailer across the courtyard, taught by M. Hutchinson Matteson—"Hutch"—a popular teacher and the church's youth pastor. "I told Nicholas he should be getting to his other class," Marino recalled. He told the boy to come back later.

Just as Nicholas left the trailer, another teacher, Susan Allen, walked in. Her next period was free, and she customarily came to T108 to take a break, grade papers, and prepare for her next classes. She and Marino chatted a bit as Marino gathered his books under his arm and braced himself for the bitterly cold walk to his next class. Allen was now sitting at the desk; Marino was standing with his back to the door.

He felt the frigid blast of outside air, then heard something thud to the floor. The impact undoubtedly was caused when Nicholas let his backpack fall from his grasp. Marino did not turn around, however. He and Allen continued talking for another thirty seconds, maybe another minute. "All of a sudden," Marino said, "I heard a real, real loud noise."

He whirled toward the sound. "At first I thought it was like an M80—like a big, big firecracker—real loud. I didn't know what it was, and so I turned around and looked."

He saw Nicholas and saw too that he was holding something. There was nothing unusual about his appearance or his expression, Marino later testified. Nicholas was, as always, "Mr. Serious," Marino said. Although Nicholas often walked around with a smile, he somehow managed at the same time to seem very sober and earnest. "He wanted to show me something," Marino said. "He was intent on showing me something."

Nicholas held what appeared to be a toy. It was black and sharply angled. Whatever it was, it had the shape of a gun, but the idea it might be a real firearm had not settled in Marino's mind. "In a situation like that, I'm a very positive individual," Marino said. "You want to think it's not what you really thought you saw or heard."

He believed it might be one of those hyperrealistic water guns that had become so popular. Or a very loud cap gun. Nicholas, wearing his usual Mr. Serious expression, pointed the thing at Marino.

"I've got something to show you," he said. "I have this really neat toy."

Susan Allen, watching from her desk, remembered thinking her own children had never had a toy like that. She too thought it might be a cap gun, or maybe a water pistol—"one of those big, long water guns; so I really didn't panic."

She told Nicholas, "We don't have toys like that in school. Right now put it up. Better give it to Mr. Marino."

"No, no," Nicholas said, "I've got to show you. It's really neat."

Sam Marino was angry. He did not like being startled that way. Whatever Nicholas had, it did not belong in school. "What is it?" Marino snapped. "A cap gun? A pop gun?"

"You'll see what I've got," Nicholas said.

Marino moved toward Nicholas, still unaware the toy was in fact a real gun. He demanded Nicholas hand it over.

Nicholas backed away.

"No," Nicholas said again. "I've got to show you. It's really neat. It works really great."

As Marino advanced, Nicholas retreated, until he had backed to the far end of the little classroom. Marino now stood roughly three feet away from the boy.

"Give it to me," Marino commanded.

"Nicholas," Allen said from behind. "That's enough. Give it to Mr. Marino."

Nicholas seemed to relent. "Here it is."

Allen thought the incident was now over, that Nicholas really did mean to hand the toy to Marino.

But Nicholas stepped back and coolly took aim.

◆ ◆ ◆

Victims of gunplay hold up articles of all kinds in their last moments in the magical belief that even a sheet of paper might save them.

Marino held up his French I textbook.

CHAPTER SEVEN

THE PURCHASE

TO BE A GUN DEALER IN America is to occupy a strange and dangerous outpost on the moral frontier. Every storefront gun dealer winds up at some point in his career selling weapons to killers, drug addicts, psychos, and felons; likewise, every storefront dealer can expect to be visited by ATF agents and other lawmen tracking weapons from their use in crime to their origins in the gun-distribution network. One must be a cool customer to stay in business knowing that the products one sells are likely to be used to kill adults and children or to serve as a terrorist tool in countless other robberies, rapes, and violent assaults. Yet gun dealers sell guns in America the way Rite Aid sells toothpaste, denying at every step of the way the true nature of the products they sell and absolving themselves of any and all responsibility for their role in the resulting mayhem. Guns used in crime are commonly thought to have originated in some mythic inner-city black market. Such markets do exist, of course, but they are kept well supplied by the licensed gun-distribution network, where responsibility is defined as whatever the law allows.

And the law, as written, allows much.

Guns Unlimited, of Carrollton, Virginia, demonstrates the kind of position every legitimate gun shop must eventually find itself in. Guns Unlimited considered itself a "good" dealer. Indeed, in the view of Mike Dick, the general manager of the company and the son of its founder, Guns Unlimited was not just a sterling corporate citizen but also a de facto deputy of ATF and a vital bulwark in the fight against crime and civil-rights abuse.

Nonetheless, Guns Unlimited sold Nicholas Elliot a Cobray M-11/9 under circumstances that led, early in 1992, to a jury verdict against the dealer on civil charges that its sale of the gun to Nicholas was negligent. The suit was filed by the husband of the teacher Nicholas killed.

Federal law bars anyone under twenty-one from buying a handgun, but Nicholas acquired his with ease through a "straw-man" purchase three months before the shootings, when he was fifteen years old. Straw-man purchases, in which a qualified buyer buys a handgun for an unqualified person, are the primary means by which America's bad guys acquire their weapons, and one the Bureau of Alcohol, Tobacco and Firearms cannot hope to put an end to, given the implicit and explicit restraints on its law-enforcement activities.

Nicholas not only knew the gun he wanted, but where to go to buy it. How he knew which dealership to patronize is not clear. Nicholas would not agree to an interview at Virginia's Southampton Correctional Center, where he is serving a life sentence. It is an easy assumption, however, that Nicholas learned of Guns Unlimited from the dealership's aggressive advertising efforts, which included TV commercials and giant billboards.

One peaceful weekend in September of 1988, Nicholas Elliot, apparently at loose ends, called his second cousin Curtis Williams, a truck driver, to ask if he would go with him to look at guns in a gun store. The two had talked about guns before. Nicholas proudly told his cousin how he had shot rifles in California with his father. Williams, in turn, told Nicholas about his encounters with weapons in the Marine Corps, which had given him advanced weapons training.

Nicholas had pestered him before about going to look at guns.

"He was calling me all the time," Williams recalled during his trial in Norfolk federal court on charges of conducting an illegal straw purchase. (Most of what follows is derived from testimony during that trial and from the subsequent civil suit against the dealer, as well as related court documents and interviews.) "We had right many conversations on the phone, but that particular Saturday I was at home stripping my floors, getting ready to take the old wax off and rewax them."

Williams lived in Norfolk, in a small bungalow with a creaky wooden porch and a front door heavily framed in decorative anti-crime grillwork. His neighborhood, shaded and neat, is known as Shoop Park, where streets are named for famous battles—Somme, Vimy Ridge, Dunkirk, Bapaume, Verdun, and so forth.

When the phone rang, Williams told his wife to tell whoever it was that he was busy—a response he should have held to.

His wife returned. "It's Nicholas again."

Nicholas. Everyone called him Nicholas, never the jauntier Nick, a reflection perhaps of his generally serious demeanor.

Williams felt sympathetic. The kid had few, if any, friends and spent most of his time with his birds. The boy was at loose ends. What would it cost to talk to him?

They exchanged greetings, then Nicholas begged him to take him to visit a gun store. Williams had put him off before and now felt guilty about it. He thought it over, again asking himself what harm it could do. It would lighten the boy's day. He could take him out for a quick trip, maybe to Bob's Gun Shop. Bob's was close, an easy shot downtown. They could hop in the car, spend a couple of minutes at the store, and then come back. It would be a nice break from Williams's work on the floors, and something nice for the boy. Williams could finish the floors when he returned.

When he picked Nicholas up, however, he realized Nicholas had a more elaborate expedition in mind.

"He wanted to go to Guns Unlimited," Williams testified. "At that particular time I didn't know where it was, but when he said Carrollton, Virginia, by me being a truck driver, I knew where Carrollton, Virginia, was."

What it was, was too far. A lot farther than Williams wanted to go. Carrollton was little more than a wide space on Route 17 in Isle of Wight County, a rural wedge of land bordered on the north by the James River and on the east by the Portsmouth-Norfolk metropolitan area. It was a long drive, easily forty-five minutes from Nicholas's house on Colon Avenue in Campostella. Ninety minutes minimum, back and forth. Extra time at the gun shop. Altogether, Williams suddenly faced an expedition that would take at least two hours.

Williams tried halfheartedly to put Nicholas off: "I don't have much gas. And besides, I'm broke."

"I'll put gas in your car. Here." Nicholas passed Williams $20.

Again, Williams gave in. "Won't take twenty dollars to get there. I'll take ten. About ten dollars will do it."

They stopped at an Amoco gas station on Wilson Road, not far from Nicholas's house, then set out for Guns Unlimited, most likely taking Interstate 264 under the southern branch of the Elizabeth River into Portsmouth, then picking up 17 for the rest of the drive. On the way, Nicholas talked about a gun he had come to admire, the Cobray M-11/9 made by S.W. Daniel.

"Man," he said, "you've got to see that; it's a nice gun."

The easy, fluid commerce of guns embraced them the moment they entered the shop. An elderly couple browsing in the store approached almost immediately and offered to sell Williams a gun in a private sale. Such transactions escape federal scrutiny altogether. In principle, the owner of a gun cannot sell it to a juvenile or out-of-state resident. In practice, however, federal law doesn't require the private seller to ask for any kind of identification or even to record the transaction.

"My husband has plenty of guns," the man's wife said. "He'll sell you a gun, if you want to buy one."

Williams declined.

He and Nicholas approached the display counters.

"Can I help you?" a clerk asked.

"We're just looking around," Williams replied.

Williams led Nicholas to a case containing a number of small, low-caliber revolvers and then did ask the clerk for some help. He asked to see a .38-caliber revolver. The clerk opened the case and passed the weapon to Williams, who then showed it to Nicholas. As the clerk watched from just across the counter, Nicholas said he wasn't interested in seeing that particular gun.

"After that," Williams testified, "Nicholas started talking, so I thought I'd let him do most of the talking to the gun salesman."

Nicholas and the clerk, Tony Massengill, a firefighter and former policeman moonlighting as a gun salesman, talked about different types of guns, about muzzle velocities, how powerful one gun was as compared to another.

Williams and Nicholas next looked at a .45-caliber handgun. The clerk, according to Williams's testimony, pulled the .45 from the counter display and handed it directly to Nicholas. They chatted a bit about the gun. Williams said they discussed "probably how many rounds it shoot and probably how hot it get, you know, after shooting so many rounds, and that kind of stuff."

This gun didn't interest Nicholas either, however. "He asked the gun salesman to show him the very next gun, which was a .357 Magnum," Williams testified.

Once again the clerk, Massengill, handed the weapon to Nicholas, according to Williams: "The gun dealer took it out from under the counter . . . and handed it to Nicholas, and Nicholas started to inspect that gun."

This was all, no doubt, great fun for Nicholas, whose passion for his birds was rivaled only by his love of guns. But he knew which gun he wanted.

Williams's defense attorney, William Taliaferro, Jr., asked whether Nicholas and Massengill talked about the .357 Magnum.

"Yes," Williams said, "how much more powerful that was versus the .45-caliber. Then after that, [Nicholas] went to the gun that we actually purchased, and he asked the gun salesman . . . he asked him, would he pull that out."

The gun Nicholas wanted to see was the Cobray, lying dark and deadly in the cabinet. Again the clerk obliged, pulling out the gun and giving it to Nicholas to inspect.

Nicholas liked it, Williams recalled. "He said he'd read a lot about it. He had books on it and everything."

Indeed, Nicholas began peppering the clerk with questions about the gun. What was the price? What was the muzzle velocity? How many rounds did the magazine hold? "They got in such a lengthy conversation about that," Williams recalled, "I just kind of moved away from them a little bit, looking around on my own."

When Williams returned, Nicholas and the clerk were still discussing the weapon. "I really don't remember the exact words, but it was, you know, about the nomenclature of the gun, how many rounds it shoot, because it's got a long clip on it, and I remember Nicholas saying we won't have to load this so often when we're in the gun range, and I said, 'Yeah.' I remember saying, 'Yeah, that's right, right.' "

The pair didn't buy the Cobray at that point. Nicholas wanted to see more guns. The clerk put the gun back in the case.

Nicholas and Williams moved to the far side of a central display counter and examined more guns there. "I don't see anything in here that I really want," Nicholas told Williams. "I'm more interested in the other gun over there."

The Cobray.

By now, of course, it had become apparent to Williams that this browsing trip had turned into something more. The fact it had become a serious shopping trip, however, did not faze Williams. He knew a lot of people who had bought guns for "juveniles," he testified. "So I didn't see anything wrong with it and I didn't know [of any] law against buying a gun for a juvenile."

Nicholas reached into his pocket and pulled out a roll containing $300, then passed the money to Williams, so Williams could pay for the gun.

When I visited Guns Unlimited in 1992, it was a small store with a showroom area about as large as a medium-size living room. The store was larger at the time Nicholas and Williams bought the Cobray and configured a bit differently, but still so small it seemed unlikely that Nicholas could have handed Williams the money without Tony Massengill being aware of the exchange.

What Massengill did see became a matter of debate—a debate that Massengill, himself, did little to resolve. He claimed he did not remember the transaction at all, although curiously a co-employee, present in the store at the time of the sale, testified later that he remembered seeing the buyers in the store even though he had not played a role in the sale. This clerk, Christopher Hartwig, also testified that he and Massengill had discussed the purchase after learning of the Atlantic Shores shootings.

Williams testified that when the money changed hands, Massengill was still behind the counter at the place where he had last talked with Nicholas, some eight or nine feet away. "He was still standing there, waiting to wait on us, looking at us."

Asked if anything blocked the clerk's view of the transfer, Williams replied no, only the center display table, on which the store had placed a stuffed bobcat. "But that wasn't obstructing any view. If the gun dealer was looking, he could clearly see Nicholas hand me the money."

(Raymond Rowley, an ATF special agent assigned to the agency's Norfolk office, testified that Williams had told him a somewhat different story during a late-night interrogation at Williams's home following the shootings. Williams had told Rowley that when Nicholas handed over the money, both he and Nicholas had their backs to the glass counter so that, as Rowley put it, "the salesclerk could not see that in fact the money . . . had come from Nicholas.")

Nicholas and Williams returned to the counter that contained the Cobray pistol and told Massengill they wanted to buy it.

Massengill passed Williams a copy of federal form 4473.

Everyone who buys a gun from a federally licensed firearms dealer must fill out this two-page form, which among other things asks the would-be purchaser if he is a drug addict, a convicted felon, mentally ill, or an illegal alien; if he has renounced his U.S. citizenship; and whether he has been dishonorably discharged from the armed forces. The form goes nowhere. It is kept in the dealer's files (provided the dealer in fact keeps such files and keeps them accurately) for later reference should the gun be used in a crime and subsequently traced by ATF. By federal law, the buyer need present only enough identification to prove that he is twenty-one or older and resides in the state in which the dealer is located. (State and local laws may add requirements.)

Williams testified that as he began filling out the form, Massengill told him, "The only thing that will keep you from buying this gun here in this store is you put a yes answer to these questions. Everything should be marked no. If you put a yes up there, that will stop you from getting the gun."

Nicholas, meanwhile, had taken the gun from the counter and begun inspecting it. He looked at Massengill. "Doesn't a clip come with this?"

Massengill found the clip and gave it to Nicholas. Nicholas walked out with the gun.

Taliaferro, Williams's attorney, asked, "Did the salesman ever say anything to you that it was against the law to purchase that gun for Nicholas?"

"No, he didn't," Williams said. "Only thing he was interested in was making that sale."

Massengill, in a deposition during the later civil trial against Guns Unlimited, testified, "I would never sell a gun to an adult that I understood was going to give that gun to a minor." In an interview late in 1992, he told me, "It would be suicide to do business like that. On a gun like that there's a profit margin of forty or fifty dollars. Is it worth taking a chance of losing your license to make fifty dollars?"

Once outside the store, Nicholas asked Williams to buy him some bullets. Williams refused. "I told him I wouldn't buy any bullets because we didn't need any bullets. I was going back home . . . to strip my floors, and we didn't need no bullets until we got actually to the shooting range, and we could buy bullets in the shooting range."

Acquiring the bullets, however, proved no great challenge for Nicholas. His mother bought them. Nicholas had told her that a friend and his father had invited him to go target shooting at a local shooting range, according to Detective Adams. They would pay all the range fees and supply the guns; all Nicholas had to do was provide the cartridges. The cartridges, Nicholas specified, had to be nine-millimeter. Mrs. Elliot was so concerned that he make friends and have a little fun in his life that she obliged. She had no idea he owned his own gun, or that he had other plans for the bullets.

Immediately after the shootings ATF agents arrested Williams and charged him with making a straw-man purchase. He was promptly tried and served thirteen months in prison. During the trial the federal prosecutor asked him, "What would ever possess someone who's thirty-six, thirty-seven years old to arrange for a fifteen-year-old young man to get a weapon like that?"

What no federal authority ever bothered to ask, however, is what would possess Guns Unlimited to allow this sale to be made, given the apparent level of Nicholas's involvement.

CHAPTER EIGHT

THE DEALER

ON A BRILLIANT MORNING IN JUNE 1992, I paid a visit to Guns Unlimited. I had arranged to meet its manager, Mike Dick, at the store at nine. His full name was J. Michael Dick and he was the son of the store's founder and owner, James S. Dick, who by then had limited his gun-dealing to sales at weekend gun shows.

My drive had begun an hour earlier in Virginia Beach, on an expressway that took me past metropolitan Norfolk, then plunged under the Elizabeth River. From the highway Norfolk looked prosperous, with a perimeter of high glass buildings, a brand-new hotel, and a festive riverside development similar to Baltimore's Harborplace. But I had been downtown several times before and knew that urban pressures had turned this portion of Norfolk into a Potemkin village. Two blocks in from the city's gleaming rim, life seemed to stop. Abandoned buildings, some boarded, some just empty, lined block after block. The streets were clean, however. There were no piles of litter, no plumes of broken glass, and no people, just a clean desolation like that of a city awaiting a hurricane.

As I traveled, the landscape gradually softened. Brittle urban architecture gave way to suburbs, then to cool green countryside. From time to time I spotted the giant cranes of shipyards and cargo wharves along the distant blue band of the Roads. I had expected

Carrollton to be a neat little Southern town of stores and a church or two arrayed along a clearly demarcated central avenue. The Carrollton I found, however, consisted primarily of a small shopping plaza on the north side of Route 17.

Guns Unlimited occupied one of the plaza's seven retail establishments, which were arrayed along a cinder-block rectangle fronted with a hot, white-gravel parking lot. A BP gas station and convenience store occupied the western end of the lot. A poster in the window of the video store immediately to the right of Guns Unlimited advertised a movie called *Mobsters;* the poster consisted mainly of eight stylized bullet holes. The only other car in the parking lot was a black-and-white Ford Mustang belonging to the local sheriff's department. The deputy glanced my way now and then, before wandering into the convenience store. As it happens, he too was waiting for Guns Unlimited to open. He had heard about a new kind of ammunition and wanted to ask about it. He was a frequent browser at the store, the clerks would later tell me—one of that class of shooter who finds guns and everything about them infinitely compelling. He was welcome, they said; it was always nice to have a patrol car parked outside as a deterrent against the daylight gun-shop robberies that as of 1992 had become a frequent and often lethal fact of life in the gun trade.

Mike Dick and his father held two of the nation's 245,000 firearms-dealer licenses, and two of the 7,500 licenses issued to residents of Virginia alone, where at the time of our meeting gun controls outside the major cities were virtually nonexistent. The lack of regulation probably traced its roots to 1776 when Virginia became the first colony to adopt a bill of rights, which included the declaration that a "well regulated Militia, composed of the body of the People, trained to Arms, is the proper, natural, and safe Defense of a free state." By the time Nicholas acquired his gun, Virginia's enthusiasm for firearms had turned the state into a massive shopping mall for gun traffickers from the North. A Baltimore police detective described Virginia to me this way: "It's the only place I know where

you can go get gas, diapers, and a gun at the same time." As one
Guns Unlimited clerk put it, during a court deposition, Virginia was
"Second Amendment" country.

A thick printout of Virginia's licensed firearms dealers, which I
bought from the Bureau of Alcohol, Tobacco and Firearms' disclo-
sure branch, captured this penchant for mixing gun peddling with
other pursuits. The list included Capt. Mike's Seafood, Ray's Used
Cars, Dale's Exxon & Grocery, Miss Molly's Inn, Miracle Chimney
Sweep, the Capitol Cafe, Forbes Window Co., Stallard's Shoe Shop,
Jenning's Music Co., Bucks Barber Shop, Glasgow Video, the Portsmouth-Norfolk chapter of the Izaak Walton League, and Camp Se-
quoya for Girls in Abingdon. Some of the business names listed in
the printout were tantalizing in and of themselves, such as Boys
Noisy Toys, The Gunrunner, Gut Pile Guns, and, my favorite, Life
Support Systems of Norfolk.

Dick was late, but two of his clerks arrived and invited me and
the sheriff's deputy inside. The shop was small, no larger than a suburban living room, with display cases arranged in a U shape and a
central table containing miscellaneous accessories and special
"safety" ammunition for use in home defense, including the Glaser
"safety" round, a bullet that ruptures on impact and scatters a multi-
tude of tiny steel balls through whomever it strikes. One medical
examiner, writing in the *Journal of Forensic Sciences*, reported on the
mysterious X ray he had made of the skull of a suicide victim. Instead of finding one or two bits of metal, he saw dozens scattered
through the dead man's brain like stars. The manufacturer calls the
bullet a safety round in the belief that its pellets are less likely to pass
through bodies and walls to injure bystanders on the other side. At
up to $3 a cartridge, Glaser safety rounds are not for practice.

The store was a fortress. The Dicks had embedded steel "tank
traps" in the sidewalk out front, this to prevent the recurrence of
what has now become a fairly routine, if hardly subtle, means of
burglarizing the gun stores of America: the use of trucks to crash
through the front wall of the store. The Dicks learned the value of

tank traps a few years ago when a thief backed a dump truck into the display windows of Guns Unlimited, then climbed out and stole dozens of handguns. An alarm system now guarded the place at night. The front door had been reinforced with steel. Steel herringbone grates covered the inside surfaces of the two large plate-glass windows. A big Pepsi machine stood against the grate just inside the door as a barrier to anyone hoping to cut through the glass to reach the door locks. As a last defense, the two clerks wore large-bore handguns strapped to their hips, one a revolver, the other a black auto-loading pistol. One clerk, dressed in black and wearing tinted glasses, told me he and his partner were careful to stand at different points in the shop so that no one could get the drop on them simultaneously. He untacked a brief news clipping from the bulletin board behind him and proudly handed it to me. The item reported how just that week a Portsmouth gun-shop owner had shot and killed a would-be robber. No charges were filed.

Mike Dick arrived in jeans and a T-shirt. He was a young man, a bit round at the corners, whose prior career was in the hospitality industry. He joined Guns Unlimited to help his father salvage the business, which had suffered badly not only from the recession but from the sudden decampment of so many military men from the Hampton Roads area during the Gulf War. The domestic gun industry as a whole had likewise experienced declining sales over the previous few years, and that March one of the country's highest-profile arms makers, Colt's Manufacturing, had filed for protection from creditors under Chapter 11. At the time of the shootings at Atlantic Shores, however, the industry was enjoying a robust surge in sales, and Guns Unlimited was thriving. As of 1990, James Dick owned three Guns Unlimited stores, including branches in Virginia Beach and Portsmouth. But he too had been forced to file for bankruptcy under Chapter 11. By the time I met his son, Guns Unlimited had scaled back to just the Carrollton store.

The company was hardly a big-time arms dealer. Financial statements filed with the U.S. Bankruptcy Court in Norfolk show that in

April 1992 it had sales of $30,000, which produced a net profit after wages, taxes, and other operating costs of only $503. The best month of the preceding dozen had been April 1991, when Guns Unlimited's revenue of $51,000 yielded a net profit of $1,752, the kind of money a big arms dealer like Interarms of Alexandria, Virginia, probably spends on lunch when wooing a major customer.

At its peak, the company advertised aggressively on television and with huge fourteen-by-forty-eight-foot billboards that featured a giant handgun and proclaimed NO PERMITS, a reference to the fact that in Isle of Wight County as in most of the rest of Virginia you didn't need a permit to buy handguns. Regulations were much stiffer in individual cities in Hampton Roads. Portsmouth, for example, required that buyers first had to get a city police permit. Guns Unlimited used the placement of its three stores to defeat these laws. In a deposition, Christopher Hartwig, a clerk until May 1991, said that if a customer at the Portsmouth store needed a gun right away, a clerk would drive the gun to the Carrollton store and meet the buyer there.

The practice came to light in a deposition given by Hartwig during the negligence suit against Guns Unlimited.

"Is that something the salesclerk would suggest or the customer?" asked Randy Singer, the Norfolk attorney who brought the suit on behalf of the murdered teacher's family. A bright, soft-spoken young man, Singer had been driving back from Disney World on December 16, 1988, with his own children safely in the car—they were Atlantic Shores students also, but had gotten permission for the trip—when he heard a news broadcast about Nicholas Elliot's shooting spree.

"I can't lie," Hartwig said. "We would do it."

But other shops did it too, he said. "Most people don't want to wait. . . . It would be like waiting two weeks to buy a nice car. You would want it today if you got the money. So they'd send the gun . . . to the other store and then all the paperwork, everything would be done right there."

This bit of gun-law arbitrage was legal. In the ethos of the gun trade, legal meant acceptable.

"Guns Unlimited is very well respected," Mike Dick assured me over coffee at the convenience store at the end of the little mall. He told me he'd been invited to join the state police firearms advisory board and had assisted ATF in numerous investigations, often calling the regional office after—or even during—suspicious transactions. "In fact, I would venture to say if you talked to the local regional office of ATF, you would find that no one in this region assists them as much as we do."

At the same time, Guns Unlimited was more than willing to sell an especially lethal weapon to an adolescent—a weapon, moreover, that its own staff had derided as serving no useful purpose. At one point in the deposition process, Randy Singer asked another former Guns Unlimited clerk what anyone would use a Cobray M-11/9 for.

"Whatever you want to use it for," the clerk answered. "Off the record, personally I wouldn't use the damn thing for crab bait."

The clerk went on to say that he would never recommend the gun for target shooting, hunting, or self-defense.

Was there anything he *could* recommend it for, Singer asked?

"Boat anchor."

Hartwig was equally disparaging: "It's good for nothing." He allowed, however, that one class of customer did seem drawn to the weapon. "Your blacks are real impressed with them. We usually joke around about it because that's the first thing they want to look at when they come in, or we get phone calls—'Do you have an Uzi? Do you have an M-11?'—because they see it on TV. They feel pretty powerful having one of those."

Nonetheless, he said, "the gun is a piece of junk."

As to whether the Cobray was any more deadly than other guns, Mike Dick, James Dick, and their clerks were in agreement. They cited one of the fundamental tenets of America's gun culture and a cherished dictum of the National Rifle Association: all guns were created equal. At bottom an AK-47 is no more dangerous than a High

Standard .22; a hundred-round Caleco semiautomatic pistol no more deadly than a Smith & Wesson .38.

Mike Dick also gave the Cobray a poor appraisal. "I hate to use this particular term, but it's a toy," he told me. "It's a fun gun for a person who wants to go out and line up a bunch of cans on a log, or to shoot at a target at very close range." He took a drag on his cigarette. "What I have a problem with is the implication that this particular gun because of what it costs or what it looks like or how many bullets it holds is inherently bad. With very little effort at all, cosmetically, that gun could be any other gun."

And yet it is cosmetics that account for some of the Cobray's appeal, as even he acknowledged.

"The Cobray is bought, I think, mainly because of its looks. It does in fact look kind of evil. And it does carry an awful lot of rounds." He was careful, however, to hew to yet another gun-camp theme: the large-capacity magazine had a sporting purpose. "Many people like to get multiple magazines or larger-capacity magazines simply to save time on reloading while they're at the range. When you're paying by the hour for range time, a lot of people do feel the need to stock up as much as possible."

Just as Nicholas Elliot knew he wanted to buy his gun at Guns Unlimited, so too have other traffickers, gang members, and killers chosen Guns Unlimited as their dealer of choice, a fact that had given Guns Unlimited something of a notorious reputation in Virginia's Tidewater region—unjustly, perhaps, but also unavoidably, given the peculiar nature of firearms retailing.

In two cases in the 1990s gun traffickers recruited straw-man buyers to shop at Guns Unlimited and purchase large numbers of guns, from high-quality Glocks to cheap Davis pistols. In both cases, according to documents in Norfolk federal court, the traffickers specifically directed their recruits to Guns Unlimited; in both cases Guns Unlimited did indeed act as an exemplary corporate citizen.

But a closer look at the two trafficking cases shows that Guns Unlimited and gun dealers in general operate in a world where profit and morality bear an inverse relationship to each other—where a truly moral dealer who followed his best social instincts at every turn would more than likely wind up on a bread line. What does it mean that even a "good" dealer can wind up promoting crime? Has gun retailing become simply too costly a pursuit for our society to tolerate?

◆ ◆ ◆

In August 1991, Amir Ali Faraz, a twenty-two-year-old student at Old Dominion University in Norfolk, Virginia, asked a friend of his, Matthew Jones, about buying "a couple of firearms." Faraz couldn't buy the guns on his own, he knew, because his permanent residence was in Pennsylvania and he had only a Pennsylvania driver's license.

This posed no great problem in Jones's eyes. About two weeks later, on August 30, 1991, Faraz met with Jones. Jones gave Faraz a Virginia driver's license belonging to a twenty-one-year-old Virginia resident, Brant Gomez Requizo, who had lost his driver's license earlier that year. Jones took Faraz to Guns Unlimited, where Faraz bought six high-caliber handguns—four for himself, and one each for Jones and a friend of Jones's who had accompanied them to the store. A week later Faraz sold three of his guns to Jones for $1,200. Faraz would later tell ATF agents that Jones had bragged he could sell the guns "for a 'big profit' in the Tidewater area to people who would take them up north and make even a bigger profit from them."

In the gun trade, buying more than one gun at a time automatically raises a warning flag; in fact, ATF requires dealers to mail in a multiple-purchase form anytime a customer buys two or more handguns within a period of five working days. Nonetheless, in the absence of specific local regulations, anyone in America can walk into a gunstore and buy a hundred handguns. The dealer is under no obligation to telephone ATF, or even to inquire why anyone would want so many guns. All the dealer must do is mail the form by the close of business on the day of the purchase. The buyer, meanwhile, is free to scoop up his hundred handguns and start selling.

ATF *will* investigate high-volume purchases, provided it learns of them. If a purchase takes place on a Saturday night, however, ATF will not see the multiple-purchase form for several days. Meanwhile, the guns will begin their rapid migration through the illicit-arms network. Guns trafficked from Norfolk, Virginia, for example, typically wind up in the hands of crooks in Washington, Philadelphia, and New York, half a day's drive up Interstate 95—nicknamed the Iron Road for all the illicit weapons that make the trip. In 1992, ATF conducted a massive tracing project to find out where the guns recovered from crime scenes in New York City had begun their travels. The agency discovered that Virginia alone accounted for 26 percent of the guns, more than any other individual state. Florida came in second, supplying 19 percent; Texas third with 11 percent; Georgia, home of S.W. Daniel, was fourth at 9 percent. Even Batman, in a December 1992 comic book, noted how easily the crooks could buy guns in Virginia. In the early 1970s most crime guns seized in New York came from South Carolina, but in 1975 the state passed a law allowing consumers to purchase only one gun per month. Although the law included a huge loophole—for inexplicable reasons it exempted purchases made at gun shows, a common source of crime guns throughout the country—it succeeded in sharply reducing the number of South Carolina guns found at New York crime scenes. South Carolina contributed only 2 percent of the New York crime guns traced by ATF in 1992. Virginia, deeply embarrassed by its role as crime-gun distributor of the Eastern Seaboard, passed a similar law in 1993. Before it took effect, however, ATF found that gun buyers in Virginia made 3,400 multiple purchases a year, or nearly ten a day. That the notification of such purchases takes place by mail in an age when virtually every ordinary consumer transaction involves some immediate form of computer verification is but one of the peculiar ironies that characterize arms commerce in America.

Mike Dick managed the first sale to Faraz and was immediately suspicious, enough so that he telephoned the ATF field office in Norfolk to alert the bureau to Faraz's purchases. (Dick also filed the multiple-purchase form.) Over the next two weeks Faraz returned three more times and bought twenty-nine more guns, selling twenty-five to Jones, according to court documents. On the last of these shopping trips Faraz placed an order for thirteen more handguns, all Glock pistols, the same guns now adopted by police departments around the country. Mike Dick telephoned ATF while Faraz was still in the store and helped choreograph an undercover operation against Faraz. Dick allowed the bureau to choose the day on which Guns Unlimited would notify Faraz that the guns he had ordered were ready for pickup. The agency chose September 17, 1991, a Tuesday.

Agents took up positions inside and outside the store and waited. At about five-fifteen that evening, a 1987 Pontiac Grand Am, registered to Faraz, pulled into the Guns Unlimited parking lot. Faraz stepped up to the counter and presented Brant Requizo's driver's license, which gave an address in Norfolk, Virginia. As an ATF agent watched, Faraz signed the required form 4473 with Requizo's name. Faraz left the store carrying the guns, then drove home, where agents kept him in sight while others contacted first Brant Requizo's mother and then Brant himself to confirm that his license had been lost.

At eight-forty, the agents arrested Faraz at his home. Faraz admitted buying the guns for Matthew Jones—Jones, he said, had agreed to pay him $6,000 for ten of the Glocks, or roughly $1,000 more than Faraz had paid to Guns Unlimited. The agents persuaded Faraz to make a monitored call to Jones and arrange to deliver the ten guns later that night. The stakeout team followed Faraz to the two A.M. rendezvous and arrested Jones.

Jones in turn told the agents that he had arranged to sell the guns to two New Yorkers and was to be paid $500 for his services.

Both Faraz and Jones were convicted of violating federal firearms laws. At Faraz's sentencing hearing on January 9, 1992, his attorney,

John Cooper, complained to the judge that the clerks at Guns Unlimited should have been able to tell from the picture on Brant Requizo's driver's license that Faraz was not Requizo. Requizo, the license showed, stood five foot five and weighed 131 pounds; Faraz was a 215-pound weight lifter. Cooper said, "There's something fundamentally strange about our society allowing somebody to go in and buy forty-eight guns within the course of a month on an ID that doesn't look anything like him." The judge, however, sentenced Faraz to seven months in prison, with two years' supervised release.

Mike Dick was proud of his role in the investigation. "I don't just send the forms in and hope it takes six months for ATF to get around to them," Dick told me. "If there is something that's obviously a problem—and this obviously was—my opinion is the best way to correct the problem from a society standpoint is to get these people off the street. If I just refuse to sell them weapons, nothing's going to happen. They're just going to go to someone less ethical than myself. And he may send the multiple-purchase form in, he may not send it in. Not all dealers are good."

Society did not make out in this deal quite so well as Guns Unlimited. The store booked at least $15,000 in sales. Yet twenty-nine of the forty-eight handguns that Faraz bought wound up in Matthew Jones's hands and thus in the gun-trafficking network, where weapons migrate quickly to their final users. (Some of the guns were kept by Jones, Faraz, and some of Faraz's friends.)

In the second trafficking case, a local college student, Dean Archer, was recruited to buy guns by a convicted felon. He made his first purchase on December 1, 1990, when he bought four handguns from Guns Unlimited—not just any guns, but four inexpensive pistols made by Davis Industries, a California company whose guns are favored by traffickers who buy them cheaply in jurisdictions with lax controls, then sell them at a steep markup to inner-city buyers.

No one at Guns Unlimited seemed overly concerned by the purchase. The clerk on duty that Saturday night did not feel moved to telephone ATF. Moreover, she sold Archer the guns on the strength of a rent receipt for a Virginia apartment and his driver's license—a New York driver's license.

When ATF learned of Archer's purchase—three days later—the agency was instantly suspicious and launched a preliminary investigation. A few days after the first purchase Archer reappeared at Guns Unlimited, this time accompanied by a young woman, Lisa Yvonne Scott. Scott bought seven cheap Davis handguns. Again ATF learned of the sale only through a multiple-purchase form mailed by Guns Unlimited. Again the form arrived three days after the purchase—more than enough time for those guns to make their way from hand to hand, state to state. And again ATF immediately assumed that something illicit had occurred.

ATF's Norfolk office called Guns Unlimited to get more details and learned that Scott had been accompanied by an unidentified male later identified as Dean Archer. By this point, however, eleven of the country's favorite crime guns were on the street.

A few days later Scott appeared again and bought thirteen Davis pistols. This time Mike Dick telephoned ATF. Nonetheless, Archer and Scott left the store with their new purchases. The total of cheap and deadly Davis pistols bought by the pair had risen to twenty-four. Four days later Scott and Archer made yet another buying trip, but at last ATF was waiting. The two were arrested and convicted.

Clearly the store had been helpful to the bureau. But why would Guns Unlimited even consider selling a handgun to a buyer presenting an out-of-state license for identification? Federal law explicitly forbids out-of-state buyers from acquiring handguns.

Dick explained that the clerk accepted the license as identification only because it had a photograph of Archer and established the link between his face and his name. A Norfolk rent receipt and an ID card from a local college established that he lived in Virginia. The fact that he was enrolled in college explained why he would have a New York license and be renting an apartment in Virginia.

Federal law grants a licensed gun dealer broad discretion to refuse a sale to anyone; a brochure mailed to licensees shortly after they get their licenses states in bold print, "Know Your Customer." Wouldn't prudence have dictated that Guns Unlimited simply refuse to sell weapons when the nature of the sale provides clear grounds for suspicion—clear enough, certainly, for the Bureau of Alcohol, Tobacco and Firearms?

"Yes, they tell me I can refuse sales," Dick said. "They tell me I have the discretion to do that. But in practical terms, that doesn't give me the right to infringe on one's civil rights."

I asked him how he felt knowing that Nicholas Elliot and various gun traffickers had specifically sought out Guns Unlimited as the place to acquire their guns.

"Well, actually, good," he said. "I don't know how to describe it without sounding . . . bad. Because I come out of hospitality, customer service is my number one concern. Period. Beyond all others. The ethnicity of an individual, in my restaurants, my hotel rooms, my store, is absolutely unimportant. I don't care what part of town you live in, what race you're of, you're going to be treated like a human being."

"But I'm not talking about race. All I—"

Dick cut me off. "But that's the point. I have a stronger black clientele than any store in Tidewater and I would bet any store in the state, and maybe any store in the Southeast, because—and word gets around—I treat people like human beings, and they can't always get that elsewhere."

One such client was Jean-Claude Pierre Hill, a young black physician from Virginia.

◆ ◆ ◆

On March 20, 1991, Hill walked into the Guns Unlimited store in Carrollton and was met at the counter by Mike Dick. Soon afterward, Hill decided to buy two stainless-steel Colt .45 auto-loading pistols, each priced at $529.99. He ordered the guns and put down a $100 deposit, then left the store. He returned on March 29 to pick up his guns and was again helped by Mike Dick. Dick brought out the two gleaming guns and let Hill inspect them, then pulled out a copy of form 4473 for Hill to fill out and sign.

ATF requires that the buyer himself fill out the top portion of the form, which asks for an address, details of the buyer's physical appearance, and other information. The buyer must also answer eight questions about his background and mental health.

Hill wrote down an address in Hampton, Virginia, said he was born at Clarke Air Force Base in the Philippines on July 17, 1961, and described himself as standing five feet six inches tall and weighing 170 pounds. At the prompt for "race," he wrote "other."

Next he answered the eight questions. The first four questions asked if he was currently under indictment, if he had ever been convicted of a felony, if he was currently a fugitive from justice, and if he used drugs. He answered no to each.

The fifth question asked: "Have you ever been adjudicated mentally defective or have you ever been committed to a mental institution?"

Here too Hill answered no.

Yet from July 25 through September 18, 1990, Hill had been a patient in an Air Force psychiatric unit, where he was diagnosed as paranoid, schizophrenic, and prone to exhibit "aggressive behavior." On several occasions Hill threatened the hospital staff, once saying, "I'm going to get you when I get out of here, I'm going to get you all."

From time to time, the hospital ordered him placed in four-point restraints. This was a prudent measure, as it happens. On the evening of August 29, 1990, Hill—at that moment unrestrained—leapt from his chair and punched a resident physician in the face, breaking the young doctor's nose. Before the staff could restrain him, Hill punched the doctor again.

He threatened to kill members of the staff. He told a nurse, "I'm going to bring my gun back when I'm released and blow your goddamn brains out, you bitch."

Hill answered the remaining questions on form 4473 and passed the form back to Mike Dick, who looked it over and asked Hill to explain what he meant by "other," in the race box. Hill said his mother was French, his father African American; to Dick, however, Hill was clearly black. Dick asked him to be more specific. Hill changed the answer to "black."

Still, something about Hill made Dick uncomfortable.

Dick remembered the case well.

"I can tell you that in that particular situation there was something wrong about him," he told me during our conversation over coffee that June morning. Hill claimed to have been in the Army, but knew nothing about how to field-strip a Colt, "one of the first things you learn in boot camp," Dick said. "I called ATF while he was in the store; I said I can't put my finger on it, but there's just something not right here.".

ATF ran a background check through the National Crime Information Center, Dick said, but found nothing. No one at the agency's Norfolk office knew of Hill or had any reason to worry about him. So Dick sold Hill the guns.

"Why?" I asked. "Couldn't you have just said, 'You worry me, I don't think you were in the Army, I'm not going to sell you these weapons'?"

"You're absolutely right, that's what I could have said. But do I trample on somebody's individual rights simply because I feel bad and ATF says I have the discretion to do it?"

In addition to the two Colts, Hill bought two extra magazines, some cleaning equipment, and 270 rounds of ammunition. He paid $1,147.87 in cash and left.

He had never signed the federal purchase form, however. And Mike Dick, despite his concerns about Hill, had not noticed the omission—even though the buyer's signature is an absolute requirement before any handgun purchase can be completed, and ATF insists the dealer witness the signature.

"I don't really have a good answer as to why I did not further pick up the signature," Dick said in testimony one year later in a Pennsylvania court. Guns Unlimited later caught the omission, Dick testified, and sent Hill a letter stating "please come in at your earliest convenience and sign this form for us."

The letter came back, however, bearing a Postal Service notice that the address did not exist.

◆ ◆ ◆

April 8, 1991, by all counts, was a stunningly beautiful day in Philadelphia, the sun bright and temperatures in the seventies. The banners along the Benjamin Franklin Parkway moved gently in the breeze. At the offices of CIGNA Corp., an insurance company, four executives gathered for a walk to a popular restaurant on the parkway, where they planned to celebrate the forty-ninth birthday of a colleague, Peter Foy, who was married and the father of two children. The lunch lasted only an hour. Everyone had chicken salad. The executives—Peter Foy, Robert Dowe, John Senatore, and Leonard Allen—had to be back at CIGNA for a one P.M. meeting.

They walked back down the parkway, Foy beside Dowe, Senatore beside Allen.

Witnesses, including a Philadelphia police officer, saw a blue Chevy Cavalier pull up at the curb. They saw the driver, a short black man, calmly exit the car, walk up behind the four men, and open fire with a large pistol. Moments later, he just as calmly returned to the car, adjusted his side mirror, and drove off. The car had Virginia plates.

Robert Dowe hadn't seen the car or its driver. He heard an explosion. "I did not see anything happen to Peter," he later testified. "The only thing I knew was that a round was fired and it was very, very close, and as I was trying to get down, I felt my—I believe I was trying to turn my head because I knew the shot was coming from behind me, and I felt my head pop. I knew I was shot in the head."

For no reason, purely at random, Dr. Jean-Claude Pierre Hill, carrying one of the stainless-steel Colt pistols he had bought a week before from Guns Unlimited, had chosen to attack the four executives. Foy, who weighed 284 pounds and stood six foot two, went down first. The .45 bullet entered the right side of his head just above his ear, then exited on the left side, leaving a massive "stellate," or star-shaped, exit wound. A hydrostatic shock wave—a pressure surge driven ahead of the bullet—fractured his skull in many places, even the orbital plates behind his eyes. The bullet macerated his brain—"not lacerated," emphasized James Lewis, a forensic pathologist with the Philadelphia medical examiner's office—"but *macerated*. The bullet basically destroyed his back portion of his lobes of the brain." Foy was pronounced dead at Hahnemann Hospital at 6:47 the following morning.

Robert Dowe too had been struck in the head, but he had been lucky. The bullet entered at his temple, exited near his ear, then reentered his body, plunging into his right shoulder and exiting through his arm. Another of Hill's bullets struck John Senatore in the arm, then continued on into his chest where it punctured a lung. Leonard Allen, the luckiest of the three, dove for cover when he heard the shots. "As I was diving," he testified, "something glanced through my hair." He was uninjured.

Jean-Claude Hill was found guilty of first-degree murder, with the caveat that the jury believed he was mentally ill.

◆ ◆ ◆

"How did you feel when you heard about this?" I asked Mike Dick. "That this guy had taken these guns you sold him, even though you had doubts, and killed somebody—the ultimate deprivation of somebody's rights? Did it cause you any sleepless nights?"

"No."

"Did you get drunk?"

"No. I did everything I possibly could have, short of compromising something I feel very strongly about. And that is, I'm not going to decide if you are a worthwhile person or not. He gave me red flags. I checked him out. Had there been anything, had ATF found mental instability in his background, had ATF said he was [dishonorably] discharged, I could have gone to him and said, 'Jean-Claude, I'm not going to sell you these guns.' But I'm not going to decide somebody's character based on my impressions of him, I'm just not gonna do it. It's not necessarily tied to any Second Amendment right to keep and bear arms, it's not tied to my right as a retailer not to do business with somebody. I just would not want to put myself in the position of deciding someone else's character arbitrarily based on my own opinion. Empowering people to do that is dangerous."

In most jurisdictions in America, however, there is little else to protect society from sales of handguns. Form 4473, far from helping to keep guns out of the wrong hands, has become a conduit for the discharge of responsibility. You would have to be naive indeed to put a yes in any of the eight boxes asking if you have been indicted, have been convicted of a felony, are a fugitive from justice, an addict, an illegal alien, have renounced your citizenship, or have ever been committed to a mental institution. In most jurisdictions no formal channel exists to check the truth of your answers. (In 1989, Virginia established an "instant-check" system that requires dealers to run a quick criminal check on every purchaser. But the system only looks for Virginia convictions and tells nothing about whether a buyer has been committed to a mental institution or is addicted to drugs.) One can argue that it is unfair to ask America's gun dealers, who after all are merely businessmen, to go beyond what the law requires of them. Nevertheless, the dealers and the gun lobby, in particular the NRA—as I'll show in Chapter Ten—played a large role in shaping the very laws that now allow gun dealers to disregard whatever qualms they may feel about selling guns to particular individuals.

The result is yet another of those curious ironies that mark America's gun culture. On the one hand, federal law clearly recognizes the dangers inherent in arming certain classes of individuals, including kids, addicts, convicted felons, and the mentally ill. Yet the law offers no practical means of eliminating those buyers from the buyer pool—nothing, that is, other than form 4473. Put another way, the law asks those people who arguably have the greatest motive to lie about their backgrounds to step forward just this once and come clean, even though doing so will automatically void the purchase they had felt so compelled to make.

Form 4473 is flimsy protection indeed for an enterprise under assault from all quarters. Mike Dick must defend against trucks. He has armored his doors and windows against burglars. He must be vigilant for traffickers, killers, and other felons seeking to buy his wares—or simply to murder him and take the guns. In the early 1990s a growing number of traffickers apparently decided that killing a gun dealer might be more efficient than recruiting a straw purchaser. In 1991, ATF's *FFL Newsletter,* which the bureau sends periodically to all federally licensed firearms dealers, warned of a rash of robberies and burglaries in Minnesota and Wisconsin. It devoted three pages to the July 29, 1991, robbery of an Ohio gun store during which the robber shot the dealer dead. The killer and two accomplices escaped with sixteen conventional guns—handguns, rifles, and shotguns—and eleven true machine guns, including two MAC-10s and an M-11 A1, a fully automatic variation of the MAC made by S.W. Daniel of Atlanta.

◆ ◆ ◆

Increasingly, gun dealers have taken to wearing guns during the workday. Mike Dick often wore one but, unlike his colleagues, kept his concealed. "The object of a concealed weapon is that nobody knows you have it," he said matter-of-factly. "I wear it about forty percent of the time and let people decide if they're going to be lucky or not." He concedes, however, that a handgun offers only limited protection. "If somebody wants to get you, you're never going to draw your weapon. They're going to start blasting before they get in the door. They're going to have surprise, and unless they're poor shots or you're very lucky, you're doomed."

All this for skimpy profits in a crumbling national industry facing ever-more-stringent controls.

"Why," I asked Dick, "do you stay in the business?"

"That's a difficult question. I come out of the hospitality industry, hospitality is my first love. I came here out of necessity to help my father. It has become a challenge to me, taking a declining business under constant siege by various aspects of society—it is a monumental challenge. My goal is to become profitable enough that at some point we can sell and I can go back to what I do best, and that is run hotels and restaurants."

I asked Raymond Rowley, the ATF special agent who investigated Nicholas Elliot's acquisition of his gun, how he would describe ATF's relationship with Guns Unlimited.

"I would say it's a good relationship," Rowley said. "We try to deal with all these firearms dealers as fairly as we can. They are selling a legal commodity. Obviously, guns can be used in crimes. We try to deal with them fairly."

Baltimore County's Col. Leonard Supenski was a bit less circumspect. Of James Dick, Mike Dick's father, he said, "That guy is a pariah. He ought to be turned out of that industry. But ATF didn't do anything—ATF should have nailed him to the cross."

ATF, indeed, plays a curious role in regulating the commerce of guns. A division of the Treasury Department, it is a bastard agency to which America has grudgingly assigned the well-nigh-impossible task of ensuring that the companies that make and distribute booze, cigarettes, and guns—together the nation's most prolific killers—pay their taxes and operate within a set of rules designed not to prevent the killing, but to keep it honest.

CHAPTER NINE

NICHOLAS

"Now you," Nicholas said.

Susan Allen had seen Sam Marino literally backing Nicholas into a corner of the classroom; she heard Marino insist that Nicholas hand over the gun. Then she saw Marino's body jump. She saw the books and folders he was carrying fly in all directions. She heard Marino cry, "My God, my God," and she watched as he fell forward.

And now this boy—this gangly black child with the sweet smile and serious demeanor, a student in her algebra class—had just turned toward her and pointed his gun at her, saying, "Now you."

She sprinted toward the door, then out and down the short flight of steps. Nicholas followed.

At first she planned to run to the school's main building to try to get help for Marino and have someone call the police, but realized that if she did so, she would lead Nicholas right to the heart of the school. She headed instead for the church.

She knew Nicholas was shooting at her. She heard one shot as she left the trailer. A few moments later, she heard another. She had the good sense to run serpentine fashion like a character in a grade-B war movie as Nicholas fired shot after shot at her back, sweeping the courtyard with a back-and-forth motion, stopping his pursuit now and then to clear a jammed cartridge. For Allen and Nicholas both, the sound was deafening. Her ears rang. His hurt.

After each shot she would pause an instant, wondering if she had been hit, waiting to see if she would fall. Then immediately she'd start running again, glancing back at intervals to see where Nicholas was and if he was still pursuing her.

Allen reached the end of the courtyard. With nowhere else to go, she made a sharp turn around the end of one of the classroom trailers. Something struck her with shocking force and knocked her immediately to the ground—with Nicholas close behind, firing at her, she had turned that corner and run face first into a utility shed.

"I hit the shed full force," she said. "I hit it, fell down. There was ringing around my ears. I fell down, and I was trying to get underneath the trailer—trying someway to get away."

Breathless and petrified, she wriggled under the trailer.

"It was not the smartest thing to do, if you think about it," Detective Adams told me.

As she lay there, she struggled for breath. She was indeed trapped. She watched Nicholas's legs as he advanced along the pavement outside.

"My God, make him stop," she whispered. "My God, please make him stop."

He took two more steps in her direction.

Then turned around.

◆ ◆ ◆

Two things had distracted Nicholas: a loud thumping noise nearby, and Sam Marino, who, wounded in the shoulder, now stood at the door to room T108. When Susan Allen had fled the room, Marino recalled, Nicholas had run past him in pursuit. "I got myself up off the floor . . . and noticed my shoulder had a tremendous ache in it." He moved toward the door, opened it, and shouted for help: "Please help me. I've been shot. I've been shot."

"All of a sudden," he said, "I looked down the steps and there he was again."

Nicholas stood only three or four feet away, at the bottom of the steps. This time he aimed a bit lower. The gun, once advertised by its manufacturer as "the gun that made the eighties roar," roared again. There was an elliptical flare. The bullet penetrated Marino's abdomen.

Marino fell onto the steps, then managed to stand again. He allowed himself to fall inside the classroom. He grabbed the doorknob, shut the door, and locked it.

Nicholas tried to open it, then gave up.

Meanwhile, the thumping had gotten louder. Nicholas knew the noise. He had heard it before during a class, when kids in a nearby trailer had been playing a game to see who could stamp hardest on the floor of the trailer.

In this case, however, the thumping was the sound made as terrified students scrambled to the rear of the trailer. On any other Friday, Nicholas would have been in that trailer, attending the Bible class taught by Hutch Matteson.

Marino, who had by now pulled himself to a window of room T108, watched as Nicholas crossed the courtyard, climbed the steps of the opposite trailer, and shot out the glass window in the door.

◆ ◆ ◆

Hutch Matteson had heard a loud explosion; like Marino, he assumed at first it had been generated by a large firecracker. He looked over his shoulder out the window of his classroom. "I saw Mr. Marino hanging out of the door yelling, 'Help. Help. He shot me, I've been shot.' At the time I didn't think that it was a real incident because I thought perhaps he was doing a demonstration for a class; so I began to walk over to the doorway of the class. As I opened the door, I took a step out and looked down the courtyard towards the church building. I saw Nicholas Elliot coming from that direction towards me. I shut the door and stood back against the wall glancing out of the door."

Nicholas was carrying what looked to be a gun. "It appeared to me at that point it was sort of like an Uzi water pistol because it seemed very small at a distance." (Cobray pistols are often confused with Uzis, police say.)

Through the glass window in the door, Matteson watched Nicholas approach. "I saw Nicholas go up to Mr. Marino. He was still hanging out of the door. He was approximately four to five feet away from him. I heard the shot go off."

Matteson turned to his students.

"I told them to get down and get back, so the class quickly started to move to the back of the trailer. One young man had the presence of mind to come up, and he locked the door."

The students—some three dozen of them—crouched at the back of the classroom, praying and crying. Matteson took up a sheltering position halfway between the students and the door and stood to see where Nicholas had gone.

"I was watching Nicholas as he came towards us. I thought perhaps he might go around the trailer. He came up to the stairway, tried the door. The door was locked. At that time, he shot the glass out and entered the room."

Nicholas walked up to the crowd of now terrified children.

"Don't do it," Matteson pleaded. "Nicholas, this is no way to handle this."

Nicholas had seen Matteson watching him through the window of the portable classroom. He knew Billy Cutter was probably in the class as well. "I don't know how I got in," Nicholas told Detective Adams. "I did not shoot the door. I did not shoot the door or the knob itself. I shot the glass in the door. I don't know how I got it open. . . . When I shot the glass, I guess it shaked the door and got it open."

Once inside, he quickly spotted Billy Cutter. Cutter had heard the shot and the sound of shattering glass, but was the last to rush to the back of the room and now lay on the floor ahead of the mound of students, fully in the open and utterly exposed. "There were chairs overturned and everything, so I would probably be about three or four feet in front of everyone else," Cutter later testified.

"Billy," Nicholas said, "I hate you, man."

Cutter was screaming, "No, don't."

Nicholas aimed the gun at Cutter.

"I know I said his name," Nicholas told Detective Adams. "I don't remember exactly what I said about him, because I was mad."

Others, however, do recall. "Billy Cutter," Nicholas said. "This is for you. I'm going to kill you."

As the other students huddled closer and wept and prayed, Nicholas pulled the trigger.

CHAPTER TEN

THE ENFORCERS

GUN AFICIONADOS MAY LIKEN THE BUREAU of Alcohol, Tobacco and Firearms to the Gestapo, but in its relationship to America's gun dealers it behaves more like an indulgent parent. This is partly the result of concrete restrictions imposed on the bureau by budget and statute, partly of an institutional reluctance to offend its primary source of investigative leads and to provoke the always cantankerous gun lobby—a legacy of the bureau's near demise in the early years of the Reagan administration at the hands of the National Rifle Association and its powerful allies on Capitol Hill.

In a 1981 congressional hearing, the bureau's then-director, G. R. Dickerson, defended the bureau, proclaiming to the House Judiciary Committee that the bureau had for the prior two years "focused over ninety-two percent of its enforcement resources on the prevention of violent crime and the pursuit of violent criminals." ATF had used aggressive, proactive tactics to enforce firearms laws, he said, including undercover stings designed to trap dealers into making illegal sales. The NRA and other members of the gun lobby saw nothing positive in these measures and charged ATF with trampling the constitutional rights of ordinary gun owners. The charge fell on sympathetic ears. In 1981, then-president Ronald Reagan announced his plan to make good on a campaign promise to abolish the ATF.

Today a chastened ATF (rescued at the last minute, as I'll show, by a most improbable angel, the NRA itself) describes its mission in more modest terms. "There's been a misconception that we're in the prevention business," said Jack Killorin, a former law-enforcement agent who now heads the bureau's public affairs office. (A plaque on the wall behind his desk identifies him as Jack "Ganja" Killorin, commemorating his role in an ATF raid against a drug dealer.) "We're not in the prevention business. We're in the business of catching those people who do wrongful acts, and causing them to be punished, and hopefully finding enough of that to create some deterrence."

Where once the bureau prided itself on running firearms sting operations, it now describes even its battles against illegal traffickers as a means not so much of halting the proliferation of guns, but of protecting and maintaining the paper trail that tracks a gun from manufacturer to distributor to dealer and finally to first purchaser. "Illegal traffickers in weapons inhibit the effectiveness of the tracing function and must be identified and put out of business," said a 1992 report from ATF's divisional office in Detroit. "The integrity of the tracing system must be preserved to ensure that valuable leads continue to be provided to law-enforcement agencies."

As things stand now, federal gun laws foster a built-in disincentive to rigorous investigation. Gun-purchase records, the most crucial element of the tracing network, remain in the hands of the dealers themselves. When riled, dealers can make the workday lives of ATF agents far more difficult. Good industry relations can mean the difference between merely having to call the dealer on the phone or making a personal visit, a significant bureaucratic obstacle for an undermanned agency. "If it were not for cooperative [dealers]," noted a 1992 report from the bureau's Detroit office, "ATF's task in locating and removing illegal firearms sources would be dealt a serious blow."

All this, however, adds up to a reactive orientation that helps bolster the culture of nonresponsibility in the firearms industry, with the unintended effect of leaving all but the most blatantly crooked dealers free to push the limits of the law.

◆ ◆ ◆

In fairness, ATF stands in an almost untenable position. It must police the nation's 245,000 licensed firearms dealers—known in the industry as FFLs, or Federal Firearms Licensees—with only four hundred inspectors, each of whom must also conduct inspections of wineries, liquor distributors, distilleries, breweries, tobacco producers, and the country's 10,500 explosives users and manufacturers. This ratio of inspectors to licensees is an improvement, by the way, over the rough-and-ready 1960s when only five inspectors faced the daunting task of inspecting the records of one hundred thousand gun dealers.

At the same time, the agency finds itself obliged by law to grant a firearms license to virtually anyone who asks for one, provided the applicant has $30 to cover the licensing fee. In 1990, 34,336 red-blooded Americans applied for an FFL. ATF denied licenses to only 75. Another 1,408 withdrew or abandoned their applications, yielding a combined rejection/withdrawal rate of about 4 percent. If the current rate of licensing continues, the number of FFLs will double through the 1990s to well over half a million licensed weapons dealers, even though the fortunes of domestic arms manufacturers are likely to continue their current decline. Increased competition for the shrinking gun-consumer dollar can only increase the already prevalent tendency among dealers to do only the minimum required by law to keep guns out of the wrong hands.

Depending on one's stance in the gun debate, the application process is either too stringent or appallingly lax. An applicant doesn't have to demonstrate any firearms knowledge, not even whether he knows the difference between a revolver and a pistol, a .44 or a .45. It is much harder to get a license to operate a powerboat on the Chesapeake Bay, to become a substitute teacher in New Jersey, or to get a California driver's license—far, far harder to get a

Maryland permit to carry a single handgun or a license to hunt in Maryland's forests—than it is to get a license that enables you to acquire at wholesale prices thousands of varieties of weapons and have them shipped right to your home. Roughly half the federal firearms licensees don't maintain a bona fide store, according to ATF, but operate instead out of their homes. Some of these "kitchen-table" dealers sell guns at gun shows, but many don't deal guns at all; they hold a license simply to buy their guns at cheap wholesale prices. A small but obviously important segment use their licenses to buy guns wholesale for distribution to inner-city arms traffickers.

"We're not in the business of putting people out of the firearms business," said Anthony A. Fleming, chief of ATF's firearms and explosives operations branch, in charge of dealer licensing and inspections. "If people qualify for a firearms license, by law we have to issue them a license."

But federal law, at least on paper, also insists that anyone who receives a license must actually engage in the business of selling firearms. In practice, however, Fleming concedes there is little ATF can do to compel a licensee to become a legitimate commercial business. "We can't force him to advertise," Fleming said. "We can't say you've applied for a license and by the end of two years you have to have at least ten sales. Your retort, immediately, would be, 'I'm open for business, I've got my door open, anybody comes in here I'm ready to sell them a gun.' There's nothing we can do about that."

He added that some licensees who operate from their homes do run sophisticated dealerships. "I've seen residential dealers with a better setup and better inventory than a commercial business. And then I've gone into commercial places and found only five or six guns in there. You wonder why they're paying rent. But they're allowed to have a license and be in the business."

A look at ATF licensing records can turn up some surprising revelations about who among us are licensed gun dealers. Licensed dealers turn up everywhere, even on the quietest streets in the best neighborhoods. My ATF printout of Maryland dealers identified 334 in Baltimore alone, yet the 1992–93 yellow pages for Greater Baltimore listed only eighteen established dealers and pawnshops. Among the dealers not listed in the phone book were two entities with the intriguing names Make My Day Guns and Shalom Services Company.

A *Los Angeles Times* reporter, David Freed, acquired the roster of Los Angeles County licensees and found the list included a Chinese baker, a survivalist, a fertility specialist, a school policeman employed by the Los Angeles Unified School District (he listed school offices as his licensed place of business), a man who told Freed he had experienced "multiple personality changes," and an agent of the U.S. Drug Enforcement Administration (he listed DEA headquarters in Los Angeles). The list also included a former soldier dishonorably discharged from the Army and arrested on burglary and concealed-weapons charges whose licensed premises was a hotel room.

My neighbors may not want to hear this, but on May 15, 1992, I set out to join this none-too-exclusive club and applied for my own Federal Firearms License. The two-page application, ATF form 7, asked which grade license I wanted. There are nine levels, costing from $30 to $3,000, the latter qualifying the holder to import "destructive devices" such as mortars, bazookas, and other weapons with a barrel-bore diameter of half an inch or more. The form asked the same nine questions about my criminal past that appear on form 4473. It also asked what other business would be pursued at my "business location," in my case, my home. I wrote "communications," typically a catchall category for journalists, advertisers, writers, and others. It also asked my business hours—I listed ten to five-thirty, Monday through Saturday. The form then asked: "Are the applicant's business premises open to the general public during these hours?"

I thought about this one. If I ever did get down to actually selling guns, of course I would admit my customers. But they would have to ring the bell first and I would have to be home, but yes—they'd have the run of the place or at least my office, where my FFL is currently openly displayed as per federal regulations. It is taped to my wall, above my official National Rifle Association membership card.

I received my license on June 22, 1992, well within the forty-five days in which ATF is required to accept or deny an application.

No one called to verify my application. No one interviewed me to see if in fact I planned to sell weapons or not. There was no federal requirement that I first check with authorities in Maryland and Baltimore about specific local statutes that might affect my ability to peddle guns in the heart of my manicured, upscale, utterly established Baltimore neighborhood. As far as the federal government was concerned, I was in business and could begin placing orders for as many weapons as I chose. In short, I could supply an urban army with modern, high-powered weapons of state-of-the-art lethality, and ATF wouldn't know anything about it. The bureau would not know, that is, unless the weapons began turning up during arrests by ATF agents or local police, or unless ATF inspectors conducted a routine compliance audit. Federal law allows ATF to do only one such audit a year of each licensee, unless the agency has a specific investigative reason for doing more.

In one crucial area, federal firearms law explicitly favors gun dealers over consumers. Any consumer who knowingly makes a false statement or representation during a firearms transaction, as Curtis Williams found when he bought a gun for Nicholas Elliot, automatically commits a felony and faces a fine of up to $5,000 and a prison term of up to five years. Yet any Federal Firearms Licensee—a dealer, manufacturer, importer, or distributor—who commits the same offense faces a maximum fine of only $1,000 and imprisonment for not more than one year. In short, the consumer commits a felony; the dealer a misdemeanor. The distinction is crucial. A dealer convicted of a mere misdemeanor can still keep his Federal Firearms License; if convicted of a felony, he cannot.

In cases where dealers are suspected of knowingly and willfully selling guns to crooks and traffickers, ATF can be a tenacious, sly, and forceful investigator. The agency is fond of saying that dealers who commit such violations will get caught sooner or later, once the ATF National Tracing Center at Landover, Maryland, detects evidence of their wayward dealings. Indeed, in the 10 percent of crimes where law-enforcement officials actually request a federal trace, the tracing network often proves an effective investigative tool both in solving crimes and for identifying renegade dealers. There is a fundamental problem with this approach, however: by the time the tracing center does get involved, the guns in question have been used in crime, typically serious crime involving assault, homicide, or narcotics peddling. ATF gets another notch in its holster, the illegal dealer is put out of business, but society is left to tend its wounds—grief, disability, surgical bills, lost income, psychic trauma, and the increasingly pervasive feeling that one is not safe in one's own home.

At times through its history ATF has tried to take a more proactive stance toward regulating the flow of firearms. The agency is immensely proud of the lawmen it counts as its ancestors, in particular Eliot Ness, the legendary commander of "The Untouchables." Walk into the offices of many senior ATF officials and you'll find a framed poster from the 1987 movie *The Untouchables*, which starred Kevin Costner and Sean Connery. The ATF press office provides reporters with a packet of background information on the bureau, including a one-page biography of Ness.

Only by understanding how ATF evolved from a tax-collection agency to the nation's sole firearms cop can one come to understand the complex relationship between the bureau and the firearms industry, and why no federal entity saw a need to examine Guns Unlimited's role in the arming of Nicholas Elliot.

◆ ◆ ◆

The Bureau of Alcohol, Tobacco and Firearms became the nation's enforcer of federal firearms laws largely by default. ATF traces its roots as far back as 1791, when Congress imposed the first federal tax on distilled spirits, an act that promptly led to the Whiskey Rebellion of 1794. Congress periodically repealed and levied alcohol taxes until 1862, when it created the Office of Internal Revenue and made the tax a formal, permanent part of the government's income. The office deployed three agents to enforce the law.

On January 16, 1919, the Treasury Department became far more deeply involved in law enforcement when Nebraska cast the last vote necessary to ratify the Eighteenth Amendment to the Constitution, banning the manufacture, sale, and transport of alcoholic beverages. The national Prohibition Act, also known as the Volstead Act for Minnesota congressman Andrew J. Volstead, placed responsibility for enforcing the amendment with the commissioner of Internal Revenue because of the department's prior role as collector of alcohol taxes and enforcer of violations of the alcohol tax laws.

The amendment may have crimped the supply of booze, but it did nothing to diminish America's thirst. Underworld entrepreneurs throughout the country sought to satisfy demand by building illegal distilleries and saloons. The amendment guaranteed them a large clientele: while it outlawed the production and distribution of booze, it allowed consumers to own, drink, and even buy alcoholic beverages without penalty. Gangs fought each other for control of the underground distilleries and distribution networks and paid a substantial portion of their profits to local officials and police to help protect their interests.

What ATF neglects to tell in its fact sheets and its biographic handout on Eliot Ness is that agents of Treasury's Prohibition Unit were themselves notoriously corrupt. They received abysmally low salaries, which Robert J. Schoenberg, author of the 1992 biography *Mr. Capone,* called an "invitation to corruption." The agents' behavior heartened the leaders of Chicago's Prohibition gangs, who found they exhibited, as Schoenberg puts it, "an almost Chicagoan capacity for corruption."

Eliot Ness urged his supervisors to let him establish a special unit of young agents not yet "bent" by mob money and influence, and in September of 1929 he founded a squad the newspapers would soon begin calling The Untouchables, for their apparent resistance to corruption. Far from shooting it out with bootleggers and walking up mean streets cradling a tommy gun, Ness and his squad used painstaking investigative techniques to pursue the Chicago gangsters, chief among them Alphonse Capone, also known as Scarface. One of their coups was to place a wiretap in a nightclub operated by Al Capone's brother Raffalo, more commonly known as Ralph.

Like the Wild West heroes who came before him, Ness was largely responsible for his own legend. In a 1957 book called *The Untouchables*, which became the basis for the TV series starring Robert Stack, Ness played up the dangers of pursuing Al Capone, even though in fact Capone and other gangsters had an overwhelming respect for the damage they would do to their own interests if they ever killed a federal agent. Indeed, Schoenberg writes, Capone explicitly warned his men not to shoot it out with Treasury agents— just to get away, if possible.

The real hero in the pursuit of Al Capone, according to Schoenberg, was an "investigative accountant" named Frank Wilson, an Internal Revenue agent who would later become head of the U.S. Secret Service, another branch of the Treasury Department. Wilson and colleagues doggedly hunted for evidence that Al Capone had failed to pay his income tax. The first step was to prove he even had an income, something Capone had consistently and effectively denied ever receiving. The agents examined some one million checks looking for any hint of money destined for Capone. A breakthrough came when Wilson discovered a ledger confiscated early on in a raid on Capone's headquarters that had been left to gather dust at the back of a file cabinet at his office.

Prohibition greatly heightened America's official distaste for guns. Gangsters rubbed each other out on street corners, in front of restaurants, from armored limousines. By the fall of 1925, as mobs in Chicago fought each other for control, the homicide rate in Cook County, Illinois, rose to more than one murder per day, a decidedly modern rate of mutual disposal. For as long as the killing remained in the family, the public was enthralled. Chicago's gangsters were

glamorous celebrities thumbing their noses at a censorious government intent on denying the public its pleasures.

The history of gun violence, however, teaches two important
maxims, whose predictive power was demonstrated yet again during
the Prohibition wars.

First, violence will always spread beyond boundaries initially
found by the public at large to be "acceptable." That is, gang warfare—or, as today, inner-city feuds between drug dealers—will inevitably expand beyond those boundaries to include bystanders.

Second, guns will always migrate from the hands of their originally intended users to those who value their use in crime. Just as the
Ingram, designed for military use, became instead the drug-gang
weapon of choice and a ghetto icon, so too the Thompson submachine gun, designed to be a "trench broom" for use in World War I,
became instead the favored tool of gangsters throughout the country
and an icon of the 1920s. In 1969, long before S.W. Daniel began
peddling its Cobray as "the gun that made the eighties roar," William
J. Helmer titled his biography of the Thompson gun *The Gun That
Made the Twenties Roar*. The gangsters' use of the gun was largely
responsible for the passage of the nation's first-ever federal gun controls in 1934, and thus for expanding the Treasury Department's
law-enforcement responsibilities to include firearms.

The Thompson submachine gun, invented by Gen. John T.
Thompson, was built in New York by Auto-Ordnance Corp.,
founded by Thompson in 1916 with the express purpose of putting
the design into production. Like the Ingram, the Thompson submachine gun was initially a failure. The Army did not yet appreciate its
value. The gun was too big to be a sidearm, too small for a field rifle,
or so went the conventional wisdom of the time. General Thompson,
like Gordon Ingram, sought to expand the market for the gun by
offering it to consumers, an effort that resulted in some unusual advertising. In a 1922 magazine ad, Auto-Ordnance merged frontier
myth with modern firepower, depicting a cowboy in furry chaps and

kerchief earnestly firing his tommy gun from the front porch of his ranch house at a group of seven bandits. The text below called the gun "the ideal weapon for the protection of large estates, ranches, plantations, etc." An article in *Army & Navy Journal* reported the gun "can be kept in the home as a protection against burglars."

Critics, however, described the gun in terms strikingly similar to those used by Col. Leonard Supenski in his critique of S.W. Daniel's Cobray pistol. In 1923, a British firearms expert described the tommy gun as "an arm that is useless for sport, cumbrous for self-defense, and could not serve any honest purpose, but which in the hands of political fanatics might provoke disaster."

The gun did not initially win many military contracts, but it captured the imagination of the Chicago gangs. The first recorded use of a tommy gun in crime occurred in Chicago on September 25, 1925, when Frank McErlane, a Chicago bootlegger, set out to assassinate a competitor named Spike O'Donnell. Police were stymied by the volume and the orderly arrangement of bullet holes left in a storefront by the attack. McErlane used the gun again just over a week later when he blasted the headquarters of another bootlegger. Here too no one was killed. A few months later, on February 9, 1926, McErlane used the gun again; this time the weapon made front-page headlines. The banner headline in the next morning's *Chicago Tribune* read, "Machine Gun Gang Shoots 2."

That day, Al Capone went to a Chicago hardware store and ordered three.

Capone first used his tommy guns on April 27, 1926, in an attack that would soon become a staple of the gangster-film genre. He and associates set out to kill a bootlegger named James Doherty. Lumbering along in a black, armored Cadillac limousine, Capone caught up with Doherty as he and two other men stepped from a Lincoln and made their way toward one of the many illegal saloons then operating in Chicago. Capone and his gunmen opened fire, killing all three men. They didn't realize it until later, but they had killed an unintended victim. It was a mistake that would, five years later, prove an important contributor to Capone's conviction for tax evasion.

One of the dead men proved to be a twenty-six-year-old Illinois state prosecutor named William McSwiggin, known as the "hanging prosecutor" for his aggressive pursuit of gangsters. In response, police raided Capone's headquarters, seizing the ledgers that Internal Revenue agent Frank Wilson would later discover at the back of a file cabinet and that would provide the first solid evidence of Capone's income.

The attack triggered an arms race. Capone's enemy, Hymie Weiss, whose gang controlled the North Side of Chicago, acquired Thompsons and, on September 20, 1926, launched a retaliatory attack against Capone, the most spectacular—if ineffective—attack of the Prohibition era, dubbed the "Siege of Cicero."

Capone's headquarters were situated in the Hawthorne Hotel in Cicero, Illinois, some two blocks from the Chicago line. Shortly after one P.M. on September 20, 1926, Capone and his associates were seated in the Hawthorne's first-floor restaurant, which was packed with other diners. They heard the telltale chatter of a machine gun somewhere down the street, but none of the screams and sounds of shattering glass that tended to accompany that kind of attack. Intrigued, they went to the windows of the restaurant—exactly what Hymie Weiss's men had intended. That first machine gun was a lure; it was loaded with blanks.

A Capone bodyguard quickly recognized the trap and forced Capone down. As everyone in the restaurant hit the floor, a convoy of ten limousines and touring cars slowly made its way up the street, machine guns and shotguns firing from every window, pumping some one thousand rounds into the room.

No one in the room was hit. Outside, two members of a Louisiana family—the mother and her five-year-old son—were slightly wounded. A minor member of Capone's gang who had been standing outside the restaurant was nicked by a bullet.

The Thompson submachine gun quickly migrated from Chicago. It turned up next during a gang war in southern Illinois, which even featured dynamite dropped from a biplane. (The bombs never went off.) Philadelphia experienced its first tommy-gun attack on February 25, 1927, New York on July 28, 1928.

The violence became more grotesque, less the "innocent" battlings of bad guys against bad guys.

On February 14, 1929, a Cadillac with a siren and gong pulled up in front of the S.M.C. Cartage Company in Chicago. Two men in police uniforms and two in civilian clothes—one wearing a chinchilla coat—stepped from the car. The officers entered the building and announced a raid, ordering the seven men inside to put their hands up and face the wall. Six of the men had ties to a gang led by George "Bugs" Moran; the seventh was a young optician named Reinhart H. Schwimmer, who had become enthralled with the mob and had stopped by that day for coffee.

The two civilians, each carrying a Thompson, entered next and began firing, instantly cutting down the seven men. For good measure, one of the gunmen then fired from ground level into the tops of their heads. The two gunmen then put their own hands up and were marched back to the car by the two men dressed as policemen.

The St. Valentine's Day Massacre marked a change in the public's willingness to accept gang violence. The brutality of the crime, the fact the men were shot in the back, somehow seemed a violation of criminal etiquette.

As other massacres followed, the revulsion grew. On July 28, 1931, gangster Vincent Coll tried to kill one of Dutch Schultz's men as he sat in front of a social club on E. 107th Street in New York. The target escaped unharmed, but the attack, quickly dubbed the Baby Massacre, left five children wounded. One, a baby in a baby carriage, later died. Coll may or may not have used a tommy gun, but the gun took the blame anyway.

Within a month, two other New York gun battles killed two girls, one eighteen, the other only five. In the latter, gunfire also killed two policemen and three of the assailants and wounded twelve other people.

Crime seemed poised to overwhelm the country. In 1932, the Lindbergh baby was kidnapped and murdered. (Capone offered $10,000 for information on who did it.) Killers of all kinds—John Dillinger, Pretty Boy Floyd, Machine-Gun Kelly (who contrary to myth never fired a gun in the course of a crime), Clyde Barrow and Bonnie Parker, Baby Face Nelson, and "Ma" Barker—rampaged over the countryside. Bonnie Parker, once again demonstrating that penchant of our heroes of violence for promoting their own legends, wrote poetry about her exploits with Clyde. One, titled "The Story of Bonnie and Clyde" and released to newspapers by Bonnie's mother, linked the pair to the mythic outlaws of the Wild West:

> You've read the story of Jesse James—
> Of how he lived and died,
> If you're still in need
> Of something to read
> Here's the story of Bonnie and Clyde.

Soon after the poem was published, police at last caught up with Bonnie and Clyde and killed them both.

One result of all this mayhem was a host of gangster movies, beginning with the 1930 hit *Little Caesar*. In 1931 alone, Hollywood made fifty gangster films. And once again myth and reality converged. On October 14, 1931, Edward G. Robinson, who starred in *Little Caesar,* sat in on Al Capone's tax evasion trial, which would end three days later and result ultimately in his being sent to a brand-new prison built on Alcatraz Island in San Francisco Bay.

A more significant result, however, was the National Firearms Act of 1934, which regulated the sale and manufacture of machine guns and other "gangster-type" weapons, such as silencers and sawed-off shotguns, and gave responsibility for enforcement to the Alcohol Tax Unit of the Internal Revenue Service. You could still buy a machine gun, but now you had to register the gun and pay a $200 tax. At the time, this was real money, more than the retail price of a Thompson, which Auto-Ordnance had reduced to $175 in its continuing quest for orders from the U.S. military. The tax remains $200 today, no longer quite the disincentive the law's crafters meant it to be.

In 1938, Congress passed the next round of federal controls with the Federal Firearms Act, which required the licensing of gun dealers and set the cost of a license at a whopping one dollar. (The National Rifle Association had argued even this was too high and should have been something nominal, say fifteen cents or a quarter.)

The next great spasm of domestic violence took place in the 1960s, with the assassinations of John F. Kennedy, Robert Kennedy, and Martin Luther King, Jr.; Charles Whitman's shooting spree from the top of the University of Texas tower, which killed fourteen people; and the overall unrest that tore the nation's cities apart in the late 1960s. This time the result was a more comprehensive set of firearms laws, called the Gun Control Act of 1968. It boosted dealer fees to $10 and required that they keep detailed records of incoming and outgoing guns. It also forbade the sale of rifles, shotguns, and handguns to felons and others deemed unfit to own guns. And taking its cue from Lee Harvey Oswald's mail-order purchase of the rifle he used to kill the president, the law banned mail-order sales of guns directly to individuals. Congress assigned enforcement of the act to the Alcohol & Tobacco Tax Division of the IRS, which became the Alcohol, Tobacco & Firearms Division.

Law-enforcement agents within the ATFD welcomed their new responsibilities. They were accomplished lawmen with a lot of nitty-gritty, dangerous experience in battling the moonshiners of the South. But officially they were employees of the Internal Revenue Service, the nation's tax collector. The images clashed. "When our law-enforcement officers were asked who they were, they would say Treasury agents," said Rex D. Davis, a former director of ATF who at the time was an assistant regional commissioner of the ATFD. In outlying field offices, the agents placed signs on their doors that said Treasury Department. "Our guys didn't want to be Internal Revenue agents."

The Gun Control Act greatly expanded the division's law-enforcement responsibilities. "There's no question the Gun Control Act of 1968 was like a breath of fresh air," Davis said. "It gave us a very important law-enforcement jurisdiction, and one that was nationwide as opposed to the moonshine and illicit-liquor enforcement, which was primarily regional, the Southern tier of states."

When Davis became director in 1970, his "hidden agenda" included separating the ATFD from the IRS. Indeed, the division's new responsibilities had begun causing something of an image problem for the IRS. When agents participated in raids or became involved in shoot-outs, the headlines inevitably described them as IRS agents, at a time when the IRS was actively promoting the value of voluntary compliance with federal tax laws. On July 1, 1972, the Treasury Department removed the division from the IRS and made it the Bureau of Alcohol, Tobacco and Firearms. (The bureau would later take to calling itself ATF, dropping the B.) Although most of the agents were delighted, a few were fearful, Davis said. "I think some people had a little trepidation. Really, what we were doing was putting ourselves out in front, and there were probably some people who felt it was nice and safe and cozy being a little thing in a great big place like Internal Revenue."

Inevitably, the new bureau found itself on a collision course with the National Rifle Association.

By 1972, the NRA was already a formidable foe, but it was wrestling with its own internal schism. In 1968 the NRA's executive vice president, Gen. Franklin Orth, committed what the association's hard-liners considered an unpardonable sin. By then, the post of executive vice president had become the most powerful position within the NRA, far more so than the presidency. Orth had dared support, in public, federal gun controls. Not just any controls, moreover, but the Gun Control Act of 1968. The ATFD's agents may have welcomed the new law, but the NRA's hard-liners loathed it. And yet Orth, in testimony before a congressional committee debating the proposed legislation, had said no "sane American who calls himself an American" could object to the bill's elimination of mail-order sales.

Orth was one of the NRA's old guard, who saw the NRA in more traditional terms as an organization devoted to promoting hunting and hunter safety, protecting hunters' rights, and protecting the environment. A growing segment of the NRA's membership, however, wanted the NRA to become a political force and in so doing to become the nation's primary guardian of the Second Amendment. To these hard-line fundamentalists, led by Harlon Carter, a former head of the U.S. Border Patrol, any gun law was an infringement of the Constitution and was to be opposed without compromise. Gradually, the hard-liners gained influence and, in 1977, at the NRA's annual meeting in Cincinnati, Ohio, won control of the board and elected Harlon Carter to be the new executive vice president. The coup, known within the NRA as the Cincinnati Revolt, set the NRA on the path it still follows today as a relentless opponent of gun control and anyone who supports it. Carter became a hero. "To the NRA faithful," wrote Osha Gray Davidson in his 1993 book, *Under Fire: The NRA & the Battle for Gun Control,* "Harlon Carter is Moses, George Washington, and John Wayne rolled into one."

The NRA chose to attack ATF as a means of diminishing the impact of the newly passed legislation. "That was a well-known strategy in Washington," Davis said. "If you're opposed to a law, the way to attack it is to attack the agency which has responsibility for it, and thereby reduce the enforcement of law."

When Davis became director, he set out at first to try to smooth relations between his agency and the NRA. "I thought it made sense," he said. "I guess probably what I started out doing was giving them too much credit. I thought that two sides to an issue through dialogue and good-faith efforts could make it a little easier on each other. But I found that not to be true."

He told the NRA's new executive vice president, Gen. Maxwell Rich, he would investigate any NRA complaints about his agency and give him a full report. "That didn't work. Their primary interest as I saw it and as I found out was in criticizing and attacking the credibility of the bureau, rather than trying to reach some accommodation."

Indeed, to Harlon Carter's NRA the new bureau was the vilest of enemies. The bureau did little to smooth relations. In March of 1978, for example, ATF agents seized four machine guns and three other weapons from the NRA's elaborate firearms museum on the first floor of its Washington headquarters, charging the weapons had not been registered in accordance with the National Firearms Act. "We didn't feel that anybody was above the law," Davis said. "We saw a clear violation." The NRA countered that the guns no longer worked and were thus exempt from provisions of the act. A federal judge agreed and ordered the bureau to return the guns. There was more to this raid on NRA headquarters than dispassionate enforcement of federal law. Davis said, with a smile, "I suspect that we would have been a little bit gleeful if we had found something a little bit more severe."

The NRA kept the pressure on Davis and the bureau. The association routinely attacked the bureau before Congress, depicting its agents as secret police who systematically trampled the rights of ordinary citizens. It cited example after example of what it alleged to be ATF abuses, including the case of Kenyon Ballew, a pressman with *The Washington Post,* who was shot in the head and paralyzed during an ATF raid on his apartment. The NRA and Gun Owners of America charged that the bureau's men barged in without reasonable cause and shot an innocent gun owner.

In fact, Ballew possessed many firearms and chose to point one at the raiding party as they entered, prompting a Montgomery County police officer to fire. The bullet struck Ballew in the head. ATF agents seized three hand-grenade casings and a supply of black powder, which together constituted an illegal destructive device. Ballew sued, but lost. The federal court found that the ATF agents "had acted reasonably" and agreed the "three grenades together with the powder seized were in combination both designed and intended to be used as destructive devices."

The NRA, however, took Ballew, by now in a wheelchair, to its annual meetings and wheeled him onstage as evidence of ATF's infamous behavior.

Despite these attacks, the bureau felt reasonably safe. When Rex Davis became director, Richard Nixon was still president, and he favored some gun controls. So did Gerald Ford. And so too did Jimmy Carter. At one point, apparently with the blessings of the Carter White House, the Treasury Department invited Rex Davis to design new regulations that would help improve enforcement of the Gun Control Act—whatever regulatory powers Davis felt he would most like to have and that could be instituted without new legislation.

Davis, delighted at the invitation, published his bureau's proposed new rules, which would have created unique serial numbers for every gun (as things stand now, guns from different manufacturers may have the same serial numbers) and established a central gun-tracing database that would include every step in the travels of every gun up to the last retailer in the chain. The database, however, would not include the names of the gun buyers themselves.

To the NRA, this was tantamount to establishing a national registration system. Outright confiscation of guns would surely follow. "The NRA went ape," Davis said. The association sent out an emergency plea to its members to write letters of protest. "We got over three hundred thousand pieces of correspondence, of which seven thousand were in favor. We had mailbags in the corridors."

Nonetheless, ATF persisted and asked Congress for the $10 million the bureau felt it would need to develop the new computer system.

"We took a beating," Davis said. "Congress not only didn't give us ten million dollars. They took ten million dollars out of our budget. So they penalized us for having the gall to initiate these programs. Needless to say, the regulations were withdrawn by Treasury, by the Carter administration, with their tails between their legs."

And ATF was left to cope with $10 million less in its operating budget.

Nonetheless, ATF still had the benefit of an administration that at least in spirit favored gun control. But Carter wouldn't be president forever.

During the 1980 campaign, Ronald Reagan made it clear where his sympathies lay. He wooed the NRA with a campaign pledge that if elected president, he would abolish the hated bureau.

The NRA and its powerful allies, including Rep. John Dingell of Michigan and Rep. John Ashbrook of Ohio, both members of the NRA's board of directors, moved in for the kill. The NRA went so far as to produce a TV documentary called *It Can Happen Here,* alleging ATF abuses. In the film, Representative Dingell appears and says, "If I were to select a jackbooted group of fascists who are perhaps as large a danger to American society as I could pick today, I would pick ATF."

What particularly irked the NRA was ATF's tactic in the late 1970s of sending agents into gun stores masquerading as illegal buyers to see whether the dealers would sell them guns or suggest that they arrange a straw-man purchase. "We were using those kinds of techniques," Rex Davis said, "because unscrupulous dealers were then, and are now, a major source for the illegal acquisition of guns." Other agencies used similar sting techniques, but only ATF seemed to catch the heat. "If the guy was a pharmacist selling illegal narcotics," Davis said, "nobody would scream at all."

During a 1980 hearing, ATF defended itself by arguing that it had in fact conducted few operations against dealers. Its new director, G. R. Dickerson, testified, "We often hear that ATF makes a practice of harassing licensed dealers in an attempt to drive them out of business. I point out to the committee in the period July 1, 1979, through April 30, 1980 . . . we had over eight thousand seven hundred firearms investigations. Only one hundred and sixty-two involved licensed dealers."

His testimony confirmed the fears of members of the gun-control camp, who charged that if anything ATF was too soft on dealers. At the same hearing the National Coalition to Ban Handguns presented a survey of 136 licensed gun dealers in New Haven, Connecticut, which found that "more than three-fourths (77.2 percent) of licensees were in direct violation of at least one federal, state, or local law or regulation. Nearly one-half (48.5 percent) were in violation of two or more firearms, tax, or zoning requirements."

The NRA and its allies kept up the pressure. By September 1981 the NRA seemed assured of achieving the destruction of the bureau. That month, at a meeting of the International Association of Chiefs of Police in New Orleans, President Reagan announced that he planned to fire ATF's firearms enforcement agents and dissolve the bureau.

The NRA was delighted; Reagan's audience was not.

Reagan had misjudged the respect accorded ATF and its firearms tracing services by other law-enforcement agencies. A slap against ATF was a slap against all law enforcement.

The administration backpedaled. Reagan still promised to dismantle ATF, but proposed now to shift the firearms agents from the bureau to the Secret Service. Everyone seemed to like this idea, including ATF agents, who, although they would have preferred an outright transfer to the Department of Justice, looked forward to joining a bona fide law-enforcement team and shedding the last vestiges of ATF's tax-collecting past.

The gun lobby now balked at the idea.

At a February 1982 hearing before a subcommittee of the Senate Appropriations Committee, Representative Dingell reiterated his "jackboot" statement word for word. Of ATF, he said, "I think they are evil." He warned, however, that shifting the bureau's agents to the Secret Service "is a little like rearranging the deck chairs on the *Titanic*." He charged that "the transfer of BATF to other agencies affords only the certainty that other agencies will be contaminated by the kind of people and behavior we have seen on the part of BATF."

The Gun Owners of America testified that the proposed transfer might make things worse than they already were "if the extraordinary powers available to the Secret Service were ever made available to the one thousand former firearms agents at BATF."

Neal Knox, head of the NRA's chief lobbying arm, the Institute for Legislative Action, testified that most of the "provisions of the Gun Control Act are purely regulatory in nature; they should be administered by a regulatory agency and not by a criminal law-enforcement organization." The NRA, he said, believed ATF should remain a freestanding agency under the Treasury Department.

The NRA's turnabout prompted Rep. William J. Hughes, chairing a House hearing on May 4, 1982, to chide, "In the confusion, the National Rifle Association, apparently with a straight but somewhat reddened face, has been able to publicly change its position and is now in the unlikely role of supporting the continuation of BATF, on the grounds that the Secret Service, to which most of BATF's functions were to be transferred, might actually take the functions seriously and not be so easy to intimidate."

The NRA, according to author Osha Davidson, suddenly saw that the shift to the Secret Service would indeed enhance ATF's prestige. "The NRA realized," he writes, "that it wouldn't be able to call Secret Service agents 'jackbooted fascists' and get away with it."

The bureau survived, but the dangers of aggressive, proactive investigation were imprinted forever in its institutional memory. "Some of the things we did were probably not the best techniques," said Bernard La Forest, a veteran agent and special agent in charge of ATF's Detroit office. The bureau, he said, took its lesson to heart: "Before you conduct an investigation of a licensed dealer, you better have some pretty good proof that there's a high probability he's engaged in some type of illegal activity."

Throughout the 1980s, the NRA continued its fight to restrict ATF's powers over dealers. In May of 1986, again with the help of powerful congressional allies, most notably Sen. James McClure of Idaho and Rep. Harold Volkmer of Missouri, the NRA succeeded in muscling through the McClure-Volkmer Act, also known as the Firearms Owners' Protection Act. A more appropriate title might have been the Gun Dealers' Protection Act. The bill banned the sale and manufacture of new and hitherto unregistered machine guns, thanks to a last-minute amendment added by Representative Hughes, but it eliminated a previous requirement that gun dealers keep records on ammunition sales. It also explicitly barred any central registry of dealer records, limited dealer inspections to once a year and only after advance notice, allowed the interstate sales of rifles and shotguns, gave private gun owners more leeway to sell guns without first acquiring a dealer's license, and, perhaps most important in terms of understanding ATF's treatment of Guns Unlimited, required prosecutors to prove that dealers charged with violating firearms laws did so "willfully."

It was this bill too that reduced to a misdemeanor the penalty for dealers found to have violated record-keeping rules, while retaining the felony charge for consumers who did likewise.

Before the act was finally passed, Representative Volkmer called it "the second most important step in the history of American gun owners. The first was the Second Amendment to the U.S. Constitution." Representative Hughes said the bill "would elevate gun dealers to a special level of privilege never before seen in the law."

ATF got the message. First came Congress's punitive $10-million budget cut, then ATF's brush with dissolution, and finally McClure-Volkmer. "I don't know what kind of syndrome it is when you get batted over the head repeatedly," Rex Davis told me, "but it certainly turns your attention away from the direction you were going."

In following years, ATF used its mandate as the nation's firearms cop to concentrate more and more resources on mainstream investigations of narcotics gangs, terrorist groups, and motorcycle gangs. From 1988 through 1992, ATF's law-enforcement divisions ranked narcotics crime as their top priority, followed by violent crime committed with firearms. "These are safe activities, and sexy activities in terms of public perception," Davis said. "With dealers, they've had their hands slapped several different ways. So it's a natural reaction."

◆ ◆ ◆

ATF remains less than enthusiastic about policing the vast dealer network. From 1975 through 1990, ATF revoked an average of ten licenses a year. The low was in 1978, with none, the high in 1986, with twenty-seven. This rate seems downright skimpy given the sheer numbers of licenses and the rate of violations discovered whenever ATF's skeleton crew of inspectors does its routine compliance audits. In 1990, for example, inspectors conducted 8,471 of these routine inspections; they found violations in 90 percent of them.

But revocation can be a tortuous process, as ATF found when in 1989 it at last moved to revoke the license of a Michigan dealer doing business as Al's Loan Office. In arresting and prosecuting Curtis Williams, the man who accompanied Nicholas Elliot to Guns Unlimited, the bureau acted with breathtaking speed; in contrast, its dealings with Al's Loan show remarkable forbearance.

In ten inspections, beginning in 1976, ATF inspectors found repeated violations of ATF record-keeping regulations, many of them serious and the kind that could have put guns into the hands of felons and traffickers. Al's Loan had failed to keep accurate records in a separate bound book of all its firearm acquisitions and sales. It had failed to make sure that customers properly completed form 4473. Moreover, the inspectors found, Al's Loan had sold guns to people prohibited by federal law from buying them.

Far from whisking officials of Al's Loan off to jail, ATF inspectors patiently sat down with them to instruct them in the proper record-keeping procedures, as they did following inspections in 1976, 1978, 1979, 1980, and 1981. After a 1982 inspection, the bureau at last flexed some muscle. It wrote the pawnshop an admonitory letter, setting out the dealer's violations. The letter, the first phase in the carefully choreographed dance ATF must go through in trying to revoke a dealer's license, warned Al's Loan that "your license is contingent on your compliance with law and regulations and that continued violations may lead to revocation of your license."

ATF agents inspected Al's records again in 1983 and again found the same kinds of violations. Again ATF wrote an admonitory letter.

The violations continued. Three more inspections took place, in 1985, 1987, and 1988, each followed by another admonitory letter.

At last ATF lost patience. On March 31, 1989, thirteen years after inspectors first discovered violations at Al's Loan, the bureau revoked its license.

The dealer protested. Under provisions governing the revocation process, the dealer requested a hearing before an ATF hearing officer. An attorney for Al's Loan argued the dealer should be allowed to keep his license because he had cleaned up his records. The attorney then presented a sample. During a recess, however, ATF inspectors examined these records and immediately found violations.

One of the inspectors testified, however, that the records did show signs of an effort to improve; he seemed more than willing to shrug off more than a decade's worth of violations. Al's Loan had testified that it had set up a new computer system to help manage its records and had fired employees who failed to keep good records of firearms transactions. "So there are some problems," the inspector testified, "but the records as presented today do show a decent and sincere attempt by the licensee to try and change his record-keeping system to meet the regulatory requirements."

The hearing officer was not moved, however, and recommended revocation, concluding: "The licensee was plainly indifferent to the regulatory requirement for conducting his firearms license operations and therefore willfully violated the regulations."

This recommendation was then passed along for the required review by the ATF regional director responsible for Michigan. The director agreed. The bureau revoked the license effective September 18, 1989.

This time Al's Loan protested to federal court, where it tried to win an injunction to stop the revocation. The judge, however, argued that Al's Loan may indeed have improved its records, but for the twelve years preceding the supposed improvement had "displayed flagrant, willful indifference" to the ATF rules. In his May 7, 1990, opinion affirming the revocation, the judge wrote: "Selling and pawning firearms is a privilege granted by the federal government and is not a right of any person. . . . Furthermore, the Court notes that we live in a very violent society where careless and violent individuals use guns to kill and maim innocent people. Those who distribute guns must be held accountable as they are the first step in preventing lawless individuals from obtaining guns."

At last Al's Loan was out of the firearms business—but the process had taken fifteen years.

◆ ◆ ◆

ATF publicly argues that the vast majority of its FFLs are honest, law-abiding citizens, and that only "one or two" go bad. Even if true, the bureau's argument would hardly be comforting given the speed with which guns migrate. A single illicit dealer can put hundreds, perhaps thousands, of weapons into the hands of would-be killers before the guns are detected by the ATF tracing network.

The fact is, many dealers do operate illegally. In fiscal 1991, ATF considered licensees to be suspects in 139 law-enforcement investigations.

The case of one Baltimore dealer demonstrates both how much damage a single maverick dealer can do, and how little time it takes for guns diverted from the legitimate distribution network to be used in crime.

On July 1, 1989, ATF issued a federal firearms license to Carroll L. Brown, then a twenty-eight-year-old postal worker and father of three kids. Initially, at least, Brown seemed intent on operating a formal, commercial gun store, going so far as to rent commercial space in an office building in Reisterstown, Maryland. A few months later, however, he stopped paying rent and broke his lease. By April the following year he had begun selling high-powered handguns from his home and from his car, without asking buyers to fill out required state and federal documentation. He advertised his wares in at least six classified ads in the *Baltimore Sun*. (In 1993, the *Sun*, recognizing the dangers of undocumented private sales of handguns, stopped accepting classified ads for firearms.)

The guns of Carroll Brown quickly fell into the wrong hands. Beginning September 20, 1990, Baltimore police began discovering Brown's guns in the course of routine calls and investigations of homicides and drug trafficking. On October 26, Baltimore officers arrested a man wearing a bulletproof vest and carrying an unregistered Astra .380 pistol. Det. Richard Young, then a member of Baltimore's Handgun Enforcement Arrest Team (HEAT), first traced the vest and learned it had been shipped to Brown from an Orlando, Florida, distributor only the day before by the United Parcel Service. The distributor also told Detective Young that it had shipped Brown two guns. The detective next checked with the distributor's parent company, RSR North of Rochester, New York, and learned it too had shipped guns to Brown—fifteen in all between July and November.

Soon afterward, Baltimore's HEAT squad and the local ATF office began a joint investigation. An ATF agent compared serial numbers from the RSR shipping invoices with records of guns confiscated during arrests made by Baltimore police. He discovered that one month earlier, on September 20, officers had confiscated a nine-millimeter pistol that had been shipped to Carroll Brown in July. Two weeks later, he found, Baltimore police had seized two more of Brown's guns, from two suspects arrested for illegal possession of handguns. One suspect, according to a federal affidavit, was a three-time felon.

On November 16, Baltimore detectives investigating a homicide conducted a search of one suspect's home and recovered a Cobray M-11/9 made by S.W. Daniel and sold by Brown. Five days later, police arrested four other suspects on handgun charges and found three more guns that had been sold by Brown, including another Cobray pistol. One of the guns, a Glock nine-millimeter automatic, had been shipped to Brown by a distributor just five days before. Another arrest one week later yielded another Cobray, this with its serial number obliterated. Technicians were able to restore the number, and police traced this gun also to Brown. It had been shipped to him about six weeks earlier.

On December 10, a man named Melvin King telephoned Brown and, identifying himself as a resident of Richmond, Virginia, asked to buy a Glock. King called Brown twice more over the next two days. On December 13, Brown agreed to meet him and sell him the pistol. Brown told King to come to a shopping plaza located about a mile from Brown's home.

When King arrived, he found Brown sitting in his 1989 Dodge, listening to a radio scanner capable of picking up police communications. Brown told King to sign what he called a "requisition blank" but told him not to write down that he was from Virginia. Brown agreed to sell King two more Glocks at another meeting they set for one week later.

Melvin King was an ATF agent. On December 20, he arrested Brown on felony charges of violating federal firearms laws. The next day Baltimore police arrested Brown again, this time on state charges. Brown pleaded guilty on March 7, 1991, and on May 31 was sentenced to twenty-one months in federal prison, later reduced to nineteen months.

The guns Brown had sold, however, continued their travels. As of January 1991 police had recovered only a tenth of the 268 handguns he had received from distributors.

Just over a week after his sentencing, at about two A.M. on a lovely spring night, another of Brown's guns made an appearance on the streets of Baltimore. A drug dealer named Ronnie Hunt had acquired a Glock .40-caliber pistol that Brown had sold to a convicted felon the previous October. Hunt and an associate cornered Sheldean Simon, a member of a local rap group called Murder Inc., and opened fire. Simon drew two nine-millimeter pistols of his own, but faced an onslaught like something from the tommy-gun massacres of the 1920s. Within seconds his opponents fired some seventy rounds of ammunition. Simon fired only once. He died after being struck by two of the forty-four rounds fired from Hunt's Glock .40.

Brown's nine-year-old daughter wrote a letter to the court to help her father: "Dear Judge: My daddy is not a bad man. He has been very good to all of us. He does his best to take care of us." Rev. James Ross, pastor of Nicodemus Baptist Church in Baltimore, wrote to the judge as well, pleading that Brown "was not intentionally trying to break the law, but that he ran his business somewhat haphazardly. He did not commit a crime of violence; he was only trying to provide a secure financial position for his children and wife."

Soon after the murder of Sheldean Simon, however, Baltimore detective Harry Edgerton told a *Sun* reporter, "As we speak, people who are out there right now, who are killed or wounded, could be the responsibility of Carroll Brown. In the end, all this gun stuff comes down to one guy who says, 'I don't want to follow the rules.' "

Among the guns Brown sold were twenty-seven Cobray pistols of the kind carried by Nicholas Elliot.

◆ ◆ ◆

On those occasions where ATF does take a proactive rather than merely reactive approach to policing America's gun dealers, it invariably discovers crooked dealers responsible for diverting thousands of weapons into criminal hands. A classic example of such enforcement, and the kind that ought to be pursued as a matter of routine, is Project Detroit, an ongoing effort by ATF and the Detroit police to trace as many guns as possible.

ATF began the first Project Detroit study with a pool of 2,342 weapons entered into the property room at Detroit police headquarters between January 1989 and April 1990. Common wisdom nurtured by an endless series of TV crime shows and detective novels holds that all weapons can be traced readily, but that is not the case.

ATF agents were able to trace only half the weapons in the initial pool. The remainder of the guns had been incorrectly identified by investigators, were too old to be traced (any weapon sold before the Gun Control Act of 1968 is essentially untraceable), had obliterated serial numbers that could not be restored, or could not be traced because of inadvertently or deliberately sloppy record-keeping among licensed dealers.

In its report on this first phase of Project Detroit, the bureau—gun-shy ever since its near demise under Ronald Reagan—was careful to note that high-volume dealers would necessarily experience more traces. It is a truism, indeed, that the bigger the gun dealer's volume of sales, the more often the guns he sells will be used in homicide, suicide, rape, robbery, assault, and gang warfare. The report said, "Just because an FFL has sold a large number of weapons that were subsequently used in crimes does not necessarily indicate the FFL is intentionally diverting weapons to the criminal element."

Yet of the five licensed dealers identified most often in the Project Detroit traces, four—including the top three—became the targets of full-scale ATF investigations. The worst offender, according to the report, was Sherman Butler of Sterling Heights, Michigan, near Detroit, whose Sherm's Guns accounted for twenty-nine traces stemming from a range of crimes that included at least two homicides. Butler's specialty was the sale of S.W. Daniel Cobrays modified to include a sixteen-inch barrel and shoulder stock, thus qualifying them as long rifles and allowing purchasers to buy them without first having to comply with stricter federal and local handgun regulations. For $125 extra, however, Butler threw in a pistol-length barrel and enough of a pistol frame—a pistol "upper receiver"—to allow buyers to quickly turn their carbines back into semiautomatic pistols.

Next in line, with twenty-seven traces, was Steven Durham, whose All Gun Cleaning Service in Detroit "provided hundreds of firearms to the most visible and most violent narcotics organizations in the Detroit metropolitan area." Durham persuaded acquaintances to fill out the form 4473s for specific handgun purchases even though these associates never actually bought the guns. Instead Durham simply filed their records and sold the guns to illegal buyers.

Three other federally licensed dealers, as a routine business practice, obliterated the serial numbers on every gun they received from wholesalers. The report estimated that together the three had sold more than three thousand firearms "and that law-enforcement officers will be recovering them in various crimes for years to come."

In all, Project Detroit led to investigations of thirteen licensed dealers—including six of the top ten in traces—and successful prosecutions against all but three. Two of the three died (one blew himself up while manufacturing hand grenades); the third, whose case was still pending at the time of the report, was a Toledo, Ohio, dealer who allegedly sold cheap .25-caliber Raven pistols to anyone, regardless of age and background. That investigation began after weapons sweeps in Detroit's public schools turned up an inordinate number of guns traced to him.

Project Detroit also turned up a new and troubling wrinkle in firearms trafficking: the use of counterfeit licenses. To order weapons from a distributor, all the law requires a dealer to do is send a photocopy of his license, freshly signed in ink. The law does not require that the dealer first have his signature notarized or otherwise validated. Nor does it require the firearms distributors who receive these copies to verify the license numbers. Distributors, driven by the profit imperative to seek as many retail outlets as possible, tend to be lax about making sure their customers are bona fide, commercial dealerships. Major manufacturers are far more picky. The same profit imperative drives them to seek out the biggest distributors with the widest reach, characteristics a fly-by-night company is not likely to possess. Smith & Wesson, for example, told me it only accepts new distributors into the fold after dispatching a sales representative to visit their operations and evaluate the quality of their records. At the same time, a company spokesman disavowed any responsibility for the customary practices of the industry. "We're not in the business of policing the laws or enforcing the laws," he told me, "other than seeing that we ourselves follow the laws."

According to Bernard La Forest, the Detroit special agent in charge and author of the Project Detroit report, one licensed dealer altered his license number several times, each time making photocopies. He gave these to associates who used them to order guns for themselves at wholesale prices. "The wholesalers thought they were dealing with eight individual dealers, when in fact it was one guy's license," La Forest said.

Any distributor who did find himself moved to check a dealer's license number would quickly find that once again the age of automation has passed the firearms industry by. No easy mechanism—no 800 telephone line, no computer-accessed data bank—exists to allow quick verification of a dealer's license number and identity. Likewise, La Forest said, ATF has no effective means of distributing an alert to dealers to watch for licenses known to be counterfeit.

The Project Detroit report failed to note what ought to be the most troubling finding of its underlying investigations: that apparently honest dealers accounted for the remaining one thousand traces, a fact that testifies again to the high costs imposed on the rest of us by even legitimate gun shops. Indeed, of the top ten dealers as ranked by ATF traces, the four who were not investigated by ATF nonetheless accounted for ten to twenty traces each, including traces involving at least four homicides. In all, Project Detroit traced guns sold by legitimate dealers from New York to Alaska and used subsequently in *at least* two kidnappings, thirty-four homicides, and hundreds of narcotics offenses—this again from only 1,226 seized weapons.

In his introduction to the report, La Forest asked: "What would the results indicate if we had the capability of successfully tracing 10,000 to 15,000 weapons seized by all law enforcement agencies in this metropolitan area?"

What the report also demonstrates is the great value of *cumula-*

tive information on the guns used in crime and the dealers who sold them. But such information is hard to come by. Until 1989, ATF couldn't even do a computer search to detail which guns were traced most. Early in 1989, two reporters from the Cox Newspaper chain found that the ATF tracing center in Landover, Maryland, possessed all the information necessary to produce such an analysis, but in hard copy. The reporters gained access to this rich seam of data under the Freedom of Information Act, then hired their own team of clerks, armed them with computers, and moved them into the center where the reporters built their own database. ATF allowed such access on the condition the team use a special computer template that prohibited its hired clerks from punching in the names and addresses of the consumers who owned the guns.

The database provided immediate revelations. For one thing, it put the lie to the NRA claim that assault weapons were not often used in crime. The study revealed a startling increase in the use of assault guns from 1986 to 1989 and found that for traces made between January 1, 1988, and March 27, 1989, assault weapons accounted for 8.1 percent of homicide traces and 30 percent of traces stemming from organized crime investigations (including arrests involving drug cartels, arms traffickers, and terrorist groups). The fourth most commonly traced assault weapon was the S.W. Daniel Cobray.

ATF wasn't able to provide such information on its own until late in 1989, when its own automated trace system began operating; as of June 1992 the agency was still struggling to rid the system of kinks.

No matter how efficient ATF's database becomes, however, it will offer only limited help in understanding the use and migration of weapons nationwide. The bureau traces only about 10 percent of guns used in crime. In fiscal 1990 and 1991 the Los Angeles police department and Los Angeles County sheriff asked ATF to conduct only 117 traces, even though in 1991 alone the city had 2,062 homicides. In most investigations involving a crime committed with a gun, police simply do not request a trace. "If they've got an armed robber and they've also got the gun, they don't care about the gun," La Forest said. "When they go to court, they say, 'This is the gun the guy had.' The question we want to ask is, 'Where'd he get the gun?' "

When police or even ATF's own agents do request gun traces, they often fail to provide the Landover tracing center with precise information. Inaccurate descriptions of seized weapons are common. The problem is especially acute for the Cobray and its look-alike ancestors, the MAC, RPB, and Ingram; it's not uncommon for a police department to list a seized Cobray as a MAC-10 or even an Uzi. Moreover, the agency requesting the trace often fails to provide accurate information about the crime in which the gun was used. Detroit's La Forest, for example, believes that easily half the Detroit guns identified as having been confiscated for "weapons violations" were actually seized during narcotics arrests. The weapons charges, he said, are merely the quickest and easiest to record in the bureaucratic process of logging evidence that immediately follows an arrest.

Taken together, the lack of comprehensive data about crime guns, ATF's ticklish political position, and explicit restrictions on the bureau's inspections and investigations, all help maintain the unimpeded diversion of guns from legitimate channels to the bad guys. Each in its own way nudged Nicholas Elliot's Cobray along its deadly path.

◆ ◆ ◆

Raymond Rowley, an agent in ATF's Norfolk office, initiated the bureau's search for the source of Nicholas's gun. He heard about the shooting on the news and quickly volunteered his help to Det. Donald Adams, the Virginia Beach homicide detective in charge of the case. Rowley ordered an "Urgent" trace, the highest of three request levels and one that typically yields a response within a matter of hours. The ATF's Urgent trace of the revolver used by John Hinckley to shoot Ronald Reagan took all of sixteen minutes.

The serial number from Nicholas's Cobray was relayed to the special agent in charge in Atlanta, Tom Stokes, who then telephoned S.W. Daniel. No one answered. It was Friday; the company operated only Monday through Thursday. But Stokes eventually managed to speak by phone with Sylvia Daniel, who, in a departure from the usual frosty relations between her company and the bureau, agreed to stop by her office on the way to the S.W. Daniel Christmas party and search the serial number herself.

The number led to a distributor, who in turn said he had shipped the pistol to Guns Unlimited. By eleven o'clock that night, Rowley, another agent, and Detective Adams were at Curtis Williams's door.

Williams went to jail. As far as federal law was concerned, however, Guns Unlimited did nothing wrong when it sold the Cobray to Williams, even under such obviously suspicious circumstances. Williams had shown the appropriate identification and had filled out form 4473 properly, dutifully writing "no" after every background question on the form.

No one thought to investigate Guns Unlimited, not even after the negligence suit filed by the family of Karen Farley yielded a judgment against the dealership early in 1992.

"We're always looking for, and sensitive to, violations of federal law, regardless of who may be the individual or entity involved," Rowley told me. "In this case, no, we did not go back and reinvestigate. Nothing that came up during the investigation of Williams pointed to wrongdoing on the part of Guns Unlimited."

But clear evidence that a dealer willfully, knowingly broke federal firearms laws can be hard to come by, said David Troy, special agent in charge of the Falls Church division and Rowley's boss.

"We don't make very many dealer cases," Troy said. "Not because we can't catch them. There just aren't many dealers who are really knowingly and willfully violating the law. But what you do have is this: you have a lot of dealers who are satisfying the letter of the law when they sell the gun, regardless of how suspicious the sale might look to a reasonable person. But they're not culpable under the law for that sale."

Troy decries the unimpeded proliferation of guns, but cautions that America's gun crisis has deeper, more intractable roots. "The fact there are guns out there is not in itself inherently bad, because a lot of people who have guns never do anything wrong with them. The problem is there are so many people out there who want to get a gun and use it in an illegal manner. If there weren't so damn many firearms out there, it would make things a little bit better. But we're talking shades of gray, here. If we had only fifty million guns instead of two hundred million, would we have less violent crime in the United States? Probably not. Because fifty million is still a hell of a lot of firearms. The point is, there are so many weapons available in the United States, and so easily obtained through legal or illegal channels, that anyone who wants a firearm can get one. Therefore, you have a hell of a lot of people who are willing to use them in a criminal manner who can get their hands on them without any exertion whatsoever."

Troy thinks something fundamental changed in American culture to make the nation more tolerant of guns and gun violence. "I don't know why it's accepted the way it is. Maybe it's like anything else. You get used to it over a period of time. If the country went from a thousand homicides to twenty-five thousand in one year, we'd have a revolution on our hands. But it's gradually built up to where we do have twenty-five thousand homicides every year. It's taken four or five generations to get there, and people have gotten used to the idea. It's an alarming thing but it's not a statistic that makes anyone do anything on a grand scale. It's a cultural thing, a value system situation.

"Guns have become so common, so acceptable, that kids know them the way you and I used to know cars. When I was a teenager, I could name every car by looking at it. I could say that's a '58 Ford, that's a '59 Chevy. Kids today can name guns. They know them by looking at them. They can pick them out just like teenagers were able to pick out cars twenty-five years ago."

Nicholas Elliot possessed this skill. But how did he come by it? How does America's gun culture foster this awareness and our tolerance of gun violence? Is *tolerance* even the right word, or have we now, in a sense, cultivated a taste for gunplay and developed the infrastructure to satisfy it?

CHAPTER ELEVEN

NICHOLAS

WHEN NICHOLAS ELLIOT LOADED HIS COBRAY before beginning his shooting spree, he selected one of the six clips he had crammed into his backpack. Each clip was long, slender, and gray, with a powerful spring that forced the stacked cartridges upward after the topmost round was fired and stripped away. The clips, also known as magazines or, in gunspeak, simply "mags," were designed to inject bullets into the Cobray's receiver much the way a kid's Pez dispenser keeps presenting new blocks of candy.

To a cynic, God may have seemed suspiciously absent from Atlantic Shores that morning. The faithful, however, believe that God did indeed intercede, at the point where Nicholas chose that first clip. Forensic investigators later test-fired Nicholas's gun repeatedly, inserting each of the six magazines. All worked perfectly, except that first one. It misfed cartridges to the gun, but only to a point about halfway down the magazine, the fifteen-round point, where it began feeding bullets correctly. By the time Nicholas broke into Hutch Matteson's class, he had emptied it of roughly fourteen cartridges, many of them ejected unfired as Nicholas cleared jam after jam.

Cutter was splayed on the floor some three or four feet in front of the rest of the students. He watched in terror as Nicholas aimed the gun in his direction. "It looked like he was pulling the trigger," Cutter recalled. "I wasn't sure. And then he was messing with the clip." The gun had jammed yet again, and now Nicholas stood before

Cutter striking and jiggling the clip, trying to get the weapon to work properly.

Still fumbling with the gun, Nicholas took a step backward. He glanced over his left shoulder.

Hutch Matteson charged him, covering the dozen or so feet at a dead run. Nicholas, busy trying to clear the jam, looked startled. He stared directly at Matteson and in that instant managed to get the gun to work.

"I was probably three to four feet away from him as that shot went off," Matteson recalled. "There was a tremendous ringing in my ear."

Matteson closed his eyes, then opened them again and continued his charge. He grabbed Nicholas by the shirt and threw him headfirst into an adjacent wall. Nicholas fell, his gun thudding to the floor. Matteson threw his body onto Nicholas and shoved the Cobray aside.

"I don't have the gun," Nicholas cried. "I give up."

Matteson struck him in the head. He stretched Nicholas's arms out on the floor, grabbed his wrists, and held him pinned under his weight.

"What in the world would make you want to do anything like this?" Matteson screamed.

"They hate me. They make fun of me. They hit me."

"Who hit you?"

Nicholas named Billy Cutter.

"Why didn't you tell me about this?" Matteson said.

As Matteson held Nicholas pinned to the floor, waiting for help, he heard Nicholas list the names of other people he had planned to shoot that morning.

◆ ◆ ◆

Rev. George Sweet, senior pastor at Atlantic Shores and president of the school, was sitting in his office when he heard someone cry, "He's got a gun, he's got a gun." Suddenly there was a lot of commotion, a lot of shouting in the outer office and in the hall. It took him a few moments to make out the words and to appreciate that something grave had occurred. Until then he had been contemplating nothing more momentous than the staff Christmas party set for that night.

Someone led him to Hutch Matteson's trailer, where he saw Nicholas pinned to the floor. He then crossed to Sam Marino's trailer and found him lying, literally, in a pool of blood. "He looked at me," Sweet recalled, "and he said, 'I'm going to die.' "

The two began praying together.

Police and medical help arrived quickly. An ambulance took Sam Marino to the hospital. Sweet followed in his car.

Marino's wounds were serious, but Sweet knew things could have been so much worse. At least no one had been killed. But just to make sure everyone else was indeed all right, the faculty at Atlantic Shores gathered staff and students together in the church auditorium to conduct a head count. Many students still had not realized a shooting had occurred, including Will and Lora Farley, whose mother, Karen, was the school's business teacher.

"I was like wondering where my mom was," Lora recalled a long while later as she sat facing a courtroom that had suddenly gone dead quiet. "We weren't really concerned or anything, but when I first entered the auditorium, this girl said to me—me and my friends were laughing and stuff because we didn't really think anything was going on—and this girl said to me, 'Someone has been shot,' but it wasn't my mom. It was another teacher, and I was like—I couldn't understand. I was like, 'Somebody has been shot at school?'

"We prayed and stuff that everything would be all right, and then we just like left it up to the Lord. We just sat there really being quiet and stuff. I asked Will—I said, 'Have you seen Mom?'

"And he said, 'No.' "

CHAPTER TWELVE

THE CULTURE

NICHOLAS ELLIOT HAD COME TO SCHOOL that Friday prepared for combat. He had filled his backpack with his gun, hundreds of rounds of ammunition, and a variety of battle accessories. The most striking thing about his cargo, however, was not the inherent firepower—although it was prodigious—but rather the weapons savvy evident in what this sixteen-year-old boy had done to the gun and its ammunition in an apparent effort to make them even more efficient at killing.

He did not carry his six clips haphazardly, but had "jungle-clipped" them using tape to bind them in pairs in such a way that the instant he expended one clip he could simply turn the pair over and jam in the other end. Each assembly was capable of providing him with sixty-four rounds of virtually continuous fire, which, barring jams, he could have pumped from the gun at a rate approaching that of a light machine gun. He had used a length of rope to fashion a combat sling for his Cobray similar in concept to slings attached to the compact Uzis and Heckler & Koch submachine guns used by antiterrorist squads to help them better control their weapons during combat. He carried a crude silencer made from a pipe wrapped in fabric, and a "brass catcher" he had made from cloth and tape, to be attached to his gun to catch ejected cartridge cases. "A gun enthusiast might use a brass catcher to catch the brass for reloading," said Donald Adams, the Virginia Beach homicide detective. "A murderer or a person about to commit a crime might use one to collect the evidence."

His six clips gave him a total of 192 cartridges ready to fire, but he came prepared for the possibility that he might use up all those rounds and need more. He carried hundreds of extra cartridges, including several boxes containing thirty-two rounds each—exactly enough to refill an expended clip. To speed refilling, Nicholas had inserted a thin, white string through the base of each magazine to produce a primitive speed loader. When tugged, Adams told me, the string would pull down the spring-driven feeder inside the magazine, thus easing the resistance. "He could hold the string down by clamping it under his foot," Adams explained. Nicholas could then insert each cartridge into the magazine more quickly and with less strain. Adams could not at first figure out what kind of string Nicholas had used. It was thicker than fishing line and very strong. After a while he decided he knew what it was: dental floss.

Finally, Nicholas modified even the bullets themselves. He filed a groove into the tip of at least one bullet apparently in the hopes of turning it into what Adams called a "dumdum," a bullet that breaks apart on impact, thereby in theory becoming considerably more deadly. Nicholas modified other bullets by drilling from the tip downward to form "hollow points." On impact, hollow-point bullets spread into lethal mushrooms that produce bigger holes and more potent neural disruption than solid rounds. Commercially made hollow-points are the bullets of choice among law-enforcement officers because they produce a lot of damage in the human body but are less likely than solid-point bullets to pass through the intended target and endanger someone else.

"This guy," Adams said, "was ready for war."

Adams knew where Nicholas got the bullets. The fact his mother bought them was troubling enough. But where does a sixteen-year-

old boy learn to modify bullets? Where does he learn to devise combat slings, silencers, and even brass catchers?

No one can know exactly how he learned it all because Nicholas
won't say. But the fact that a child can acquire so much lethal knowledge should surprise no one who is acquainted with America's gun
culture and the manufacturers, marketers, writers, and others in the
so-called gun aftermarket who make knowledge about how to succeed at murder so readily available to anyone willing to thumb to the
back of a gun magazine or take a weekend stroll through the nearest
gun show.

◆ ◆ ◆

Homicide, or rather the homicide fantasy, is the engine that drives
America's fascination with guns. Target shooters spend hour after
hour firing into human silhouettes. Practical shooting competitions
held nationwide test civilian competitors' ability to hit targets after
leaping from a car. Occasionally such meets conclude in an explosive finale, with entrants firing away at a distant target consisting of
dynamite and a gasoline-filled barrel. In this milieu, guns used in
grisly crimes actually wind up gaining popularity. After the assassination of John F. Kennedy, sales of the otherwise undistinguished
Mannlicher-Carcano rifle used by Lee Harvey Oswald soared. Hundreds "were immediately bought by souvenir-seekers who wanted to
get the feel of the weapon that had brought down the president,"
wrote Robert Sherrill in *The Saturday Night Special*. Even the murder
of schoolchildren boosts sales. After Patrick Edward Purdy opened
fire on a schoolyard in Stockton with his AKS, a semiautomatic version of the now-infamous AK-47, sales of the gun and its knockoffs
boomed. Prices quadrupled, to $1,500. Guns Unlimited felt the
surge in demand. "I didn't sell an AK until Stockton in California;
then everybody wanted one," said James S. Dick, the owner of Guns
Unlimited, in a deposition.

A *New York Times* reporter once asked the marketing director at

Intratec, a Miami company that makes an assault pistol similar in spirit to the Cobray, how he felt about the widespread condemnation of his company's weapons. Like the Cobray, the TEC 9 is a handgun of "dirty" design, meant to evoke a submachine gun. It has a perforated barrel sheath, akin to those that appear on full-scale machine guns. "I'm kind of flattered," he replied. "It just has that advertising tingle to it. Hey, it's talked about, it's read about, the media write about it. That generates more sales for me. It might sound cold and cruel, but I'm sales oriented."

Intratec was so oriented to sales that when California banned assault weapons and included the Intratec 9 on the list, Intratec sidestepped the law through the simple maneuver of changing the gun's name to TEC-DC-9. Gian Luigi Ferri bought two in Las Vegas and, on July 1, 1993, took them to the thirty-fourth floor of a gleaming San Francisco office building. He killed eight people, wounded six, then shot himself to death. Like Nicholas, indeed, like so many of our very many spree shooters, he carried an excessive amount of ammunition, some six hundred rounds. He had acquired the guns legally. "Everything was by the book," said a Las Vegas police officer.

The passion for lethality suffuses the process through which guns and ammunition are conceived and made. Manufacturers routinely test their prototypes not by firing them at tin cans, but by blasting away at blocks of Jell-O–like goo—ordnance gelatin—intended specifically to simulate human tissue. Their enthusiasm for gore can lead to some vivid advertising. In the March/April 1992 issue of *American Handgunner,* a magazine for the civilian firearms consumer, the Eldorado Cartridge Corp. ran a full-page ad for its Starfire cartridge under the bold headline "IF LOOKS CAN KILL." The ad called the Starfire the "deadliest handgun cartridge ever developed for home or personal defense, and hunting" and went on to describe how the bullet expands on impact "resulting in a massive wound channel." Its deep penetration, the ad crowed, "helps assure fast knockdown."

During one of several visits to a gun show in Frederick, Maryland, I stood at one dealer's table beside a man and his young son who, like me, were intently watching a promotional video produced by Power-Plus, a maker of exotic ammunition. The narrator, dressed in a dark T-shirt and speaking in that laconic backcountry drawl that characterizes today's notion of toughness, demonstrated his company's rounds by firing a sample of each into a fresh block of yellowish gelatin, with the camera then cutting to offer a close side-view of the depth of penetration and the jagged wound channel coursing through the translucent plasma. Each round was more destructive than the last, until the narrator fired a sample of the company's Annihilator high-explosive bullets, which slammed into the gelatin, exploded, and knocked the quivering block from its stand. Anyone wondering who might use such a bullet need only look to John Hinckley, who used a similar bullet marketed under the brand name Devastator in his attack on Ronald Reagan. Only one of the bullets he fired did actually explode, much to the benefit of Reagan, who did not even realize he had been shot, but to the lasting detriment of James Brady, in whose brain that one bullet happened to perform as intended.

The Power-Plus narrator moved on to demonstrate the company's Multi-Plex rounds, which launched anywhere from two to four bullets from a single cartridge. An Alabama mail-order ammunition dealer described these bullets in its catalog as "an outstanding choice for home defense."

As if all this weren't enough, our narrator next demonstrated the effects of the company's bullets on a pail packed with clay. This time those of us watching were treated to the additional audio enticement of hearing the wet slapping sound of the clay as the bullets entered, fragmented, and ruptured the surrounding muck, gouging caverns the size of pumpkins.

"Still watching, Son?" the father asked softly, his hands resting on his son's shoulders.

His son, clearly entranced, nodded slowly.

Gun shows are marvelous places to capture a feel for America's

gun culture. The moment I stepped from my car, I saw a middle-
aged man with a well-developed paunch sauntering toward the
show entrance. He was dressed in a short-sleeve shirt and loose,
wrinkled slacks and looked like a TV producer's dream image of the
average suburban American male—except, that is, for the black Colt
AR-15 assault rifle slung over his shoulder.

The show occupied two buildings at the Frederick County fairgrounds. A few men walked the aisles wearing little signs on their
backs listing the guns they owned and wanted to sell. Another man
had stuck a FOR SALE sign in the barrel of the rifle dangling at his
back. Seated behind battered fold-down tables, dealers sold guns,
books, accessories, and ammunition, even those hard-to-find .50-
caliber rounds needed for long-range sniper rifles and battlefield machine guns. Several dealers sold books on how to kill and, for those
who knew how already, how to do it more effectively, including
books on how to make silencers, military manuals on how to make
booby traps, black-covered Army manuals on how to make "improvised munitions," and a nifty little tome courtesy of the Pentagon on
how to brush up on your sniper skills.

One dealer offered a Browning heavy machine gun complete
with tripod. A thin, balding clerk wearing a black T-shirt commemorating the 1992 "Machine Gun Shoot" told me the gun worked
and asked, was I interested?

"I don't have the tax stamp," I said. (I was referring here to the
$200 transfer tax any adult must pay before acquiring a machine
gun, a silencer, or any other weapon restricted by the National Firearms Act of 1934.)

"No problem getting one," he said. "If it's the cost—think how
much money you'd spend if you had a boat. You fill that tank, that's
what? Fifty bucks each time you go out?"

Elsewhere in his booth he displayed an S.W. Daniel Street-
Sweeper shotgun, a Cobray M-11/9, and on an adjacent table the
Cobray's full-auto RPB-made ancestor, its price reduced to $410
from $598 as a special deal for this show only.

"Looks new," I said, referring to the RPB. "Has it been fired?"

"That's the display gun. All the rest, new in the box."

"How many have you got?"

I hadn't meant to be cagey, but he gave me a sly grin all the same. "How many you need? I got lots and lots."

◆ ◆ ◆

For an advanced course in dealing death, all Nicholas Elliot would have had to do was turn to the back pages of his treasured gun magazines, where advertisers peddle all manner of lethal know-how. One afternoon I sat down with my checkbook and the classifieds from a current issue of *American Handgunner* and scanned the ads as would, say, a presidential assassin.

I wrote to the Kinetic Energy Corp., at a post office box in Tavernier, Florida, to learn about its products, which it called the "world's deadliest handgun ammunition." A week later I received a badly typed one-page photocopy listing the company's cartridges and, to the probable delight of police officers everywhere, touting their ability to penetrate bulletproof vests. Kinetic wrote, for example, that its nine-millimeter bullet "will penetrate the Kevlar Type IIA bullet proof vest and make a 1½ inch diameter hole through 1600 pages of a dry phone book protected by the Kevlar vest from a distance of 45 feet."

Kinetic felt moved to add three rather ill-crafted lines to the very end of the flyer. "Any one including the worst of criminals can purchase a kevlar bullet proof vest. More and more of the criminals are commiting hold ups and home invanisons [sic] wearing these vests."

I also sent three dollars to Lafayette Research of Varnell, Georgia. This company proposed not to sell me deadly ammunition, but to teach me how to make my own. A week or so later I received from Lafayette a set of directions on how to make exploding bullets. The two-page instructions, clearly produced on a none-too-sophisticated computer printer, began with the warning: "This plan is for information only!!"

This disclaimer struck me as less than convincing, however, in light of another warning that followed closely thereafter: "Warning: Always wear proper safety equipment including protective eye wear whenever in the vicinity of moving machinery or tools such as drills!!"

Explicit, step-by-step instructions followed, detailing how to drill out the nose of a .44-caliber bullet, pack the hole with oil and a BB, then reassemble the cartridge. On impact, the steel BB is rammed backward into the softer lead of the bullet, thus causing the bullet to shatter.

Despite the "information only" disclaimer, the directions included machining tolerances down to a few thousandths of an inch.

One *American Handgunner* ad was especially compelling to my inner terrorist.

"MEN OF ACTION AND ADVENTURE," it hailed.

This was Paladin Press of Boulder, Colorado, offering me a fifty-page catalog of books and videos on "new identity, improvised explosives, revenge, firearms, survival, and many other outrageous and controversial subjects." I sent in my dollar and soon afterward received a catalog chock-full of books every red-blooded American really ought to be reading.

Inside I found dozens of books that promised to turn me into a major neighborhood asset. Here, for example, were *Breath of the Dragon: Homebuilt Flamethrowers; Improvised Land Mines: Their Employment and Destructive Capabilities* ("Just in case your future includes a little anarchy," the blurb reads); *Ragnar's Guide to Home and Recreational Use of High Explosives* (with the author's techniques "a single individual can easily dig a dry well, redirect creeks, blow up bad guys and perform a host of otherwise impossible chores of immense benefit to mankind"); *Hit Man: A Technical Manual for Independent Contractors,* purportedly written by a practicing professional named Rex Feral; and *Death by Deception,* on how to turn ordinary objects like computer modems and showerheads into deadly booby traps.

Here too I found the How to Kill series by John Minnery, all six books now packaged in one handy 512-page volume called *Kill Without Joy: The Complete How to Kill Book,* whose chapters according to the catalog "provide gruesome testimony to why these books have been banned by certain countries around the globe." The catalog calls this a how-to history of murder, but quickly inserts its catchall disclaimer, "For information and academic purposes only!"

I ordered *Kill Without Joy.* Paladin, the L.L. Bean of mayhem, delivered it shortly thereafter.

The book begins: "The object of this study is to instruct the reader in the techniques of taking another human life, up close, and doing it well." It includes a chapter called "Smothering" and offers a few tips on decapitation. "If the subject's execution is to be ritualized, kneel him down, hands tied behind his back. Pass the blade of the weapon lightly over the back of his bowed head. This causes the muscles to stiffen."

Interested readers can find the book in the rare-book collection of the Library of Congress in Washington, D.C. Not because it's at all rare, however. "For security reasons," a librarian there told me. "A book like that wouldn't stay on the shelf for long."

Paladin Press merits closer examination. It represents the distillation of the attitude of nonresponsibility that prevails in America's gun culture and that so influenced the evolution of Nicholas Elliot's gun. At a time when America is struggling with a rising tide of violence, Paladin Press enthusiastically peddles primers on how to produce such violence. Its books are well-known to police and federal agents across the country, who have found them in the libraries of serial killers and bombers. Paladin, moreover, is but one company, albeit the most visible, in a little-known industry nurtured by America's infatuation with violence and sheltered by the free-speech guarantees of the First Amendment. Often referred to as the "gun aftermarket," the industry includes scores of small companies devoted to peddling murderous know-how of all kinds, including at least one guide to torture. That such an industry exists at all demonstrates how deep the roots of our infatuation with guns and violence descend.

◆ ◆ ◆

Paladin Press keeps a low profile in Boulder, a town whose pronounced leftward lean prompts many residents to refer jokingly but pridefully to the city as the People's Republic of Boulder. A business columnist for the *Boulder Daily Camera,* the city's newspaper, had never heard of the company. Nor had anyone at the city's public broadcasting radio station. Paladin occupies several small, nondescript buildings a few blocks north of Pearl Street, the city's chic pedestrian mall. No sign announces the location, just a small plaque by a side door to the main building.

The company, however, makes no effort to discourage inquiries. Its owner, Peder Lund, is unabashedly candid about the 450 books he sells and his motives for doing so.

"I prefer to make decisions about publishing based on what we want to publish and what our customers want, rather than acceding to any particular desire for respectability," he told me. With a gravelly laugh, he added, "Why bother? It's not on my agenda."

Lund is a midsize man with dark hair, steady blue eyes, and a deep, assured voice. Although his roots are Scandinavian, at first glance he leaves an impression of Irishness. His nose is on the long side of pug, his ears are cantilevered outward in a mildly elfish way. As always, a fully loaded .357 Magnum revolver rested on the right-hand surface of his desk, in full view.

Lund and a partner, Robert K. Brown, founded Paladin in 1970 after both had served with the Army's Special Forces in Vietnam. The two first met in Miami in 1964 where Lund was working on a plan to lead a group of amateur soldiers into Castro's Cuba to rescue some refugees and to capture the whole heroic saga on film. "It was a harebrained scheme hatched by harebrained people, myself included," Lund said.

Brown advised Lund not to get involved. The plan stalled of its own accord.

In July 1964, Lund joined the Army and in December 1966 went to Vietnam, where he served as a second lieutenant and company commander. He joined the Special Forces in July 1967. He fought in the Central Highlands until July 1968 when the Army tried to transfer him to the U.S. to run a training company. "It was a waste of talent," he said. He quit the service, did odd jobs, until he and Brown founded Paladin in 1970, taking the name Paladin not from the lead character in the old TV series "Have Gun Will Travel," but from a class of medieval knight that rode about the countryside correcting injustice.

Paladin Press had no particular interest in righting wrongs, however. "The point," Lund told me, "was pure profit."

Initially Paladin concentrated on subjects in which Lund and Brown felt they had some professional expertise, such as guerrilla warfare and firearms. Paladin's first title was *Silencers, Snipers and Assassins* by J. David Truby, a book Paladin still sells.

Brown left Paladin in 1974 to found *Soldier of Fortune* magazine, also based in Boulder. Paladin branched into other topics. Lund had noticed an increasing interest in survivalism during the last days of Jimmy Carter's administration. Lund moved to capitalize on the trend and published *Life After Doomsday*, a guide intended to help individuals, families, and small groups survive after a nuclear holocaust. Lund also published *The Great Survival Resource Book*, a consumer's guide to the tools of survival. The book evaluated weapons, water-filtration systems, and other products.

In 1980, Paladin expanded beyond the survival movement with *Get Even: The Complete Book of Dirty Tricks,* a half-serious primer on nonlethal revenge by an author using the name George Hayduke, a name more widely recognized as that of the maverick environmentalist in Edward Abbey's *The Monkey Wrench Gang.* Lund approached Hayduke with the idea, he said, "because I realized there was a great deal of frustration among people against institutions that screwed them." *Get Even* remains a Paladin staple, its top seller as recently as the autumn of 1992; Hayduke became one of its star authors, identified in Paladin's catalog as the "Master of Malice."

Nicholas Elliot might have produced a better silencer if he had read Paladin's catalog and ordered Hayduke's *The Hayduke Silencer Book: Quick and Dirty Homemade Silencers*. "These simple, effective silencer designs are your passport into the world of muffled mayhem," the catalog says of the Hayduke classic. "And best of all, they can be made right at your kitchen table with common items found around the house." Or, Nicholas could have picked any of seven other books advertised on the same page, including several more how-to primers on silencers and books on the history and fundamental design requirements of effective sound suppression.

Lund declined to tell me his company's profit or revenue, other than to say that over the previous decade revenue had doubled. The company, which employed fifteen people full-time, seemed to provide him a comfortable living. He owned a $45,000 Range-Rover free and clear and said he customarily spent up to five months of every year at a cottage Paladin owns in Britain's Cotswolds. For the rest of the year, he lived in a house in Boulder Canyon with a skeet and rifle range off one of its several decks and a one-story indoor waterfall.

Paladin's books have exposed the company to business trials not typically faced by small companies. Printers have refused to print its books. Magazines have declined to accept its ads. Two different banks asked Paladin to take its business elsewhere.

Even Paladin betrays a certain lawyerly squeamishness about its books. The first page of *Kill Without Joy*, for example, disavows any responsibility for "the use or misuse of the information herein." Most of Paladin's books and catalog blurbs include the caveat "For Information Purposes Only."

But surely, I argued, Lund knew that some customers would try out the advice and instructions included in his books, particularly *Kill Without Joy*.

"I understand someone could conceivably misuse the information," Lund said. "I know that. Absolutely. There's no question in my mind about it. But I am not responsible for someone misusing information."

"Why publish the book at all?" I asked. "Does the world really need a five-hundred-page book on how to kill?"

For the first and only time during my visit, Lund flared with anger: "If you want to pin me down on moral culpability, I cannot accept it. I cannot accept it."

Besides, he argued, Paladin published much more than books on how to kill and bomb. He cited books on military history and self-defense, and a handbook for law-enforcement officers.

Paladin's eclectic tastes can lead to some odd juxtapositions in its catalog. For example, *Streetwork: The Way to Police Officer Safety and Survival* appeared on page forty-four of one of its catalogs. According to Lund, its author was a San Diego police officer. *Kill Without Joy* appeared two pages earlier.

Paladin readers are not crooks, Lund said. Many customers, he argued, buy his books as a "cathartic," a means of harmlessly working off frustrations with bosses, ex-wives, and intractable institutions by imagining acts of violence and revenge. "I think there are many, many Walter Mittys on our mailing list, people who live in a fantasy world."

Michael Hoy, owner of Loompanics Unlimited of Port Townsend, Washington, another mail-order publisher with a taste for handbooks on violence, told me he doubted Paladin's books or his own triggered any crimes—although he was quick to add that a "couple hundred" of his own customers were already in prison. Once a week he prepared a special catalog just for them by tearing out pages on improvised firearms and other topics that prison officials tended to frown on. He did not believe that killers needed to read such books as *Kill Without Joy,* which Loompanics buys from Paladin and resells. "I just don't think that's how serial killers operate, reading books and all."

One Loompanics offering is *Physical Interrogation Techniques* by Richard Krousher. The book, according to a Loompanics catalog, "tells you the best ways to tie and bind a subject for physical interrogation, where to obtain tools and devices needed, and even how to get the guy to torture himself while you're out for coffee."

Hoy's own lead-stomached staff refused to proofread it, so he took on the task alone. "It's a pretty gruesome book," he told me. "I was pretty sick of that stuff myself by the time I was done." Nonetheless, by the time we spoke in December 1992 he had sold 5,500 copies.

A big fan of Lund and his company, Hoy gushed, "It's just a joy doing business with Paladin Press."

Paladin seems to have a good many satisfied customers. Many write fan mail to the company, applauding both its efficient service and its daring. A San Antonio customer wrote: "I've got to give you credit, you offer controversial, often shocking literature that is invaluable to all Americans. It's a pity that all mail-order companies don't follow your example."

Here are three of the five books this particular customer ordered, along with excerpts from their catalog descriptions:

Expedient Hand Grenades, *by G. Dmitrieff. "Almost anyone can now master the art of constructing an effective hand grenade. One of America's leading ordnance designers makes it simple with easily understood instructions that describe the equipment and methods needed to make two optimum models: the fragmentation and incendiary grenades."*

Improvised Explosives: How to Make Your Own, *by Seymour Lecker. "With ease, you can construct such devices as a* *package bomb, booby-trapped door, auto(mobile) trap, sound-detonated bomb or pressure mine, to name just a few."*

The Mini-14 Exotic Weapons System (*no author listed*). *"Convert your Mini into a full-auto, silenced, SWAT-type weapon that is capable of field-clearing firepower. Note that this conversion process requires no machining or special tools. Once completed, it takes just five minutes to drop in the Automatic Connector (the book's secret) or remove it as needed. It's that simple!"* [*The Mini-14, made by Sturm, Ruger & Co., is a semiautomatic rifle.*]

An urgent need for revenge apparently prompted a customer in Valdosta, Georgia, to write for a copy of George Hayduke's *Get Even.* "I have a lot of people that need to get screwed for a change!" this customer wrote. At the bottom, he added: "Rush please! They are way past due!"

A Wallingford, Pennsylvania, parent was less than thrilled, however: "Take our son's name off your mailing list immediately. You should be stopped from sending your publication through the mail to minors."

Bomb squad members are some of Paladin's most motivated customers. Joseph Grubisic, commander of the Chicago police bomb and arson section, told me he put himself on Paladin's mailing list and bought any new book on explosives in order to be prepared for future encounters with the fruits of the book's instructions. As a training exercise, members of each shift build hoax bombs (without explosives) and pass them along to colleagues on other shifts, who then attempt to defuse them. Often, Grubisic said, the shifts design their bombs using Paladin books as a guide.

Investigators often find books from Paladin and its competitors in the possession of bombing suspects. "Hundreds of times," an ATF bomb expert told me.

Although a direct connection between the books and bombs is almost always difficult to prove, ATF agents now routinely look for such books in their searches of suspects' homes and use them to buttress their cases in court. The connection can be close. A few years ago a religious zealot tried bombing an X-rated drive-in theater in Pennsylvania by attaching fourteen explosive charges to the posts that supported the screen. Only one charge went off. The ATF lab analyzed the remaining explosives and discovered the contents matched a formula from *The Poor Man's James Bond*, published by Desert Publications of El Dorado, Arkansas, but sold both by Paladin and Loompanics. The lab was even able to cite the page. When agents searched the suspect's home, they found the book.

These "burn-and-blow" books may pose the gravest danger to their own users. Any bomb recipe is dangerous, no matter how precise. Even a change in the weather can cause a devastating change in chemical reactions needed to make such explosives as nitroglycerin. Some published recipes are flat-out wrong, particularly, experts say, in *The Anarchist's Cookbook*, published by Barricade Books of Secaucus, New Jersey, and sold by Paladin. ("It's kind of like the *Physicians' Desk Reference*," one assistant U.S. attorney told me. "Every self-respecting terrorist has to have *The Anarchist's Cookbook*.") The experts won't say exactly where the errors lie, preferring to pick up the pieces of wannabe bombers rather than innocent civilians.

Even the marketers of such books acknowledge their dangers and flaws. Mr. Lund told me he is fully aware the *Cookbook*'s recipes contain dangerous errors: "They're wrong. No doubt about it." But he added, "There are so many copies of that book extant, I don't see how not selling another one is going to be in any way redeeming." Billy Blann, owner of Desert Publications, said anyone who tries to act on the directions in Desert's book *The Poor Man's James Bond* takes a great risk. Most of his customers, he said, are "closet commandos" who just like to read on the wild side. "Anybody who fools with this stuff," he said in a profound Arkansas twang, "has got to be a fool."

Or, bomb investigators fear, a child.

That Wallingford, Pennsylvania, parent wrote to Paladin after his son received a copy of *The Anarchist's Cookbook* and, while trying out one of its recipes, blew off the tip of one finger. In August 1992, two boys in Athens, Tennessee, set off two powerful bombs in a city park. In a search of one suspect's home, investigators found *The Poor Man's James Bond,* Volume II, complete with little pink Post-it notes marking crucial pages. In San Juan Capistrano, California, three young boys were seriously injured when a pipe bomb they were making in one boy's garage exploded. Members of the Orange County bomb squad searched the boy's home and in a freezer found a high-explosive solution made from a recipe in the *Improvised Munitions Blackbook,* Volume III, another book published by Billy Blann's Desert Publications and sold by Paladin and Loompanics. "We're talking some bad-news stuff," said Sgt. Charles Stumph, commander of the squad. "He was just taking it through the cooling process, and he was a thirteen-year-old kid."

Park Elliott Dietz, a forensic psychiatrist and FBI consultant in La Jolla, California, studied Paladin Press and its peers. In 1983 he set up a dummy company, Hawkeye Industries, through which he corresponded with Paladin and other companies in what he calls the "violence industry." He used this oblique approach, he said, "because I thought these people were dangerous. Some of them are."

He no longer placed Paladin in that category, however. "Paladin is so aboveboard in selling the worst of information for profit that there's no need for any subterfuge with them." His scrutiny earned him a dedication in one of Paladin's books—George Hayduke's *Payback: Advanced Back-Stabbing and Mudslinging Techniques.* Hayduke's dedication reads, in part: "Park Baby, this book's for you."

Dr. Dietz estimates that he is called on to serve as a forensic psychiatrist in fifty to seventy-five criminal cases a year. When he interviews defendants, he said, he asks about the movies and TV shows they watch, the books they read. "And when one asks them," he told me, "one learns that a large proportion of offenders of the type I'm asked to see are aware of and interested in these materials. I've come to expect bombers, killers using exotic weapons, mass murderers, and political-extremist offenders to have a level of familiarity with the violence industry, including Paladin Press, equivalent to the familiarity of sex offenders with pornography."

The effect of Paladin's books and pornography is similar, Dr. Dietz argued. "People with a preexisting interest in tying and torturing women gravitate to such pornography. People with a preexisting interest in mass destruction gravitate to titillating descriptions of that."

His work brought him into contact with at least two multiple murderers who had read books by Paladin and its competitors: George Banks, who killed thirteen people in Wilkes-Barre, Pennsylvania, and Sylvia Seegrist, who killed three people and wounded seven in Media, Pennsylvania.

In an article in the *Journal of Forensic Sciences*, Dr. Dietz argued that books sold or published by Paladin—in particular the How to Kill series, *Get Even*, and *The Poor Man's James Bond*—may have been the inspiration for the Tylenol killings of 1982 and subsequent product-tampering cases. As early as 1972, he wrote, *The Poor Man's James Bond* described how cyanide could be substituted for the drugs in medicinal capsules. The first murder using cyanide in capsules occurred in 1982 in Chicago, in the Tylenol case. Nine other murders followed, six more in Chicago, three others in 1986 in Seattle and Yonkers, New York.

In 1973, Dr. Dietz's report continued, Paladin's *How to Kill* suggested adding acid to eyedrops. A few years later a pharmacist allegedly used a similar technique.

In 1981, *Get Even* described a novel means of contaminating a bottled drink. Four years later, someone used the approach in a Santa Clara, California, grocery store.

In 1983, Paladin's *Hit Man* noted a way of tampering with tea bags to make them deadly. Four years later, Dr. Dietz wrote, a New

Jersey man was convicted of placing similarly contaminated tea bags in a grocery store.

"One of the usually ignored concerns about this industry that I would underscore is the effect of exposure on vulnerable members of the community," Dr. Dietz told me. "It's the same concern that I have always emphasized ought to be foremost in our thinking about the effects of pornography. It is not relevant what effect if any either pornographic or violent materials have on college-educated, nonantisocial, non-substance-abusing, nonpsychotic persons. What is relevant is the effect on uneducated, substance-abusing, antisocial, or psychotic persons with little or no family or community control, in circumstances where they think they have no witnesses."

In fact, he argued, vulnerable readers migrate to such material and may incorporate the "worldview" of the publication into their thinking. "My concern," he said, "is not just that one can learn to build a better bomb this way, but also that through sufficient immersion in this subculture one comes to find a greater need to build the bomb."

I asked Peder Lund what he thought of Dr. Dietz's views.

"I really can't be bothered by him," he said. Dr. Dietz, he said, had seized on a few aberrant cases to postulate a link between Paladin's books and crime. "If you take two hundred thousand people, statistically you're going to find two or three who don't wear underwear, four or five who cultivate bonsai trees, six or eight who've shaved their heads. There's no statistical validity to the man's conclusions. It's as if you went to a party last night and met five people who were divorced and decided the divorce rate had gone up catastrophically."

Lund dismissed Dr. Dietz's product-tampering theory as "conjecture." On the reports of bomb injuries from books published by Paladin and others, Lund said, "As a human, I feel very sorry for anyone who's put through any physical suffering. As a publisher and as a pragmatist, I feel absolutely no responsibility for the misuse of information."

Paladin is merely a vehicle for conveying information, he said. "We are not encouraging illegal activity."

No one, at least no one I could find, has sued Paladin over the ways people put its books to use. "And I think it would be a travesty of the legal system to do so, don't you?" Lund said. "Do you sue General Motors because a kid runs over his schoolmate in a stolen car? Do you sue the manufacturer of a hammer because a child picks it up and bashes his little sister's head in? I can't see any clear-thinking person holding someone responsible for conveying information."

The U.S. Supreme Court agrees. "The general rule is, people do have a constitutional right to engage in speech which might cause serious harm or danger to others," said Bruce Ennis, a First Amendment attorney. Speech, or a written work, can be deemed illegal only when it is virtually certain to lead a listener or reader to an immediate act of violence. "These are difficult standards to meet," said Floyd Abrams, considered a leading expert in First Amendment law. "They are *supposed* to be difficult."

Even bomb investigators, the people who most often encounter the fruits of the violence-industry's advice, oppose banning such books. "You can't say they can't print this stuff," said Joe Grubisic, commander of the Chicago bomb squad. "I don't like it, but I really don't know what the solution is. I don't want a police state."

No problem would exist, argued Sergeant Stumph of Orange County, if Paladin and its peers simply chose not to publish their violence primers. "It'd be so nice if the big R-word would just come into play, if some of these people would just take responsibility for their friggin' actions."

Jack Thompson, a Miami lawyer whom the ACLU picked to be one of its 1992 Arts Censors of the Year, took a less indulgent view. That Paladin can continue to sell a book like *Kill Without Joy*, he said, is evidence of a lack of prosecutorial initiative. "The ACLU has been very successful in convincing an entire generation of prosecutors that you can't do anything about this stuff," he said. The majority of

Americans, he argued, want the likes of Paladin Press "aggressively pursued and prosecuted, but they've been abandoned because of a lack of will by the government at every level."

Some books even Paladin will not publish, Lund told me. He will not accept anything racist or "scatological." He will not publish advice on altitude-sensitive detonation devices. "We don't want to be the scapegoats for an investigation of an airliner coming down," he said.

He also said he would not publish books on poisons—although in fact several books in Paladin's catalog, including *Kill Without Joy*, include tips on the subject. He countered that these references were very general. "We try to avoid publishing specifics."

But why this scruple if Paladin's customers are just Walter Mitty types in search of a psychic release?

Lund tipped back his chair. "Perhaps I can't tell you accurately," he said slowly. "I find it very offensive, poisoning. Because it's something done by the devious, it isn't a direct-confrontation kind of thing."

"Bombs are pretty devious," I suggested.

"We all have our boundaries, wouldn't you say?" His voice was mild, but his gaze turned perceptibly cooler. "Perhaps my boundaries are different from yours. My boundaries are different from many people's."

◆ ◆ ◆

The "aftermarket" bazaar offers far more than mere advice. Dozens of large and small companies peddle all manner of accessories capable of turning your neighborhood bully into a Rambo-esque urban warrior. U.S. Cavalry, a mail-order company in Radcliff, Kentucky, offers "military and adventure equipment," including laser sights, a "sleeve dagger" meant to be strapped to the user's arm or leg (complete with "blood grooves" ground into its triangular blade), a plastic hairbrush with a knife embedded in the handle, and all the accessories needed to turn your Mossberg Model 500 shotgun into a tactical assault gun with front and rear "assault grips," folding stock, and a perforated barrel shroud that gives the weapon the look of an exotic machine gun.

The lushest source of weapons and accessories remains *Shotgun News,* the thrice-monthly advertising tabloid in Hastings, Nebraska. The front page invariably includes half a dozen ads from companies offering to help people acquire their own federal gun-dealer licenses ("Confused? Call Bob or Jennie today!"). The rest of each issue consists of 150 or more onionskin-like pages of classified and display advertising directed at gun dealers, collectors, and shooters of all tastes. In July 1989 the newspaper carried an advertisement offering the "Whitman Arsenal," consisting of the seven weapons and accessories that Charles Whitman brought with him on August 1, 1966, when he climbed the twenty-seven-story clock tower at the University of Texas and spent the next ninety minutes firing away at anyone who happened to fall within his sights. He killed sixteen people, including a receptionist and two tourists in the tower; he wounded another thirty-one. The ad offered the guns along with a copy of the *Life* magazine edition that covered the shooting and called the incident "the most savage one-man rampage in the history of American crime."

Shotgun News also carried ads placed by an Athens, Georgia, company for products designed to convert semiautomatic weapons to full-auto machine guns, a company later included in ATF's wide-ranging effort to discover how the Branch Davidian cult in Waco, Texas, managed to acquire enough firepower to repel the 1993 ATF raid on the compound.

When I opened the July 10, 1992, edition of *Shotgun News,* to which I had subscribed, I found an advertisement for a Nazi tank—"a rare opportunity to own a fine piece of German artillery." A Chillicothe, Ohio, broker of vintage military vehicles offered the tank for $145,000. "There's no difference between owning a tank and a Ferrari except four inches of armor," he told me during a visit to his office. Oddly enough, such ads may be among the most innocent in the publication. Private buyers of tanks tend to be history-loving souls and members of the Military Vehicle Preservation Association, which doesn't allow live guns of any kind at its various meets.

Once notorious for running quasi-legal and occasionally racist ads, including an advertisement placed by the Ku Klux Klan, *Shotgun News* has grown more circumspect, at least in terms of its published policies. It now includes a notice that it no longer accepts ads for silencer parts, plans for making explosives and booby traps, "plans, videos or books" for full-auto conversions, and such burglar-friendly tools as lockpicks, slim-jims, and books on how to pick locks. Nonetheless, my April 1993 issue contained an advertisement from a Sun City, Arizona, company offering instructions for converting Chinese SKS semiautomatic assault rifles to full-auto operation. Another company, Jonathan Arthur Ciener Inc. of Cape Canaveral, Florida, "Manufacturer of the Finest in Suppressed Firearms," ran a full-page ad offering sound-suppressed handguns and rifles, and separate silencers for a variety of assault weapons including the MAC-10 and MAC-11 and Nicholas Elliot's gun, the Cobray M11/9.

During a reporting journey unrelated to guns, I inadvertently wound up at the fountainhead of aftermarket suppliers, the huge annual "surplus" show in Las Vegas, also the source of much of the cheap merchandise we encounter in "dollar" and Army-Navy stores and in low-rung direct-mail catalogs. Some thirty thousand retailers from around the world visited the show, shopping its four thousand booths for bargains in bulk quantities of those ubiquitous purple-haired trolls, cheap plastic toys, and other merchandise. But I found dozens of dealers selling a darker sort of merchandise, including surplus night-vision scopes like the one used by the serial killer in the movie *Silence of the Lambs,* dummy hand grenades, combat knives, police badges, and black caps emblazoned with the law-enforcement acronyms we see routinely in newspaper photographs of raids conducted by ATF, DEA, and the FBI. "It's perfectly legal," an attendant at one of the cap booths told me. These caps and badges, along with the magnetic blue or red police-style flashing lights offered in U.S.

Cavalry's catalog, can turn anyone into a convincing replica of a bona fide lawman.

At one of the largest booths at the Las Vegas show I encountered Jim Moore, chief executive officer of Military Supply Corp., LaCenter, Washington, who told me he sold uniforms and other equipment to armies around the world. He was also selling .50-caliber long-range sniper rifles. In fact, he said, he had one up in his room at the Las Vegas Hilton at that very moment. He flipped to a page in his catalog that contained a sketch of the bipod-mounted rifle. "It's called reach out and touch someone at two thousand yards," Moore said. "Would you like to come out and shoot it?"

He later canceled the demonstration. The colonel was a victim of jet lag, Moore explained; he had napped through the afternoon.

The aftermarket has so much to offer that Nicholas Elliot need not have gone to all the trouble of making the combat accessories police found in his backpack. With a little effort, he could have ordered them directly from S.W. Daniel's mail-order catalog. It offered a brass catcher, complete with see-through bag and Velcro fastener; an official Cobray "assault sling," wrist strap, and rear sling collar ("Get Super Control By Adding These Accessories," the catalog said); "fake" silencers; slotted barrel extenders; and flash suppressors, designed to keep that all-too-detectable muzzle flash to a minimum. For $127.95 Cobray enthusiasts could also order a screw-on barrel-and-grip assembly to make the Cobray M-11/9 resemble "the fabled Thompson" machine gun. Instead of jungle-clipping his magazines with tape, Nicholas could simply have ordered a plastic magazine joiner tailored to the purpose. S.W. Daniel named this product Double Trouble.

The catalog asked, "Can You Imagine 64 Rounds?"

Two institutions share much of the responsibility for cultivating the anything-goes attitude of firearms makers and the aftermarket bazaar. They have declared themselves each other's enemy, but together both served as a kind of cultural cheering squad, nudging Nicholas Elliot and his Cobray along their path to Atlantic Shores.

The first is the National Rifle Association.

To people who dislike guns, the NRA is the Great Satan. They see its influence in every act of gun-related legislation and in every political race. Although its impact on electoral politics has been greatly inflated, the association has indeed been influential in lobbying against firearms regulation, as when it diminished the authority of the Gun Control Act of 1968 by promoting the McClure-Volkmer Act. Where the NRA has been most influential, however—and where its influence has been least acknowledged or appreciated—is in defining the vocabulary of the firearms debate and thus, in a sense, winning the debate before it even began.

The NRA accomplished this bit of intellectual gerrymandering by deftly marketing an ideology that posits any and all firearm regulation as a direct challenge to the U.S. Constitution and, by inference, to America itself. In this ideology, all guns are equal, be they Cobray pistols having no utilitarian value or the Glocks now embraced by so many police departments; guns are to be kept in readiness to repel invaders or—and this is a real prospect to the hard-liners who run the NRA—to resist the U.S. government itself; regulation of firearms is necessarily the first step toward confiscation of all firearms. Soon after I joined the NRA in 1993, I received my official NRA "Member Guide," which stated the NRA's position in unequivocal terms: "Any type of licensing and computer registration scheme aimed at law-abiding citizens is a direct violation of Second Amendment rights, serves no law enforcement purpose, and ultimately could result in the prohibition and/or confiscation of legally owned firearms." In a 1975 fund-raising letter to NRA members, retired general Maxwell E. Rich, executive vice president, warned of the true consequences of gun control: "My friend, they are not talking of 'Control'; they want complete and total 'Confiscation.' This will mean the elimination and removal of all police revolvers, all sporting rifles and target pistols owned by law abiding citizens." He asked, "What would the crime rate be if the criminal knew our police were unarmed . . . ?"

At times the NRA has even sought to link support for firearm regulation to Communist sympathies, as in 1973 when the NRA's *American Rifleman* magazine described the "Rules for Revolution," a never-authenticated document purported to set out the principles by which Communist cells could attain world control. The tenth rule, the magazine said, called for "the registration of all firearms on some pretext, with a view to confiscating them and leaving the population helpless."

On this battlefield anyone who advocates firearms regulation finds himself immediately on the defensive, forced into arcane debate over the exact meaning of the Second Amendment, and branded an enemy of The People.

An important effect of the NRA's propaganda was to arm even the least articulate of gun owners with a snappy response that allows them to readily deflect unfriendly challenges from the unpersuaded and at the same time to avoid having to think about what kinds of firearms regulations might indeed ease the national crisis. (To the NRA, of course, guns are not the crisis. People are. More jails and swifter prosecution will solve the problem of gun violence.) In this intellectual desert, the mere act of possessing or manufacturing a gun, even a Cobray M-11/9, becomes a noble and patriotic undertaking.

The NRA was not always the paranoid, Constitution-thumping entity it is today. Nor is its current radicalism shared by the great mass of its members, many of whom simply join to take advantage of the organization's broad array of grass-roots services or merely to get the NRA hat (mine is black with the NRA eagle insignia stitched in gold thread). The NRA is not the monolithic, omnipotent force of popular imagination. It is two organizations, and only by understanding this can one come to understand the fervor with which the association opposes even the simplest efforts at impeding the flow of guns from the good guys to the bad.

The NRA was founded in New York in 1871 by William Conant Church, a former *New York Times* war correspondent and soldier, and Gen. George Wingate, with the rather modest goal of sharpening the marksmanship skills of the New York National Guard and Guard units in other states by promoting a system of rifle practice and establishing rifle ranges. It remained a small, struggling organization until 1905, when federal legislation allowed the United States to sell surplus military weapons at cost to rifle clubs and made the NRA responsible for determining which clubs were qualified to acquire the guns. A 1911 amendment allowed the government to donate the guns to such clubs free of charge. Needless to say, NRA membership began to rise.

The association began attempting to influence legislation in 1934, in response to the increased clamor for firearms regulation that resulted in the National Firearms Act, which banned the sale of unregistered machine guns and sawed-off shotguns. The act was the NRA's first defeat, but also its first victory. As originally proposed, the act would have regulated the sale of pistols and handguns as well. But the NRA objected and, in its first demonstration of how a relative few ardent loyalists can shape a nation's laws, launched a lobbying and letter-writing campaign that convinced Congress to limit the retrictions to "gangster" weapons.

By 1946, the association had all of 155,000 members. In 1956, the NRA amended its New York State charter to include a set of objectives broader than those it had outlined in 1871. Now it sought "to promote social welfare and public safety, law and order, and the national defense; to educate and train citizens of good repute in the safe and efficient handling of small arms," and, broadly, "to encourage the lawful ownership and use of small arms by citizens of good repute."

The NRA was still largely a sportsman's organization, promoting target shooting, hunting, and hunter's rights. It might have kept to this moderate course if not for the assassination of John F. Kennedy in 1963, which prompted a horrified and heartbroken nation to call for gun control. The NRA, now galvanized by a threat to its members' favorite pastimes, began attacking controls and pressuring legislators to oppose them, while sidestepping the fact that Lee Harvey Oswald acquired his rifle by mail through an advertisement in the *American Rifleman*. Nonetheless, Congress passed the Gun Control Act of 1968.

The NRA's hard-liners, who despised the Gun Control Act, began working to ensure that such an infringement of the constitutional right to bear arms would not occur again. And soon the bald, bullet-headed figure of Harlon Carter took the helm. He was the perfect leader for an organization steeped in the myths of the American frontier. As an officer and later chief of the U.S. Border Patrol, he came as close to being an Old West lawman as anyone could in the twentieth century.

But he also symbolized the darker aspects of America's enthusiasm for guns. For Carter was a convicted murderer.

In 1931, when he was seventeen, Carter shot and killed a Mexican boy with his shotgun under circumstances that prompted a jury to convict him of murder. Carter claimed he killed the boy in self-defense, after he brandished a knife. An appellate court overturned the conviction, charging the lower-court judge had improperly instructed the jury as to what constituted a valid claim of self-defense. The charges were never refiled.

After Carter and his allies seized control of the NRA in the 1977 Cincinnati Revolt, the NRA heeled sharply to the right. It shifted emphasis from promoting the shooting sports to battling firearm regulations, a shift made official in 1977 when the association amended its New York State charter to include the goal of promoting "the right of the individual of good repute to keep and bear arms as a common law and constitutional right both of the individual citizen and of the collective militia."

A study conducted a few years earlier by the Institute for the Future, Menlo Park, California, for Remington Arms Company, warned that the NRA's "right-wingers are becoming increasingly isolated from the society of today." The report continued: "Dismissing unpleasant information about guns in society and denying integrity to those who are concerned about guns, they manage to survive in a bunker decorated with white hats and black hats, in a make-believe world of American 'sacred rights,' ancient skills, and coonskins."

Nonetheless, by 1978 the NRA claimed 1.2 million members. By 1983, its membership had increased to more than 2.6 million and was growing at three thousand a week.

But the NRA had moved so far to the right, had become so ardent in its opposition to any and all firearms regulation, that it soon began to lose some of its closest friends outside the organization. Most important, it alienated the law-enforcement community. In the late 1980s it opposed legislation aimed at outlawing armor-piercing ammunition and at banning such assault weapons as the MAC-10 and the Cobray. When police agencies dared criticize the NRA, their officials came under withering return fire. One of those attacked was Joseph McNamara, the widely respected chief of police in San Jose, California. (As of 1993 he was a fellow at the Hoover Institution studying ways to halt illegal drug distribution and was working on his next police novel.) In a 1987 advertisement for Handgun Control Inc., McNamara charged that the NRA leadership "has repeatedly ignored the objections of professional law enforcement," thus making police work "more difficult—and more dangerous." The NRA, in its own advertisements, accused McNamara of favoring legalization of drugs, a course he had never endorsed. At one point, someone sent him a bull's-eye target bearing his image. "I'll tell you," he said. "That target was shot full of holes."

Until the NRA began its attacks, most law-enforcement agencies considered the NRA their ally, McNamara said. Their allegiance, he said, reflected a fundamental misunderstanding of the NRA's attitudes and mission. "The NRA had gotten by for a lot of years on an image that wasn't really accurate, that they were supportive of law enforcement." The attacks on police chiefs, he said, "educated law enforcement as to their true colors."

Then the unthinkable occurred: the NRA began losing membership. From 1989 to 1991, its membership shrank from almost 3 million to about 2.5 million. Newspapers across the country began running stories that the NRA had lost its punch. The embattled association launched a campaign to restore the popular conception of its influence, drawing on frontier imagery to help. The annual meeting that was to mark its comeback was deliberately staged in San Antonio, home of The Alamo. The historic site, according to Osha Davidson, author of *Under Fire,* "was the touchstone of all those American values the gun group liked to claim as its own: an uncompromising attitude, unabashed love for this country, and a readiness to fight her enemies—no matter what the odds."

The NRA stepped up spending to bolster its influence, calling itself "The New NRA." Its political action committee—the NRA Political Victory Fund—spent $1.7 million on the presidential and congressional campaigns of 1992, more than twice as much as the $772,756 it spent in 1988. Between the 1990 and 1992 election cycles, the Victory Fund increased its spending more than any other registered PAC. The NRA also stepped up its lobbying expenditures. In 1992 it spent $28.9 million, 43 percent more than in 1988.

The centerpiece of its image-burnishing campaign, however, was a membership drive of unprecedented expense. The best way to refute reports of the NRA's demise was to boost membership to record levels. The NRA set out to do so, and to spare no expense. In 1992 alone, PM Consulting, the direct-mail company chosen to manage the drive, spent $25 million—$10 million more than budgeted. The NRA lured members with all manner of appeals and devices, including no-fee credit cards, gun-safety videos for kids, even a "Sportsman's Dream Gun Sweepstakes," in which the grand-prize winner stood to receive ten different hunting rifles and ten all-expenses-paid hunting trips. For the first time, the NRA enlisted the help of firearms dealers, offering them a substantial share of the $25 new-member fee for each recruit they managed to sign. For-profit gun shows waived their admission fees for anyone who joined the NRA on the spot.

The drive worked. In 1992, the NRA had a net gain of 616,000 members. As of October 1993, its membership had risen to a record high of nearly 3.3 million. The NRA was indeed bigger than ever before, but its campaign to boost membership and bolster its member programs had resulted in a 1992 operating deficit of $31.6 million, larger than ever in its history.

Despite all this spending and the surge in membership, by the middle of 1993 the NRA still seemed to have lost important ground. The association remained estranged from the nation's law-enforcement community. And it faced a series of unaccustomed setbacks. In 1993, Virginia passed its one-gun-a-month law, despite the $500,000 the NRA spent to defeat the legislation. Connecticut passed an assault-gun bill that outlawed the sale of certain assault guns, including the AR-15 made by Colt's Manufacturing, headquartered in Connecticut's own "Gun Valley." New Jersey passed an assault-gun bill. The New York assembly did likewise. Politicians and pundits began talking of a "sea change," a new distaste for gun violence as pervasive as the antigun mood of the late 1960s. One New York assemblywoman, Naomi Matusow, won her seat in 1992 after campaigning with an explicitly anti-NRA slate. "It may just be," she said, "that the NRA had cast a longer shadow than the reality."

Far from adapting to the changing mood, the NRA continued its shift to the right. In 1993, a hard-right faction headed by Neal Knox, a former NRA executive who heads his own firearms lobbying group, further consolidated its hold over the NRA's board and helped win a seat on the board for Harlon Carter's widow, Maryann Carter. The board already included such hard-liners as Robert K. Brown, cofounder of Paladin Press and publisher of *Soldier of Fortune* magazine, but Maryann Carter's election symbolized a return to first principles. No gun controls; no compromise. The "New" NRA seemed a reincarnation of the old NRA of Harlon Carter's day.

The NRA went on the offensive. It saw in the shifting national mood an opportunity to raise money and membership by sounding an especially urgent alarm. A four-page ad inserted in gun magazines showed President Bill Clinton and Sarah Brady shaking hands and on the verge of an embrace. "If you still need convincing reasons to guard your guns," the ad said, "here's a couple." Striking a familiar note of hysteria, the ad cried: "All conditions are ripe for 1993 to be the worst year for gun owners in American history. No holds are barred. No one's guns are safe. No one's hunting is protected. No one's ammunition is off limits. No one's firearms freedoms are secure."

It is a mistake, however, to think of the NRA as one uniform block of hard-right, pro-gun zealots. A survey by Louis Harris in 1993 found that of those NRA members captured in the sample, 59 percent supported registration of handguns and 49 percent favored limiting handgun purchases to one a month.

Why this division in attitude between the leadership and the ranks? And how does the NRA manage to avoid blowing apart from internal pressures?

For one thing, turnover among the rank and file is high. In the 1992 membership drive, for example, the NRA actually recruited more than one million new members, but lost more than half a million. Such turnover helps account for why the hard-core faction is able to retain control, despite a far more moderate member pool. For under the bylaws of the NRA, only members who have maintained their membership for five years in a row, or who have acquired a life membership, are permitted to vote in elections of board members. Thus only a small percentage of members are eligible to vote. And a small percentage of these ever bother to use the privilege. Those who do vote tend to be the most ardent of the NRA's Constitution-thumpers. They field slates of hard-line candidates in each board election and campaign aggressively to see that these candidates win.

To mollify the nonvoting ranks, the NRA provides a broad array of practical services. NRA-certified instructors provide shooting courses and teach gun safety to adults and kids. Celebrated hunters tour the nation conducting NRA hunting seminars. The organization runs shooting camps for kids and for advanced shooters hoping for a berth on the U.S. Olympic shooting team. It helps shooting clubs establish skeet ranges and provides grants to affiliated state shooting associations.

The NRA of political legend is a relatively small group of insiders who control the NRA's propaganda and lobbying apparatus and adhere to what is at heart a radical, Libertarian political orthodoxy—yet cloak their beliefs in familiar images that evoke mainstream American values and history. Eagles abound in NRA literature. The NRA cap bears an eagle. The NRA's gun-safety program is named Eddie Eagle. The NRA's famous bulletins, crafted to rouse the membership to write their legislators in response to some immediate threat, are called Minuteman Alerts. NRA executives lace their remarks and columns with allusions to the American Revolution, patriotism, and frontier history. At the NRA's 1993 annual meeting in Nashville, executive vice president Wayne LaPierre told the crowd, "You know, a couple of hundred years ago a group of citizen-patriots met at a bridge—Concord Bridge. You are no different from them. Because every day somebody still has to go to that bridge and stand there to defend freedom."

During the same annual gathering, a John Wayne impersonator, Gene Howard, addressed a separate meeting of the NRA's board. He wore a red cowboy shirt, brown leather vest, and a blue kerchief—tied at his neck in John Wayne fashion—and recited two of his own poems. One, titled "Do You Want My Gun," reprised Cold War themes:

> Today the majority of us are not politically correct
> And what do the liberals want us to put in check?
> That's right, our guns, they want us to turn them in.
> For as long as we have them socialism cannot win. . . .

Curiously, Howard then shifted battlefields and identified the NRA cause as nothing less than a fight to restore religion to America:

> For today freedom of religion is no longer a right,
> But a battle ground for which we must fight.
> So if you ask me for my gun, the answer is no!
> Try to take it, and if there's a hell, you'll know.

Central to the NRA's rhetoric is opposition to the American media—both the press and the entertainment media—which the leadership perceives as antigun. In his Nashville speech, Wayne La-Pierre called the news media "a force that dwarfs any political power or social tyrant that ever before existed on this planet." In a column in the June 1993 *American Rifleman*, NRA president Robert K. Corbin called the offending media "thought police" and warned such media "can unwittingly be manipulated by hidden, far-more-sinister forces."

In 1993 the association launched a formal assault on television violence, joining a broad popular attack that culminated early in the year in a network decision to air content warnings before especially violent shows. The NRA's attack, however, contained a curious twist. In testimony before a Senate Judiciary Committee hearing, NRA lobbyist Susan R. Lamson complained that violent television shows unfairly stigmatized guns and gun owners. "This steady diet of stereotypes coupled with gratuitous criminal violence provokes a widespread bigotry against law-abiding gun owners and fuels the drive for restrictions that impact the law-abiding."

◆ ◆ ◆

The media—and I include here the gun press—bear at least equal responsibility for nurturing firearms violence in America. Gun writers, TV and movie producers, and the daily press directly and indirectly stoke demand for exotic firearms and accessories and orchestrate the bloodthirsty mood that infuses the gun culture.

The gun writers know what their readers want. The newsletter *Gun Tests* routinely rates the penetration power of handguns and ammunition the way *Consumer Reports* compares new cars. *American Handgunner*'s 1992 "Combat Annual" reviewed six new high-caliber revolvers, calling them "The Ultimate Manstoppers!" Regular issues of the magazine are full of tales of combat tactics and police shoot-outs, part of a running series by Massad Ayoob, the magazine's star reporter. "Gory True Story," teased the cover of the October 1991 issue. "REAL-LIFE TERMINATOR! Soaking up bullet after bullet, a cop-killing PCP freak just won't die! Massad Ayoob's chilling account on page 70."

Gun writers often skirt the gory reality of gunshot injury by driving euphemism to new heights, deftly avoiding the words *kill, murder,* and *death,* using instead such etymological eunuchs as *knockdown, stopping power,* and—this is my favorite—*double-tap,* meaning to shoot a guy twice. (Double Tap also happens to be the name of a Virginia Beach gun store, whose sign features a black human silhouette with two red holes over the heart.)

To the gun press, no firearm is unworthy of praise, not even the Saturday night specials made by the now defunct RG Industries, one of which was used by John Hinckley when he shot James Brady in the head. In its "Combat Annual" *American Handgunner* included a defense of RG's guns written by Mark Moritz, special projects editor. Moritz, who noted that his first gun was an RG, tested a .22-caliber RG revolver against an expensive Smith & Wesson .22, comparing their performance in both head and body shots.

The RG was a little slower.

However, Moritz wrote, "even out of the box we are only talking about two-tenths of a second for multiple headshots at the relatively long range of seven yards."

Moritz won't win any awards for sensitivity in journalism. Early on in the story, in an angry denunciation of the "slimebucket" lawyers who sued RG Industries out of business after the Reagan-Brady shootings, he wrote: "When John Hinckley shot James Brady, with an RG .22 revolver, his wife, Sarah, head spokesnut at Handgun Control, Inc., sued RG. She was offended that her husband was shot with a cheap, low-powered gun. I guess she wanted him to be shot with an expensive, high-powered gun."

A writer for *American Survival Guide* even had nice things to say about S.W. Daniel's Ladies' Home Companion shotgun, the gun the Maryland state police ballistics expert refused even to test-fire. "When we first came across the Ladies' Home Companion at a large gun show earlier this year, we found it a highly interesting and unique firearm," the author wrote. He never commented on the inappropriate name of the weapon. The gun's heavy trigger pull, he wrote, "makes the LHC a very safe gun."

The Cobray M-11/9, Nicholas Elliot's gun, gets its share of praise too. *The Gun Digest Book of Assault Weapons* included a chapter on the pistol and its heritage. The author described it as "a plinker's delight and the bane of all tin cans, milk jugs, clay pigeons and other inanimate objects." He saw its primary practical value as being home defense. "Appearance alone should cause most burglars and intruders to consider instant surrender if brought before its muzzle."

In the closing paragraphs, the writer waxed nostalgic: "It is nice to know the Ingram family of submachine guns still is living and well. Because of their use on television and in the movies, they are justifiably famous."

◆ ◆ ◆

America's entertainment media provide the last ingredients to the perverse and lethal roux that sustains our gun culture. Today's TV producers and movie directors have not only adopted and amplified the elemental messages of frontier myth—in particular the notion that only a gun can set you free—but so deified guns as to promote the use and proliferation of specific kinds of weapons. Just as *McQ* promoted the Ingram, so too *Dirty Harry* promoted the Smith & Wesson Model 29, and "Miami Vice"—in addition to also promoting the Ingram line—such assault weapons as the Uzi and Bren 10. Dr.

Park Dietz, the La Jolla forensic psychiatrist, studied the effect of "Miami Vice" on gun prices and demand and found that the appearance of the Bren 10 in the hands of Sonny Crockett (Don Johnson) in the early episodes of the show immediately boosted demand for the weapon. Dietz has argued that "Miami Vice" by itself "was the major determinant of assault-gun fashion for the 1980s."

Dr. Dietz told me he believes America's news and entertainment media—its action movies, "reality" shows, news broadcasts, novels, and newspapers—play a far greater role in stimulating the country's bloodlust than any other source, including underculture publishers like Paladin Press. "Nothing evil or disgusting known to man lacks a guidebook," he told me. "But it's not only Paladin producing them. Today Hollywood studios market more widely a more graphic version for the illiterate than Paladin would be capable of generating or selling. Whereas ten years ago someone wanting to know how to more effectively rob a bank or kill with poison or booby-trap a crack house would have to consult a more experienced offender or go to a library or bookstore, today they need merely turn on HBO. And so a lower intellectual grade of offender has been given access to what only those who could read or communicate had available in the past. That's not Paladin's doing. That's Hollywood's doing."

Clearly, the role of movies and television in stimulating violence can never be quantified. Their impact, however, seems obvious. Consider how the phrase "Make my day" migrated from the movie *Dirty Harry* to car bumpers from coast to coast, even to a presidential speech, and, in slightly altered form, to the dialogue in a Disney "Duck Tales" cartoon. Recall too how sales of the Ingram submachine guns boomed after *McQ*, how *Dirty Harry* jolted sales of the Smith & Wesson Model 29. Add to this the American Psychological Association's estimate that by the time a child finishes elementary school he will have watched eight thousand murders on television.

Early in 1993 I again visited the Frederick County gun show and, while loitering at a booth offering sawed-off shotguns, silencers, and submachine guns (including a MAC-10 for $595), listened in as a young boy peppered the dealer with questions. The image was pure Rockwell, but with a rather dark contemporary twist. The boy wore a baseball cap with the beak lifted high off his forehead. He had freckles and ruddy cheeks, and glasses that had slipped a bit down his nose. His jacket was new, and too big. Instead of trying out the stethoscope of some kindly Rockwellian doctor, he caressed the smooth metal finish of a Heckler & Koch submachine gun. He paused before a Barrett Firearms .50-caliber sniper rifle, which reared above the table on its bipod barrel rest. This was the gun Jim Moore had offered to show me in Las Vegas.

"Is this the same gun they used in the movie?" the boy asked the dealer.

"Right," the dealer said. *The Navy SEALs.*"

The boy touched the rifle. "He used this to shoot through a building," the boy said with the kind of reverence once reserved for home-run baseballs.

"You shoot this at a building, it'll take off a pretty good piece," the dealer agreed.

The boy pointed at the powerful scope mounted on the rifle. "And he used this to see through the building."

The dealer kept a straight face.

The power of the entertainment media in fostering the appeal of guns became especially clear to me one afternoon when I and my daughters visited a video store in hopes of renting *Peter Pan*. My two-and-a-half-year-old was immediately distracted by an almost life-size cardboard cutout of Mel Gibson and Danny Glover in their *Lethal Weapon* roles, with Mel Gibson's arm and his trademark Beretta extended into space. My daughter closed her hands around the Beretta, then pulled away, making her hands into the shape of a gun. She held them out before her in a position astonishingly like the isosceles combat stance used by police and their TV counterparts and, while imitating as best she could the sound of a gun, fired two pretend shots at her older sister. This was sibling rivalry, American style.

Our movies and TV shows do far more damage than simply

boosting the appeal of weapons, however. They teach a uniquely American lesson: when a real man has a problem, he gets his gun. He slaps in a clip, he squints grimly into the hot noon sun, then does what he's gotta do. The training begins early. In the summer of '92, for example, I watched a TV commercial for the Super Soaker water gun, then the rage among pint-size assassins. The commercial offered a chilling parallel to the kind of real-life revenge killings carried out every day in the streets of America's inner cities:

Two nerdy boys show up for a pool party at the home of a snooty preppy girl named Buffy. She shuts the door in their faces.

They return, however, this time dressed in black suit jackets, white shirts, black ties, black fedoras, and of course dark glasses, exactly like the Blues Brothers as portrayed by John Belushi and Dan Aykroyd, except that in place of black slacks the boys wear gaudy swim trunks. One boy solemnly opens a briefcase. His friend reaches in and pulls out the Super Soaker. "Oh, Buffeeee," he calls in a mocking, nasal voice. She turns. He fires. Buffy is so shocked she spills her glass of punch over her face and torso.

The punch, of course, is dark red.

It was this lesson, above all, that Nicholas Elliot absorbed: when all else fails, maybe a gun can solve your problem.

CHAPTER THIRTEEN

NICHOLAS

TWO DIFFERENT TEACHERS TOLD LORA FARLEY that her mother, Karen, was either tending to a wounded teacher or comforting a teacher who had been chased. Both scenarios seemed plausible to her. That's the kind of woman her mother was, always giving and always getting involved. "I was like, 'Well, that sounds right too. I can see her doing both of them, but I don't know how she could do it at the same time.'"

Soon afterward, a teacher asked Will and Lora to come out into the hall.

"And one of my teachers was standing there and she was staring off . . . like out into where all the trailers were. She like gave me a hug and then they said, 'Take them back in the auditorium.'

"So we went back in the auditorium, and then about ten or twenty minutes later, they came and got us and they took us into Pastor Sweet's office, and my pastor was there." (The Farleys were members of a different church but sent their kids to Atlantic Shores.) "They never said that, you know, your mom has been shot or your mom is dead. They just—my pastor was crying, and then, I mean, we just sort of knew what had happened."

◆ ◆ ◆

Sweet was at the hospital waiting as Sam Marino underwent emergency surgery. One of his assistants telephoned him there. "George, you need to get back here right away."

"Why?"

"They found Karen Farley and she's dead."

◆ ◆ ◆

"She came at you?" Det. Donald Adams asked Nicholas as their conversation proceeded.

Nicholas nodded.

"Did she say something to you about the gun?"

"She did say something, but I didn't really hear her."

"Then what did you do? You didn't want her to take the gun, so what did you do?"

"It went off again."

"Do you know how many times?"

"Once, I think. I'm pretty sure once."

Adams spent the next few moments trying to pin Nicholas down on exactly what had occurred and in what order. Periodically his mother inserted questions and urged Nicholas to tell the truth.

"I know I went in there and she wanted the gun," Nicholas said. ". . . She was saying something, but I didn't hear her. She was coming at me and the gun went off."

Mrs. Elliot asked impatiently, "You didn't hear what she was saying?"

"I'm not deaf," Nicholas said.

But he could not remember.

◆ ◆ ◆

Bill Farley learned of his wife's death about two o'clock that afternoon from his pastor, who arrived accompanied by a female police officer. The Virginia Beach police had not found Mrs. Farley until ninety minutes after the shootings when the head count determined she alone was missing. A teacher saw her through the window in her trailer, but could not reach her because the door was locked. One of the Virginia Beach officers rushed over and broke the glass with his baton.

"It was unbelievable," Farley said, recalling his reaction. "Nobody gets shot at a Christian school. It's in a church building. Come on, get real. People don't get killed in church."

Detective Adams believes Karen Farley may have walked in on Nicholas as he was preparing his weapon before his return to the trailer where he encountered Sam Marino and Susan Allen. When police found her, she was still wearing her winter coat. The first bullet had struck her forearm before entering her torso, suggesting to investigators that she had raised her hand either to ask for the gun or to plead for her life, or perhaps merely in another of those magical efforts to defend against the bullet.

Nicholas fired twice, investigators found.

The first shot knocked her down. Next, they deduced, Nicholas walked over to her body and shot her again, firing downward at point-blank range—"execution style," as the local press put it. The bullet passed through her body and lodged in the trailer floor. The formal cause of death as stated by the state medical examiner was "gunshot wounds of trunk perforating heart. Internal hemorrhage."

The gun contained a half-empty magazine, one of the six fully loaded thirty-two-round magazines that Nicholas had brought with him to school. "It's the only magazine of all the six that misfires," Adams said with a touch of awe. "If he'd gotten one more round off, it would have stopped misfiring and he could have done whatever he wanted at that school."

The next night, Lora and a friend, Jennifer Cook, picked out what Lora's mother would wear for her funeral. They also wrapped Christmas presents that Mrs. Farley had hidden in a closet. Months later, in March 1989, Lora and Will would find yet another cache of presents salted away ever so secretly.

"I just try to think about the good times that we had together," Farley told me as we spoke in the living room of his home. "I miss her, I wish she was still around." He had remarried, but clearly the pain remained acute. He is a gravel-voiced man of the old school, but as he described his life after Karen's death, his voice broke. "She was a person I spent almost twenty years of my life with. She was the mother of my children. We all have to go on and make the best of it, but it's really hard. We were real close. We didn't have any friends, like lots of people have friends—you know, where they have 'Bob and Carol' over all the time. We didn't have anybody like that. We were each other's best friends. I didn't have anyone to talk to."

The more Farley learned about the gun and the way Nicholas had acquired it, the angrier he became.

◆ ◆ ◆

Soon after Nicholas Elliot's arrest, the state of Virginia formally charged him with one count of murder, four counts of attempted murder, and fourteen other related offenses. Three months later, in April 1989, Nicholas's mother filed a $1 million lawsuit against Atlantic Shores Christian School, alleging the school should have known about the harassment aimed at her son, and had failed to monitor his emotional adjustment, thereby contributing to what the lawsuit describes as the "mental breakdown" that prompted Nicholas's shooting spree. She later withdrew the suit.

On October 31, 1989, during a court hearing, Nicholas pleaded guilty to killing Karen Farley and to thirteen of the remaining charges. In return for his plea, the state agreed to drop the five least serious charges. During the hearing the prosecutor detailed the evidence against him. Nicholas sat at the defense table with his fingers in his ears.

On December 12, almost one year to the day since the shootings, Nicholas attended his sentencing hearing. The defense presented three character witnesses, including his mother and his barber, Jimmy Edney, who lived just across the street from Nicholas. Edney testified that he had known Nicholas ever since the boy had moved onto the block. He described how Nicholas had done his grocery shopping and tended his lawn after he had returned home from a stay in the hospital. "I wasn't able to handle it," Edney said. ". . . I never had any trouble out of him. He always correspond to me very well."

Judge Alan E. Rosenblatt found the testimony unconvincing. "These were offenses that were deliberately and cold-bloodedly thought out by Nicholas Elliot," he told the court. "If the gun had not jammed, there's no question in my mind I'd be presiding over a mass murderer." He described Nicholas as a "time bomb" that had finally exploded. "In this court's opinion," he said, "he's a time bomb that could go off again."

He asked Nicholas if he had anything to say before he pronounced sentence.

Softly, almost too quietly to be heard, Nicholas said, "I'm sorry for what I did."

"I'm sure you are, Mr. Elliot. But it's too little, too late."

He sentenced Nicholas as an adult to life in prison for the murder of Karen Farley. He added another 114 years for the remaining felony charges, then suspended fifty of them. Even at this, however, Nicholas would be eligible for parole fifteen years later, in 2004. He was assigned to the Southampton Correctional Center in Capron, Virginia.

His mother held a Bible throughout the hearing. "My child did not get justice," she said afterward. "He's just a child."

◆ ◆ ◆

Curtis Williams too had been convicted and sentenced. His trial, in March 1989, brought out details of how Nicholas Elliot had acquired his gun that William Farley had not known. One afternoon, after reading fragments of testimony in a local newspaper, Farley decided to explore the possibility of suing both Guns Unlimited and S.W. Daniel. "Number one, I just wanted to get the attention of the gun shop, to say, 'hey, you all have done something wrong. And just because ATF didn't do anything to you doesn't mean it was right, it just means you did it and got away with it.' "

He himself kept a handgun for home-defense; Karen Farley too had practiced with it. But the Cobray was different, Farley said. "There's just no reason for that kind of weapon to be sold in the United States. If you need something like that to protect your home, you better move."

He approached Randy Singer, a young Norfolk attorney whose wife taught part-time at Atlantic Shores and whose children were enrolled at the school. Singer and his family had been returning from a trip to Disney World when they learned of the shootings from a news report on the car radio. "One thing that struck me about Bill," Singer said, "was that he was looking for something good to come out of this tragedy."

Singer told Farley that he too had begun to think there might be grounds for a lawsuit. Farley hired him. In August 1989, Singer filed a negligence and product-liability lawsuit in Virginia state court charging Guns Unlimited with negligence in selling the gun to Nicholas, and charging S.W. Daniel with having indiscriminately marketed an unreasonably dangerous gun, one whose risks far exceeded its utilitarian value. The suit was one of an increasing number of such actions brought in courthouses around the country, including one filed by the family of actress Rebecca Schaeffer, the murdered costar of "My Sister Sam," against the dealer who sold the murder weapon. The Schaeffer case was settled before trial, however. Farley did not want an out-of-court settlement. "Bill was in this case for the principle of the thing from day one," Singer said. "His feeling has always been that if this case can make gun dealers follow the spirit and letter of the law, then all the better."

The lawsuit progressed slowly. The first judge assigned to the case became ill, and soon died. The usual paper combat of motions, cross-motions, and discovery proceedings dragged on for nearly two years. The case finally went to trial in January 1992. In his opening remarks, carefully tailored to avoid alienating a jury from the heart of Second Amendment country, Singer said, "This is not a case about gun control. The plaintiff is not here today asking you to adopt some new statute or legislation. This is a case about existing laws."

He presented testimony from Lora and Will Farley, Curtis Williams, James Dick, ATF special agent Raymond Rowley, and others, including Col. Leonard Supenski, the Baltimore County police firearms expert. Supenski testified that in the hands of a juvenile, a gun like the Cobray was "death waiting to happen."

Judge John K. Moore struck his testimony from the record, calling it inflammatory and prejudicial.

At one point, Beverly Cook, principal of the Atlantic Shores Christian School, took the stand to describe the impact of the shootings on the Farley family. Karen Farley, she said, had been the force that held the family together. It was Cook's daughter, Jennifer, who spent the second evening after the shooting with Lora wrapping the presents and choosing Karen Farley's funeral garb. The scene was so wrenching, Cook said, obviously fighting tears, that she was concerned for her own daughter's mental health, how the trauma would affect her. At one point Cook herself visited the Farley home. "I left physically ill. It wasn't the same home. It was darker, or I may have perceived it that way. Lora was boiling hot dogs while I helped Will with his schoolwork. It wasn't alive like it had been. I just thought, this is *one* night, it's tearing *me* up. They have to face this every night."

On Valentine's Day she called Bill Farley to check on him before going out to celebrate with her own husband. He was home by himself.

"I feel like Bill was just on automatic pilot for those months afterward," Cook said. "He'd tell me he was fine, but I never felt that he was."

Things got tougher still for the Farleys.

Bill Farley lost his job, found another, and lost that one too.

"Within a six-month period," he told me with a rueful laugh, "I lost two jobs and a wife."

He told the court, "I really couldn't imagine my children having a better mother than she was."

The jury ruled in Farley's favor, which in itself constituted something of a landmark in the history of firearms legislation, but the jury awarded the family only $105,000. "I was real happy that we won," Farley said, "there was no question about that. The main thing we were interested in was winning. I *was* disappointed in the award, and there's no question about that either. I have no idea what they were thinking about, with the numbers they came up with. I just have no idea what they had on their minds."

Still, he said, he accomplished his goal. "I definitely got the attention of the gun store. But we didn't get their attention as well as we had hoped. I gave it my best shot. I felt something needed to be done. We did all we could do."

In one respect, however, the suit had failed entirely.

Long before the trial Judge Moore cut S.W. Daniel free of the case. In an order sustaining arguments made by S.W. Daniel's attorneys, Moore wrote that reigning legal theories concerning negligence and product liability dictated that the "plaintiff must first show 'goods were unreasonably dangerous for [the] use to which they would ordinarily be put or for some other reasonably foreseeable purpose.' "

One way to establish unreasonable danger would have been to prove that the gun was defective. But Farley, the judge wrote, had not made any such allegation. And even if he had, he might have had difficulty persuading the court a defect existed.

"Unfortunately," Judge Moore wrote, "the weapon worked."

CHAPTER FOURTEEN

THE NEW TYRANNY

WHEN ONE FOLLOWS THE PROGRESS OF A single gun from design to homicide, the gaps in existing firearms regulations become painfully obvious. We accomplish little in this country by enacting bans on assault weapons and establishing waiting periods without first addressing the regulatory vacuum that allows manufacturers, distributors, and dealers to shrug off all responsibility for the diversion of guns from legitimate gun-distribution channels. An effective body of firearms laws must recognize an obvious truth obscured thus far by our cultural indulgence in the romance of guns and the effective propaganda of the gun lobby: when guns are easy to get, the wrong people get them easily.

Buying a gun should be the most difficult consumer ritual in America, instead of one of the easiest. Toughening acquisition will not harm legitimate gun owners. The right laws, in fact, can only help them. The right laws can reduce the incidence of impulsive teenage suicides. The right laws can limit the firepower of street guns and undoubtedly save the lives of a few innocent bystanders. The right laws, moreover, can give even gun buffs a greater appreciation of the dangers inherent in the weapons they buy and demonstrate society's conviction that owning a gun imparts a monumental responsibility to the owner. The right laws could at last bring firearms into the twentieth century in terms of consumer-product safety. Who knows, someday our firearms manufacturers, so adept at devising ever more lethal weapons and ammunition, may even come up with a childproof gun. My Cuisinart food processor can't be started without first taking a series of deliberate steps; how nice if the same could be said for the guns sold now to women and men for self-defense. Toughening the buying of a gun will not harm responsible users any more than toughening the licensing of hunters and boaters has harmed them. If anything, toughening the process will improve the fast-diminishing reputation of shooters, dealers, and manufacturers alike by reducing the "gun-nut" aura that now taints even those good souls who take pride in improving their marksmanship or who live in such desperate neighborhoods that gun ownership really is their only hope of self-defense.

Most important, toughening the process will staunch the free flow of weapons to the bad guys and others who simply should not own guns. Sure, some will acquire guns through burglary just as they do now. Others will drive trucks through the front walls of gun dealerships. And no matter how strict dealer licensing is, there will always be renegade dealers willing to sell guns into the black market. Likewise, there will always be gun manufacturers who tailor their designs deliberately to the demands of felons. But street crime typically is a crime of opportunity. So too is juvenile homicide. Kids have always fought and will forever do so, but the ready acquisition of guns by kids is a new phenomenon. Even our increasing suicide rate, according to the studies I cited earlier, may be associated with too-ready access to guns, allowing the despondent to blow their brains out upon the least dark whim.

The firearms industry has resisted regulation, disavowing any responsibility for the widespread costs and harm produced by its wares. But then, it has always been adept at ignoring the paradoxes inherent in the production and marketing of weapons. It develops ever more lethal weapons while at the same time insisting that guns are not inherently dangerous. It claims the moral high ground by describing its wares as tools of salvation for those afraid to leave their homes, but somehow deftly manages to sidestep the fact that one reason most of us are afraid to venture forth is that someone with the same gun is going to leap out from behind a bush and shove the barrel down our throats. And that's if we are lucky enough to encounter the old-fashioned crook who merely wants our money, not the snappy new model who likes to sneak up behind us and put a bullet in our brains so he can use our credit cards for a couple of hours without fear of interception.

The NRA's greatest coup has been in constantly bleating that gun controls cannot and will not work, while working feverishly to ensure that indeed whatever regulations are enacted are so full of exceptions and gifts to the downtrodden dealers and manufacturers that they could not possibly have an impact. Notice, please, that wherever possible in this book I have avoided using the phrase *gun control*, a term the NRA has conflated with paranoid visions of jackbooted agents kicking down the doors of honest gun owners.

If one parts the curtain hung by the NRA, one sees that in fact firearms regulations can and do work, when given half a chance.

South Carolina, as I mentioned earlier, was a primary source of crime guns seized in the Northeast until it passed the nation's first law limiting sales of handguns to one a month. It quickly fell to the bottom of ATF's list of states feeding firearms to New York. The National Firearms Act of 1934 sharply reduced criminal use of machine guns. The bad guys undoubtedly turned to other, more readily available guns, but at least when they used the guns, they fired one shot at a time. If still able to acquire machine guns from hardware stores and pawnshops, our felons and gang members would undoubtedly have done so, and the drive-by shootings we read so much about today would have taken far more innocent lives. Patrick Purdy's attack on the Stockton schoolyard, for example, might have killed even more children had he used a true, fully automatic AK-47, rather than its semiautomatic equivalent. Machine guns made a comeback in the 1980s, but only because such manufacturers as RPB and S.W. Daniel placed guns on the market that could readily, if illegally, be converted from semiautomatic to fully automatic operation.

The Gun Control Act of 1968, however much reviled by the NRA, succeeded in establishing the national tracing network that law-enforcement agencies now take for granted. Strict gun controls in Washington, D.C., helped reduce gunshot homicides in the city by 25 percent from 1976 through 1987, but did not alter the rate of homicide involving other kinds of weapons or the homicide rate in neighboring Virginia and Maryland. This improvement, of course, was erased by the 1990s, when Washington experienced a wild surge of homicides that caused the city to be dubbed the murder capital of America. Although the National Rifle Association likes to point to this as one example of how gun controls cannot work, the real lesson is rather different. Gun controls in a single city cannot possibly succeed when that city is surrounded by regions with few or no controls.

Existing federal laws contain gaping loopholes that allow the free flow of guns from legitimate channels to the bad guys. We have seen, for example, that a consumer who makes a false statement in filling out form 4473 commits a felony; a dealer who does likewise commits only a misdemeanor. Dealers must keep detailed records of their sales of guns from their stores, but a private citizen can sell a gun to a friend with no restriction. A dealer operating at a gun show must follow all federal regulations, but a private citizen at an adjacent table can sell guns from his personal collection without so much as a signature. Federal law prohibits certain classes of individuals such as convicted murderers and dope peddlers from buying guns, then relies on those same individuals to exclude themselves by giving honest answers on form 4473. This last curiosity would be comical if not for its lethal effect.

These gaps in existing federal law, and the utter lack of uniform regulations governing most other aspects of firearms transactions, create insane juxtapositions of regulation and deregulation at those points where federal and state laws intersect. Guns Unlimited, as I've shown, played regional variations in the law to its advantage, selling customers a handgun in one jurisdiction, but completing the paperwork and delivering the weapon in another, less-regulated locale. In Maryland, state law requires that anyone who buys a handgun from a legitimate dealer must wait seven days before he can actually take possession of the gun; yet, as per federal law, if he buys that same gun from a private seller, say after seeing it advertised in the classified ads of his local newspaper, he can receive the gun immediately.

On December 14, 1992, Wayne Lo, a Montana boy attending Simon's Rock College in Great Barrington, Massachusetts, bought a semiautomatic Chinese ancestor of the AK-47, called an SKS, simply by presenting his Montana driver's license and plunking down $150. Before the McClure-Volkmer Act, he could not have bought the gun so readily. The Gun Control Act of 1968 had banned interstate sales. Even if Lo had established residency in Massachusetts, he still could not have walked away with the gun. Under Massachusetts law, he would have had to apply for a firearms identification card and wait thirty days for a background check. The McClure-Volkmer Act, however, allowed sales of rifles and shotguns to out-of-state buyers if the sale is conducted in accord with the laws of the buyer's home state. Regulations in Montana are notoriously lax. Lo used the gun that night to kill a professor and a student, and to wound four others at the college. He had acquired the ammunition by mail directly from a North Carolina ammunition supplier. This transaction too was a dividend of the McClure-Volkmer Act, which repealed the Gun Control Act's ban on interstate and mail-order sales of ammunition directly to consumers.

The lack of a uniform system of federal regulations allows traffickers to shop jurisdictions for the easiest commercial conditions.

When South Carolina instituted its one-gun-a-month law, for example, Virginia became the number one source of crime guns found in the Northeast. Early in 1993, Virginia passed its own one-a-month law. Although the new law's impact was not immediately apparent, it seemed certain to reduce the traffickers' interest in Virginia. The trafficking will not stop, however. Just as many guns will make their way to the bad guys as ever before. The East Coast buyers will simply spend their money elsewhere, most likely Georgia, Ohio, and West Virginia.

That the nation needs a detailed, uniform code of firearms regulations ought to be, by now, beyond rational dispute. The fact is, many states have already passed firearms regulations far stricter than anything Congress has ever seriously debated. As of 1989, for example, twenty states already required that consumers first get some kind of license or purchase permit before acquiring a handgun; nineteen had a handgun waiting period ranging from forty-eight hours to up to six months.

The Second Amendment certainly poses no obstacle, despite the NRA's rhetoric. As written in the Constitution, the full amendment reads: "A well-regulated militia, being necessary to the security of a free State, the right of the people to keep and bear arms shall not be infringed." The amendment may indeed guarantee individuals the right to bear arms. Then again, it may not. At this point, only a definitive ruling by the U.S. Supreme Court can resolve the matter. I for one remain intrigued by the "well-regulated" portion, which the NRA omitted when it displayed the rest of the amendment on the front of its Washington, D.C., headquarters. One gun-camp scholar has gone so far as to suggest that "well-regulated" means equipped with rifles that shoot straight. In his book, *The Samurai, the Mountie, and the Cowboy: Should America Adopt the Gun Controls of Other Democracies?* David Kopel argues that "in firearms parlance 'regulating' a gun means adjusting it so that successive shots hit as close together as possible." He writes that " 'regulated' was an exhortation to competence, not an invitation to bureaucracy." His conclusion, one he describes as "plausible," is that a "well-regulated militia" meant "an effective citizen militia whose members hit their targets." Kopel presents this notion three hundred pages into a detailed, heavily footnoted volume published by the Cato Institute that on first read may seem unbiased and almost scholarly. It is always important, however, to read anything on the gun debate carefully with an eye to capturing distortion and undisclosed bias. Kopel raises his true flag on page 152 where he cites research by "criminologist Paul Blackman." Blackman may indeed be considered a criminologist in some circles, but he is also the NRA's director of research. And Kopel, as I later found, is an NRA activist and gun columnist. Nowhere, I might add, did the book divulge Kopel's true identity.

I happen to side with established constitutional scholars who believe the document was designed to be applied at any time in the future with full relevance and authority to accommodate even such once-inconceivable developments as women's suffrage and the abolition of slavery. I cannot help but wonder how James Madison would react upon reading a week's worth of the Metro section of the New York Times, especially at year-end when the Times and most other big-city papers present their running tallies of the year's homicides.

All the noise and dust generated by the debate over the true meaning of the Second Amendment obscures a fundamental question: Who cares? I recognize that here I am inviting the NRA to do a little joyful editing and display this sentence in one of its ads or better yet in one of its emergency Minuteman mailings. (I say now, it's okay, boys, you have my permission.) In fact, the Second Amendment does not, and never has, prohibited robust regulation of firearms, not even the NRA-conjured bogey, national registration of firearms.

Rather than viewing federal firearms regulation as the first step toward tyranny, as the NRA propagandists propose, we should see it as a means of ensuring that we can still enjoy the liberty we do have. We live now under the increasing restrictions of a particularly pernicious kind of tyranny that has sharply proscribed the contours of our lives. We do not go out at night without first considering the risks involved in doing so. Already many of us consider vast portions of America off-limits to us because of the potential for gun violence. We run red lights at lonely intersections. We choose our gas stations with care. We park as closely as possible to the entrances of our favorite malls. We avoid certain automated teller machines. When we pull up at our neighborhood 7-Eleven store, we look carefully through the display windows to see if the place is being held up. We do not intercede when we encounter an altercation among teenage boys because one or both may have a gun. We don't dare yell at drivers who drive too fast through our neighborhoods. When our cars are hit from behind, we keep driving until we reach the nearest police station. In happier times this was called leaving the scene of an accident; now even my insurance company advises the practice.

Today when we send our kids off to school, we experience a brand-new kind of anxiety, the fear not that some bully will rough them up and steal their lunch money, but that they will be shot dead. What are we to advise our children today when they come home complaining of harassment by the school bully? Do we teach them how to fight, as Ward Cleaver might have taught "the Beave," or do we buy them Kevlar vests and tell them to stay low? Should we buy our kids Raven pocket semiautomatics? A 1993 survey by Louis Harris found that four out of ten students said the fear of violence had sharply altered what they did with their free time and whom they picked to be their friends. These students lived in rural, suburban, and urban neighborhoods. Fifty-five percent said they wished their schools had metal detectors. In a related survey, Harris found that 59 percent of adults saw the dangers from guns as "serious" as or "more serious" than car crashes. Even the NRA's rank and file seem troubled. Thirty-four percent of the NRA members captured in Harris's survey agreed "young people's safety is endangered by there being so many guns around these days."

I read with rueful delight a 1993 cartoon by Mike Luckovich of the *Atlanta Constitution,* which showed an Arab terrorist squad in a bomb-packed car receiving some last-minute advice before heading for America. "Remember, carry a map. If you get lost, you may end up in a bad neighborhood. If someone rear-ends you, don't get out. They may be armed carjackers. Keep your doors locked. . . ."

In 1975, a congressional subcommittee asked the NRA's Harlon Carter if he felt it was preferable to allow felons, drug addicts, and the mentally ill to acquire guns, rather than to establish a means of checking the backgrounds of all buyers. Yes, Carter responded, it was "a price we pay for freedom."

We are advised today by the NRA and the likes of Paxton Quigley not to fight like the devil to free ourselves from the new tyranny of the gun, but to arm ourselves. The more guns the better. To anyone raised in the Vietnam War era, surely, this position has a disconcertingly familiar ring. For what is the NRA doing but reshaping that sad old maxim "We must destroy the village in order to save it."

We must endure tyranny—the new tyranny of the gun with its concomitant loss of dignity, honor, and compassion—in order to avoid tyranny.

I propose a five-part omnibus law that will use the word *ban* only once—yes, I apologize, I betray a rather antiquated bias here: I do happen to believe that silencers should be outlawed, even those registered by police and law-enforcement agencies. However hard I try, I simply cannot foresee a practical use for silencers that would conform to our society's belief in due process and the rule of law.

If enacted in its entirety, with none of the almost-criminal loopholes that have marred existing laws, I guarantee my proposed regulations, which I like to think of as the "Life and Liberty Preservation Act," would sharply impede the flow of guns to kids, felons, and irresponsible shooters, with no significant impact on those upright citizens who keep guns for self-defense, for plinking, or for hunting. If anything, today's patchwork of laws has made things far more difficult for the legitimate shooters, something the shooters tend to blame on gun-control advocates, the media, and other "gun grabbers." In fact, the blame belongs with the NRA itself, which bears so much responsibility for the disarray in firearms regulation that exists today.

I propose, for example, to abolish all barriers to the interstate transportation of firearms. Wouldn't that be nice, those of you who hunt or who for professional reasons feel a need to carry a gun? (I refer here to private detectives, bodyguards, and the like, not hit men.) In fact, I suggest that the nation's first step ought to be the wholesale repeal of every state, county, and municipal firearms regulation currently on the books. The NRA is quite right in pointing out, ad nauseam, that New York and Washington, D.C., have some of the toughest gun-control laws in America, and two of the highest per capita homicide rates. Erase these ineffective regulations—but immediately replace them with a formal, rational federal code that at last recognizes guns for what they are: the single most dangerous, socially costly, culturally destabilizing consumer product marketed in America.

Herewith, the Life and Liberty Preservation Act, its provisions divided into three parts governing the distribution, purchase, and design of firearms:

I. DISTRIBUTION

Any serious effort to halt the mass migration of weapons to illegal hands must first concentrate on the firearms distribution network, in particular, the role played by retail dealers. As things stand now, it is simply too easy to get a license to buy and sell guns. As a first step, Congress should repeal all provisions of the McClure-Volkmer Act, except the machine-gun ban.

The Life and Liberty Preservation Act would then:

- Sharply increase the cost of the basic gun-dealer license to $2,500 and designate this a one-time business-entry fee. This alone would sharply reduce the number of Americans who now hold Federal Firearms Licenses. At $30 the license has proven too tempting for would-be felons to pass up.

- Require that before receiving a license, a prospective gun dealer first present proof that he has met all local and state regulations governing the operation of a business. For example, he would be required to show proof that his dealership satisfied all local zoning requirements.

- Require every dealer to take a course designed to familiarize him with all federal firearms laws, with the ways in which buyers try to evade the laws, and with proper techniques for protecting firearms and ammunition from robbers and burglars. The law further would require that dealers demonstrate a basic working knowledge of firearms and firearms law by passing a licensing examination, as doctors and lawyers must. The dealer would have to attend a refresher seminar every three years to revalidate his license. These seminars would brief dealers on new changes in federal regulations, new court precedents, and the latest patterns in firearms trafficking.

- Provide, for the first time, an objective definition of what it means to be "engaged in the business" of dealing firearms. Any dealer who wished to retain his license would have to prove that in his first year of operation he had revenue from gun sales of $1,000 or more. As proof, he could simply file a duplicate of his dealership's annual IRS filing.

- Establish a scale of penalties for failure to keep accurate records. If, for example, ATF discovered that a dealer had failed to record the disposition of firearms sought in three ATF traces conducted in any one year, ATF could immediately revoke his license, subject to administrative appeal. Any dealer who refused to cooperate with an ATF trace request, even once, would likewise lose his license.

- Require mandatory inspection of the business premises of all new licensees. The dealer's license would remain provisional until the dealer passed such an inspection, or until six months had elapsed, whichever came first.

- Require that consumers who buy guns from private sellers fill out a form 4473, just as they would if buying from a licensed dealer. In this case the sellers would send a copy directly to their regional ATF office. (Notice I said *regional* office—the same place where multiple-purchase forms currently end up. I emphasize this to calm those who may be inclined to leap from their chairs and condemn this measure as an effort to build a central database of gun owners.) The actual transfer of the weapon would take place in the presence of a licensed dealer. Such a service would not be that different from the role now played by dealers who act as middlemen in mail-order sales of firearms. Consumers cannot receive mail-order firearms directly, but must designate a local dealer, who then formally transfers the weapon, keeps the form 4473, and records the transaction in his acquisition and disposition book. Dealers should not object to my proposal. The new purchaser is highly likely to turn around and buy ammunition and other accessories from the dealer.

- Require that ATF issue to licensed dealers a primary display license and a set of formal, embossed duplicates to be signed by the dealer and notarized before being mailed to the distributor. Distributors in turn would be required to verify the dealer's license number and name before sending him any guns. A distributor would accomplish this by calling a toll-free number at ATF's licensing center, punching in his own license number, waiting for a prompt, then entering the dealer's number and name. A tone would signal that the license was valid. An ATF computer would keep a digital record of the call and file it for later retrieval when inspectors got around to doing their routine compliance audit of the distributor's business.

Manufacturers would likewise have to verify the license numbers of distributors.

The primary benefit of these distribution regulations would be to shrink the number of licensed dealers to a core group of those willing to take the time and energy to establish bona fide businesses. These dealers, in turn, would benefit from reduced competition and by capturing as customers those consumers who became kitchen-table dealers just to buy guns at wholesale prices. Dealers who remained in the business would have a greater incentive to keep good records and to turn away clearly questionable buyers. Private sellers too would be less inclined to sell their guns to such buyers. The measures, moreover, would greatly bolster the tracing network.

It would be unfair, of course, and exceedingly naive to expect that dealers would suddenly become priestly arbiters of firearms distribution, rejecting customers who looked felonlike or who sweated too much or whose eyebrows twitched a tad too often.

My law would at last remove from their shoulders the weighty burden of screening customers through a measure that many ardent gun owners tell me they would be more than willing to accept. . . .

II. PURCHASE

The Life and Liberty Preservation Act would require that all prospective gun buyers age twenty-one or over first acquire a license-to-purchase. Yes, we are talking here about licensing gun owners. To qualify for the license, each consumer would have to pass a criminal background check and take an ATF-certified course covering firearms law, the use of deadly force, and safe gun-handling, and including lectures on the most common forms of firearms accidents, the importance of cleaning a gun, and how best to keep that gun out of the hands of children. It would be nice, but certainly not mandatory, if such a course also included a film or some other means of demonstrating the damage real bullets do to real people. Scare films of the kind I envision here were a staple of driver's education classes at my high school: one image, of bodies strewn around a head-on wreck caused by a drunk driver, stays with me even now just as vividly as ever.

These purchase provisions also would:

+ Require license applicants to demonstrate minimum proficiency with a handgun and a rifle. An appropriate firearm would be supplied to them for use during their training course. (Many firing ranges already provide rental guns, even machine guns.) Licensees would have to renew their licenses and undergo a new background check every five years, but the renewal process would be accomplished simply by mailing ATF a form attached to the original license. ATF would charge a licensing fee meant to recoup some of the program costs. The license would, of course, include a photograph of the holder, and such vital statistics as his age, height, weight, and the color of his eyes.

+ Allow successful applicants to acquire guns in any state and to transport guns to any state. A rigorous licensing program would allow states and cities to lessen their vigilance and thus alleviate a good many of the headaches now endured by hunters, private detectives, and even state and local law-enforcement officers when they travel or relocate from one part of the country to another.

+ Designate the use or manufacture of a counterfeit license a felony, with a mandatory sentence of five years in federal prison.

+ Prohibit minors, as now, from acquiring handguns and rifles, and set the minimum age for purchases of both at twenty-one. (Currently federal law allows a minor to acquire a rifle when he turns eighteen. He must be twenty-one to buy a handgun.)

+ Limit purchases of handguns to one a month. The law, however, would also establish a mechanism for exempting collectors and others with a compelling reason for buying more than one handgun at a time.
+ Establish a waiting period of ten working days, both to provide a cooling-off period for consumers intent on killing themselves or others in a fit of passion, and to allow ATF to verify that the purchase license is still valid. A fresh criminal-record check would be unnecessary. The law would include a provision for emergency exemptions in situations where a gun buyer can demonstrate an immediate threat to life and limb if he cannot have his gun immediately. The Brady bill's five-day waiting period will provide a welcome pause in gun transactions, but only for five more years, after which the pause will be eliminated and replaced by an instant criminal background check. This is an optimistic expectation given the complexity of developing any computer system capable of searching the databases of fifty states in any period of time even broadly qualifying as "instant."
+ Enact a nationwide version of the parental-liability laws now in force in Florida and California, which hold parents criminally liable if their children wound themselves or others using an improperly stored firearm.

These purchase provisions would, at the very least, compel consumers to recognize the grave dangers and responsibilities inherent in owning a firearm. The buyer-licensing program alone would save lives simply by requiring consumers to learn about the weapons they hope to acquire.

III. DESIGN

The Life and Liberty Preservation Act would include provisions aimed at restricting the firepower of consumer guns, improving the design of guns to make them safer for the people who buy them, and producing for the first time hard statistics on what makes, models, and calibers of guns are most often used in given crimes. These provisions would ban the sale or transfer of silencers, limit the magazine capacity of civilian firearms to ten rounds, and forbid the sale and possession of empty magazines having capacity for more than ten. The law also would take the long-overdue step of increasing the tax fee for transferring machine guns to $500, from the $200 fee established in 1934.

In addition, these design provisions would:

- Amend the Consumer Product Safety Act to include firearms and thus grant the Consumer Product Safety Commission authority to monitor firearms accidents and firearms defects, and to order the mandatory recalls of defective or unsafe guns. This measure would go a long way toward at last compelling firearms manufacturers to build safer guns, in particular child-safe guns. At last an official oversight agency could ask that most obvious of questions: If aspirin bottles can be childproof, why not guns?

- Require that police departments report to ATF the manufacturer, model, and serial number of every gun they seize in the course of their operations, along with a description of the primary criminal charge that prompted the seizure. Such a massive tracing effort would for the first time provide an accurate count of just how many guns are used in crime each year, and which models the crooks choose most often. The data would be published quarterly and annually in the *Federal Register,* complete with the name of each manufacturer, the caliber, and the model. The nation's firearms industry would undoubtedly protest this provision, but it would provide the great benefit of at last establishing in quantifiable, objective terms the direct relationship between the production of guns and their use in crime. It would, for example, provide hard numbers on just how often criminals use assault-style weapons like the Cobray M-11/9.

◆ ◆ ◆

The Life and Liberty Preservation Act doesn't have a chance in hell of being passed.

Even the simplest regulations meet outraged opposition from the NRA, the Second Amendment Foundation, and the Gun Owners of America. Theirs is a reflexive opposition based on the rather paranoid belief that any step toward firearms regulation must necessarily take us one more step down the road to federal confiscation of America's guns and, willy-nilly from there, to tyranny and oppression. Yet survey after survey shows that most Americans favor rigorous firearms regulations. The 1993 Harris survey of adults found that 52 percent of us favored an outright ban on ownership of handguns, provided consumers could petition a court for special permission to own one. Sixty-seven percent favored limiting "the purchase of guns by any one person to one a month." Eighty-two percent favored a federal law requiring that all handguns be registered with federal authorities.

Given all this support, why does America still stand virtually alone in the world as the nation with the fewest and least effective limits on the proliferation of guns?

The answer, I think, is that even those of us who favor strong regulation lack the conviction of those who oppose such laws. The vociferous few dominate the debate and shape the laws to suit their interests while the rest of us stand by and cluck at news of the latest homicidal spree.

Robert Sherrill in his 1973 book, *The Saturday Night Special,* suggested that all this mayhem might satisfy something deep within the American soul. "We enjoy it more than we will admit," he wrote. "We experience the assassination of a Kennedy with all the wailing gusto that an Irish wake deserves. We are honest enough to admit, by implication at least, that gunplay involving some of our lesser celebrities doesn't always, or uniformly, make us feel nearly so depressed. . . . We are like the old Wobbly who, shortly after Huey Long's assassination, told a colleague, 'I deplore the use of murder in politics, but I wouldn't give two cents to bring the sonofabitch back to life.' "

The assassinations of the sixties were a unique and in a sense nonthreatening form of gun violence. We in the TV audience could congratulate ourselves on being safe because we, after all, were not in politics. Even the race riots in the last third of the decade seemed containable phenomena. Most of America watched from secure living rooms with a collective shaking of heads. I can remember watching the news in the weeks before one of my family's annual trips to visit relatives in South Dakota. Although I did briefly wonder whether the world could remain intact, I assured myself there would be no riots in the town of Arlington, South Dakota, where my grandparents lived behind still-unlocked doors. I trusted the turnpike system to neatly whisk me past the smoldering remains of Newark and Detroit. Many Americans did buy guns in those years, enough to produce that largest-ever increase in gun sales, but the fact is, most of us fortunate enough to live outside the ghetto were as safe as rain. Many of us, no doubt, even saw a positive side to letting *those* people duke it out among themselves. This sense of remove from the battlefield has long been one of the fundamental obstacles to reasonable, effective gun legislation; it explains why our able representatives on Capitol Hill only feel empowered to crimp the free flow of guns when some hitherto unimaginable act of carnage demonstrates beyond doubt that violence knows no geographic or racial border.

Many of our most ardent supporters of firearms regulation became so a bit late, after the grotesque tragedy of gunshot violence had already speared their lives. Pete Shields founded Handgun Control Inc. after his son was shot dead in the infamous Zebra killings in San Francisco. Sarah Brady joined the cause after her son picked up a family friend's revolver. A Sandston, Virginia, woman, Beryl Phillips-Taylor, began her crusade when she received a mailing from the NRA addressed to her son, who had been shot dead by a classmate two years before. "Hell flew in me," she told a *Baltimore Sun* reporter. "There is a misconception by the general population that murder happens to others. The truth is that murder has no barriers. It can happen to your child just as easily as it happened to mine."

Today more Americans of all races, classes, and ages are being touched by gun violence than ever before. The gunplay, indeed, seems to come closer and closer to home. In the course of my pursuit of Nicholas Elliot's gun, I learned that the brother of an old high-school friend had been shot dead following an argument. On hearing this I remembered an afternoon in my teen years when this friend led me to his father's bedroom and pulled a large auto-loading pistol from under the mattress, just to show me. I felt a mix of excitement and terror and asked him to please put it back. Another friend, an avid shooter, told me over lunch how as a college student he along with two friends had been kidnapped at gunpoint, but managed to escape. In June 1993, when Gian Luigi made his assault on a San Francisco law firm, a friend of mine was hard at work in his office a few floors above. In March 1992 a wealthy young bachelor who lived a few doors from my house was murdered in his company parking lot, shot once in the back of his head apparently by a car thief who wanted his $85,000 BMW. On the day the man's mother put her dead son's house on the market, the for-sale sign was emblazoned with cheery balloons and an extra signboard that called the place an "American Dream Home."

The spreading violence evokes the forecasts made by AIDS researchers in the early days of the epidemic. As the disease gained momentum, forward-looking doctors warned that a time was fast approaching when the disease would cease to be a "gay" crisis; that every American, regardless of race, income, or sexual inclination, would soon know someone who was dying of the disease. The same, I think, can now be said of gun violence.

So what are we to expect in coming years if we continue on our current course? Will things get better on their own, and this era take its place beside the great hard times of history? Or will conditions simply worsen? Many of us already send our kids to child self-defense courses. When, I wonder, will some enterprising company introduce the first bulletproof vest for kids?

Prophecy is a dangerous pursuit, but some trends seem certain to continue gaining momentum for a good while to come. We will see, for example, a proliferation of more advanced and lethal variations on legal weaponry, such as guns with built-in laser sights and ever-more-powerful handguns, including more models built to fire .50-caliber bullets, the largest caliber allowed for unrestricted sale.

We will witness, and soon, firearms massacres conducted in realms we now naively consider off-limits to even our most craven killers. Schools are now accepted killing grounds—what Nicholas Elliot did is old hat. Post-office massacres do not surprise us either. The link between postal workers and random gun violence is now well-established in contemporary mythology, causing us all to contemplate that trip to the post office just a little more carefully than we did in the past. Law firms have been done. So have playgrounds and public pools.

What remains? Well, churches certainly. Funerals. Grocery stores. Museums. Baseball games. Hospitals—well, perhaps not hospitals. Most major urban hospitals have already felt the unaccustomed sting of violence in their sterile corridors and have already stepped up security.

We can in the next few years expect to see metal detectors turning up at the entrance doors of an ever-wider array of institutions, such as malls, emergency rooms, elementary schools, and fast-food shops located in perilous neighborhoods. This last may be of limited value, however. Another neighbor of mine was held up at the drive-through window of a Wendy's restaurant located a few blocks from our homes. She had been hungry when she drove up to the window. When a robber pointed a gun at her head as she waited in line, her appetite disappeared.

The question is, when will we as a culture get the point?

In discussing this book with my editor and her marketing associates, we all came to the same conclusion. This book would never lack for a promotional tie to a national news event because a new massacre was bound to occur within the viable lifetime of the book, and this massacre would be more horrifying than the last.

When will we as a culture stop seeing gun ownership as a God-granted right, so precious as to be nurtured and preserved at the cost of thirty thousand corpses a year; when will we at last demand that all those armed patriots out there first demonstrate a little responsibility and recognize that while they are in the woods waiting for that eight-point buck to wander within range, a newly released felon in Nebraska is buying a gun to blow his ex-girlfriend away, a kid in East Baltimore is tucking a .45 into his belt to defend his lunch money, a toddler in Chicago is aiming the family gun at his baby brother, and a drunken husband in Beverly Hills is climbing the stairs to teach his wife a lesson she will not soon forget?

We can solve the problem of firearms violence. The National Rifle Association and its homicidal allies in Washington would have us believe otherwise, but we can solve this. We have solved other equally intractable, even comparably lethal, problems. We have awakened to the dangers of smoking to the point where smokers are now an embattled minority. We have virtually eliminated polio, smallpox, and the German measles. We have controlled highway litter and sharply reduced the presence of lead in our lives—atmospheric lead, that is. Anyone who has been to a recycling depot lately and seen young and old dutifully sorting colored glass from clear cannot help but marvel at how much we as a culture have changed our wasteful ways.

The nation's success in reducing the death rate from traffic accidents provides the best model of what could be done with guns.

Through a combination of lower speed limits, increased enforcement of drunk-driving laws, public service advertising campaigns, strict regulation of car safety, and nationwide monitoring of the causes and characteristics of traffic accidents, the death rate has declined to the point where public health researchers expected it to fall, by the turn of the century, below the death rate from firearms.

America's gun crisis cannot be solved just by limiting the proliferation of guns and mandating responsibility on the part of gun owners. Solving the problem requires far more fundamental change. Where now our cities consider it an accomplishment simply to keep school-kids from getting killed, we must have excellent schools that cause hope to blossom. A true, full-scale National Service program might be a good start, offering interesting and creative jobs in far-flung portions of the country. Safe, clean housing for America's poor would be nice too, in place of the somber, stinking temples of despair that ring most of our biggest cities. Vital too is federal recognition that times have indeed changed, that women do raise families all by themselves, that many couples need two incomes just to survive, and thus that access to good, safe, nurturing day care ought to be near the top of the nation's domestic agenda, rather than at the bottom. All these are, or should be, obvious requirements. And these are just the minimum. We will have to fix much more in America if we are to slow the rise and expansion of gun violence.

The place to start is with guns themselves, and the time is now. There will be no better time. There will be far worse times.

Unfortunately, as the history of federal gun legislation so clearly demonstrates, a dramatic worsening may be necessary. The tommy-gun massacres brought the first federal controls; the riots and assassinations of the sixties brought the second. What will bring the third, in a country so stunned by violence that we now expect and accept armed rampages as if they were natural phenomena like hurricanes and tornadoes? "Maybe that's the answer," said David Troy, the special agent responsible for ATF law-enforcement in Virginia. "Right now you have people who are involved in violent crime and firearms violence who were never touched by it before. Maybe there is a watershed coming in the United States. We haven't gotten there yet."

More firearms atrocities will occur. In America today, this is a given. The greater atrocity, however, is to stand back and allow the gunslingers of America free play while the rest of us cower under the new tyranny of the gun.

CODA

AT THE TIME OF NICHOLAS ELLIOT'S rampage, business was
brisk for James Dick and Guns Unlimited. This was before the Gulf
War exodus of his customer base and the general slackening of firearms sales that later forced Dick to file for bankruptcy. Business was
so brisk that within a year of the shootings Dick decided to expand
the Guns Unlimited empire and open his third store.

One must be cool indeed to be a gun dealer. The site Dick chose
was a small shopping plaza on Kempsville Road in Virginia Beach.

The Atlantic Shores Christian School was across the street.

CODA

AFTERWORD TO THE VINTAGE EDITION

IN SEPTEMBER 1993, when I completed the original manuscript for this book, I was certain significant reform of America's firearms regulations was a long way off and that a package like my Life and Liberty Preservation Act had little chance—to be more precise, "no chance in hell"—of being enacted. But much has changed, and I have since come to believe that progress toward rational regulation may in fact be inexorable now that America seems at last to have awakened to the obvious and mounting social costs of allowing the unimpeded flow of arms to kids, crack addicts, felons, and fugitives.

In August 1994 President Bill Clinton helped his Congressional allies muscle through a new crime bill containing a long-overdue ban on nineteen specific models of assault weapons and related guns. Among the specific models banned were the Intratec pistol used by Gian Luigi Ferri in his attack on a law firm in San Francisco; the semi-automatic AK fired by Patrick Purdy in Stockton; and the Cobray M-11/9 adopted by Nicholas Elliot for his attack on the Atlantic Shores Christian School.

A more significant but little-known portion of the crime bill substantially tightened regulations governing firearms dealers, requiring that license applicants be photographed and fingerprinted and that the dealers comply with all state and local laws governing firearms dealerships, including zoning regulations. The law also dictated that ATF must provide to local law-enforcement agencies lists of firearms dealers in their territories. These requirements alone will begin to reduce the ranks of that vast army of "kitchen table" dealers who supply so many guns to America's crooks.

In May 1994, President Clinton used his executive powers to halt the import of Chinese SKS rifles, ancestors of the AK-47 and once the standard infantry rifles of the Chinese, North Vietnamese, and Soviet armies. Chinese exporters, some with direct connections to the Chinese military, pumped the rifle into this country at such high volume that throughout much of 1993 a shopper could buy one for well under $100. As a consequence of its low price and its ready availability under regulations governing the sales of long rifles, the SKS became the only rifle to make ATF's 1993 and first-quarter 1994 lists of the top ten weapons most commonly traced by America's law-enforcement agencies. It was an SKS that Wayne Lo used in his massacre at Simon's Rock College in Massachusetts.

The most important legislative advance toward public safety, however, was the activation of the Brady law early in 1994. News reporters, forced by space constraints to describe the bill in journalistic shorthand, managed to create the widespread impression that it merely established a five-day waiting period. In fact, the bill took a revolutionary step down the road to rationality.

Prior to the Brady law, a fundamental paradox governed firearms regulation. Everyone in America, even the most zealous NRA fundamentalist, has long agreed that certain people—felons, fugitives, and so forth—should not be allowed to buy guns. Yet Congress, until it passed the Brady law in 1993, never took the necessary next step of establishing a practical means of eliminating those very people from the marketplace. Society's only brake on the wholesale distribution of firearms to killers and robbers was the rather flimsy form 4473, which, as I showed on pages 113–14, asked illegitimate buyers to disqualify themselves at the point of purchase and stayed in dealers' files unvetted by anyone.

Brady's major accomplishment was to establish for the first time in American history a uniform minimum background check on all handgun purchasers and thus take the responsibility for screening buyers from the hands of America's gun dealers. Brady exempted states such as Maryland, California, and Florida, which already had some form of background-check system. But elsewhere, where sales of handguns hitherto had been virtually unregulated, prospective buyers now had to wait five days while local law-enforcement officials conducted a background check.

Such checks constitute a powerful limit on distribution of firearms to the wrong people. In 1991, Florida began an instant background-check program. The process takes an average of three and a half minutes, but in 1993 alone the program unconditionally barred 7,534 purchases of firearms by known crooks. It blocked another 13,274 purchases attempted by persons who had been arrested for "dangerous crimes" but whose cases had not yet been fully adjudicated. The program also intercepted 854 purchases attempted by buyers wanted under felony and misdemeanor warrants.

The fact that so many felons, fugitives, and other dangerous souls still try to buy guns from licensed dealers, despite such checking networks, indicates the extent to which they had become accustomed to the easy access afforded in the past by form 4473. Old habits, apparently, die hard.

A couple of vast gaps still remain in America's system of firearms regulation. People spurned by legitimate dealers can turn to other avenues of firearms access that remain wide open, the most notorious being the private marketplace, where gun owners remain free under federal law and most state laws to sell handguns and rifles from their personal collections to any adult they please without so much as asking to see a driver's license. Even the new Brady law does not apply in such sales. Like most federal gun-sale laws, Brady regulates only transactions conducted through federally licensed dealers. "It's not even a loophole," one Colorado law-enforcement official told me. "It's a chasm."

One Saturday in the summer of 1994 I paid a visit to Happy's Flea Market in Roanoke, Virginia. Sellers of collectibles rent space inside the defunct Happy's Recreation Center on a more or less permanent basis, but on weekends anyone with something to sell can pay a fee and set up shop in the field out back. At the end of the last row I found a jovial man selling rifles and several high-quality pistols, including a Smith & Wesson 9 millimeter and a Colt .45. At another table, this one erected in front of a large RV, I found a woman sitting before a table strewn with what at first appeared to be the usual flea-market fare. As I got closer, however, I saw that her merchandise included a few high-quality handguns and one cheap derringer. Two men at two other tables sold rifles. In still another row, a sullen man stood before a flame-red Ford Fairlane, idly flipping the cylinder of a small-caliber pistol. Both the pistol and the Fairlane were for sale.

That afternoon I drove north a hundred miles or so to Harrisonburg, Virginia, to visit a gun show under way at the fairgrounds just south of the city. Dozens of federally-licensed gun dealers had spread their guns atop folding tables. As federal licensees they were obligated to obey all federal and state regulations governing firearms sales, including Virginia laws requiring an instant background check on handgun purchases and limiting such purchases to one a month. The same laws, however, did not apply to a young man and his female companion, who walked the aisles with signs pinned to their backs advertising two German Lugers and an M-1 carbine for sale. Nor did these laws apply to a man who had settled in a chair at one end of an empty table, where he had opened his attache case to display four handguns offered for private sale. Outside, at an adjacent flea market, another six men were peddling their personal weapons. Anyone, with any kind of record, could have bought a handgun here. A three-hour drive would have brought the buyer to Washington or Baltimore, two cities where murder has eclipsed stickball as a pursuit of the young.

Accountability continued its traditional absence from America's gun trade. Certain guns, most notably the inexpensive Raven, Jennings, Davis, and Lorcin pocket semi-automatics, are well known to police as weapons commonly used in crime. In the first quarter of 1994, the Lorcin L380, a .380 caliber pistol, was the most frequently traced weapon in America—traced more often than the Smith & Wesson .38 revolver, produced and distributed over the years in numbers that dwarf the Lorcin's production. Next in line came the Davis .380, Raven .25, Lorcin .25, Mossberg Model 500 shotgun— an emerging favorite among crooks—and the Jennings .22. The manufacturers clearly know the extent to which their products are implicated in the country's serious crimes because they field the calls from ATF's tracing center. Yet they continue to produce the weapons, distributors continue to buy them, and dealers—even some who work full time as police officers or police department armorers—continue to sell them. No public means exists for regulating the design of such guns, or their manufacture and distribution. We have outlawed the importation of such weapons from foreign manufacturers, but otherwise we leave such matters to the good conscience of our domestic producers, because they are, after all, red-blooded American companies.

Privately, the big manufacturers complain that they are misunderstood, that the liberal media distort their beliefs. They argue that they are simply producing legitimate products; that their responsibility ends when the guns arrive at the warehouses of their distributors. The distributors, in turn, say their responsibility ends when the guns reach the retail dealer. And the dealers say they cannot police the behavior of their buyers. A gun, as Shane said, is just a tool, only as good or as bad as the person who wields it.

However frivolous these arguments seem when juxtaposed with year-end tallies of America's gun-shot dead, they nonetheless tug resilient strands from that web of beliefs that define America and Americans: the free market, self-determination, the right to keep and bear arms, an armed populace as a check against tyranny.

But reform of America's firearms regulations will continue. One day a truly rational system of firearms laws will exist, because such a system *must* exist. It is the only rational course, and for a culture like ours that still prides itself on common sense and rationality, it is an inevitable course. Stranger things have happened in the world. The Soviet Union collapsed. Israel and the PLO settled their feud. A truce was declared in Northern Ireland amid talk of an end to the Troubles. And America at last seemed to have awakened to what doctors and the American Cancer Society had said all along, that tobacco is indeed inherently dangerous, that smokers ought to be isolated, and that tobacco companies ought at last to begin bearing the social costs incurred by smoking.

A similar sea change seemed under way with regard to guns. Gun buy-backs and swaps began to proliferate, providing little direct impact on crime but helping to raise consciousness about guns and their prevalence in America. Major newspapers around the country launched multi-part investigative reports on guns and the gun trade. Grassroots organizations, similar in design and spirit to Mothers Against Drunk Driving, began forming in New York, Los Angeles, and elsewhere. And for the first time, large masses of individual citizens began marching for firearm-regulation reform. In Maryland, marchers advanced on Annapolis, the state capital, in support of new gun legislation. In San Francisco, some one hundred thousand people marched down Market Street at the center of the city on the one-year anniversary of Ferri's law firm rampage. By the fall, grassroots activists were planning a "Silent March" on Washington. They proposed to set down an empty pair of shoes for every man, woman, and child killed with a firearm, and to array these shoes in a single line ending at the Capitol steps. Public service ads, including one featuring President Bill Clinton, began urging a reduction in violence. Granted, no gang leader in South Chicago is likely to pay much attention to such ads, but, like gun buy-backs, they help energize the plasma of public opinion and reinforce the still all-too-novel idea that firearms violence is unacceptable.

Increasingly, victims and gun-control advocates have turned to the courts to try to force the firearms production and distribution network to a higher level of accountability. In the spring of 1994, a civil jury in Texas—a state known for its tolerance of guns—assessed a $17 million penalty against Remington Arms Co. after finding that the company knew of a design defect in one of its rifles, a defect which cost the plaintiff one of his feet. Just over $2 million of the award represented actual damages; the rest were punitive damages. In 1994, the Center to Prevent Handgun Violence, an affiliate of Handgun Control Inc., went so far as to file a lawsuit against Intratec, alleging the TEC-9 pistol used by Ferri was an unduly hazardous product.

I have often thought that such lawsuits could show the way to the ultimate solution to the problem of limiting the flow of guns. Suppose once again America repealed all its gun laws—but now imagine replacing those laws not with my Life and Liberty Preservation Act, but with a single federal law assigning to gun manufacturers strict liability for the use of their products. In other words, suppose Congress made America's gun industry financially responsible for every time a firearm was used to injure or kill someone. Justifiable shootings by police or by citizens defending themselves would of course be excepted.

The NRA and its libertarian core would get what they have sought all along: unrestrained access to firearms. Manufacturers could build and sell any weapons they chose, distributors and dealers could sell them to anyone, including felons, fugitives, drug addicts, and children. But all parties in the distribution chain would now have to accept legal and financial responsibility for such libertine commercial behavior.

I guarantee that within a breathtakingly short period of time, the manufacturers, distributors and dealers of America would by themselves establish a more stringent, more efficient, more highly automated system of distribution restrictions than anything ever dreamed of by Handgun Control Inc. Suddenly all firearms would be childproof, perhaps with built-in combination locks; the manufacturers' advertising would concentrate on assuring the market that guns were as macho as always—just different. All pistols would include magazine safeties, which deactivate the firearm when the magazine is removed, thus ensuring that no one gets hurt if someone forgets there is a live round still in the chamber. Manufacturers doubtless would require gun buyers to present some kind of prior medical authorization—a kind of prescription—to assure them that the buyer was not insane, depressed, despondent, or otherwise likely to contemplate murder and suicide. The first thing the manufacturers would do is make gun proficiency and safety education a mandatory requirement for gun ownership. In short, with one bold stroke America could eliminate all the bizarre and dangerous behaviors of the firearms trade, and do it in a distinctly American, free-market way.

For now, however, society at large continues to absorb all the costs: to bury its children, heal its wounded, endure its mounting grief and embarrassment—all costs so blithely charged to our account by America's firearms industry.

In early August 1994, Sylvia and Wayne sent licensed dealers, including me, their latest catalog. It arrived well after the House and Senate had each passed its own crime bills containing a ban on the Cobray and other assault weapons, but before the two bills were finally reconciled and passed by the full Congress. On the catalog's cover was a photograph of a private jet. A woman in white steps from the aircraft, guarded by three armed men. A headline over the photograph reads THE LEGEND CONTINUES.

—ERIK LARSON
September 1994

SOURCE NOTES

ABBREVIATIONS USED

ATF   Bureau of Alcohol, Tobacco and Firearms

ATF-CR1   ATF Case Report. Case no. 93215 85 1526P. Federal Records Center, Atlanta.

ATF-CR2   ATF Case Report. Case no. 93215 85 1526P-Supplemental. Federal Records Center, Atlanta.

EE-ASC   Estelle Elliot vs. Atlantic Shores Christian School. Virginia Beach Circuit Court. CV 89-1022.

ET-SP   Earl Taylor, et al. vs. Snell Publishing, et al. Fulton County Superior Court, Atlanta. Case D-26477.

GAO   U.S. Government Accounting Office

NES   Nicholas Elliot. Statement to police, December 16, 1988. Police case no. 88-222747. Page numbers refer to locations in court documents or in transcripts of testimony commissioned by author.

PA-JH   Pa. vs. Jean-Claude Pierre Hill. Superior Court, Philadelphia. No. 4178, Philadelphia, 1992. Court transcript.

US-AF   U.S. vs. Amir Faraz. U.S. District Court, Norfolk. CR 91-154-N.

US-CW   U.S. vs. Curtis Williams. U.S. District Court, Norfolk. CR-88-145-N. March 1, 1989.

US-DA   U.S. vs. Dean Archer. U.S. District Court, Norfolk. CR 91-4-N.

US-PEG   U.S. vs. Pablo Escobar-Gaviria, et al. U.S. District Court, Jacksonville, Florida 89-29-CR-J-16. Indictment, February 24, 1989, 12, 13, 14.

U.S.-SWD   U.S. vs. SWD Inc. and RPB Industries Inc. U.S. District Court, Atlanta. CR-86-22A. Federal Records Center, Atlanta.

VA-NE   Virginia vs. Nicholas Elliot. Circuit Court, Virginia Beach, Virginia. CR89-1681. Page numbers refer to locations in court documents or in transcripts of testimony commissioned by author.

WF-SE   William Farley vs. SNUG Enterprises (t/a Guns Unlimited). Circuit Court, Virginia Beach, Virginia, CL 89-2047. Page numbers refer to locations in transcripts commissioned by author. Testimony with no page citation means I culled the testimony from a videotape of the trial made by Court TV in New York.

Chapter One: Introduction

1   On a bitter, cold . . . Norfolk Virginian-Pilot, March 1, 1989, A1.

1   A single homicide . . . Here I refer to Patrick Purdy's January 17, 1989, assault on a school in Stockton, California, which killed five children, and James Oliver Huberty's attack on a McDonald's restaurant, which left twenty-one people dead.

3   I acquired . . . License, form 8. ATF.

4   I discovered . . . "Putting Guns Back Into Criminals' Hands." Violence Policy Center, 1992.

4   I learned too . . . "Accidental Shootings: Many Deaths and Injuries Caused by Firearms Could Be Prevented," GAO, March 1991; "Compilation of Statutes Administered by CPSC." U.S. Consumer Product Safety Commission, April 1992.

4   One evening . . . Georgia Sport Shooting Association, American Legion Hall, Smyrna, Georgia, November 21, 1992.

Chapter Two: Nicholas

6   Virginia Beach alone . . . Printout of Virginia and Maryland Federal Firearms Licensees. ATF, May 12, 1992.

7   The Atlantic Shores Baptist . . . George Sweet, interview.

7   The church school . . . Richmond Times Dispatch, December 18, 1988, 1.

7   As of December 16 . . . *Norfolk Virginian-Pilot,* correction, April 21, 1989.

8   "As far as I know . . ." George Sweet, interview.

8   He had dyslexia . . . Complaint. EE-ASC.

8   A Virginia Beach psychiatrist . . . Judge's notes. VA-NE.

8   Another psychiatrist . . . Sentencing hearing. VA-NE, December 12, 1989, 18.

8   He told Det. Donald Adams . . . NES, 8.

9   "Like fire . . ." George Sweet, interview.

9   Billy would call . . . (Billy Cutter), testimony. VA-NE, February 28, 1989, 105, 107, 114.

9   At six foot one . . . Ibid., 106.

9   "There was some slapping . . ." Duncan Wallace, testimony. VA-NE, December 12, 1989, 16.

9   Dr. Wallace found . . . Ibid., 12.

10   As Nicholas left . . . (Billy Cutter). VA-NE, 112.

10   "I can't take . . ." NES, 44–45.

10   At lunch . . . William Farley, interview.

10   His locker . . . Det. Donald Adams, interview.

11   One told . . . *Norfolk Ledger-Star,* December 18, 1988, 1.

11   Even the guns . . . NES, 42.

11   His mother worried . . . NES, 43–44.

11   When she arrived . . . NES, 2.

12   His mother, during . . . Estelle Elliot, sentencing hearing. VA-NE, 6.

12   In California . . . Duncan Wallace. Ibid., 17.

12   On arriving . . . Estelle Elliot. Ibid., 10, 11.

12   "The public schools . . ." Ibid., 7.

12   "She said something . . ." NES, 20.

13   "I've heard . . ." NES, 21.

13   When Adams asked . . . NES, 63.

13   This was clearly evident . . . Karen Farley, videotape.

13   The morning of December 16 . . . William Farley, interview.

14   She had begun . . . Ibid.

14   "Do you think . . ." *Norfolk Virginian-Pilot,* December 10, 1988, D1.

Chapter Three: The Lethal Landscape

16   "I know several . . ." Anthony Cobb, letter to author, February 2, 1993.

17   Over the last . . . The statistics in this paragraph may be found in: American Academy of Pediatrics, Policy Statement, *AAP NEWS* (January 1992): 22; Garen Wintemute, "Firearms as a Cause of Death in the United States, 1920–1982," *The Journal of Trauma* 27:5 (May 1987): 532; *Los Angeles Times,* May 17, 1992, 1; Department of Justice, Bureau of Justice Statistics, Special Report (July 1990).

17   A relatively new . . . Gary J. Ordog, et al., "Gunshot Wounds in Children Under 10 Years of Age," *American Journal of Diseases of Children* 142 (June 1988): 618–22.

18   No one knows . . . American Academy of Pediatrics, Policy Statement, 20.

18   The story is less . . . Michael Pertschuk, interview.

19   Over the most . . . "Civilian Firearms: Domestic Production, Importation, Exportation and Availability for Sale, 1899–1989," ATF.

19   As of 1989 . . . Ibid.

19   One study of . . . American Academy of Pediatrics, Policy Statement, 20.

19   A July 1993 poll . . . Louis Harris, "A Survey of Experiences, Perceptions, and Apprehensions About Guns Among Young People in America," LH Research Inc. (July 1993): 12, 13.

19   The Harris poll . . . Ibid., 12.

19   A University of North Carolina . . . Laura S. Sadowski, "Firearm Ownership Among Nonurban Adolescents," *American Journal of Diseases of Children* 143 (December 1989): 1412.

20   From 1965 to 1990 . . . "Crime in the United States," FBI, Uniform Crime Reports, 279.

20   Anyone inclined . . . *Baltimore Sun,* July 20, 1993, 1.

20   In 1985 stray . . . *New York Times,* December 31, 1990, A25.

20   In 1987, America's . . . Lois A. Fingerhut, "International and Interstate Comparisons of Homicide Among Young Males," *JAMA* 263:24 (June 27, 1990): 3292–93.

21   A landmark study . . . Arthur L. Kellermann and Donald T. Reay, "Protection or Peril?" *New England Journal of Medicine* 314:24 (June 12, 1986): 1557–60.

21   A Pittsburgh . . . David A. Brent, et al., "The Presence and Accessibility of Firearms in the Homes of Adolescent Suicides," *JAMA* 266:21 (December 4, 1991): 2989–95.

21   In 1987, Dr. Garen . . . Garen J. Wintemute, "Firearms as a Cause of Death in the United States, 1920–1982," *Journal of Trauma* 27:5 (May 1987): 535.

21   A 1986 study . . . Jeffrey H. Boyd, "Firearms and Youth Suicide," *American Journal of Public Health* 76:10 (October 1986): 1240–42.

22   He established . . . Franklin E. Zimring, "Firearms, Violence and Public Policy," *Scientific American* (November 1991): 50.

22   In one of . . . John H. Sloan, et al., "Handgun Regulations, Crime, Assaults, and Homicide," *New England Journal of Medicine* 319 (1988): 1256.

23   "WHAT WILL IT TAKE . . ." National Rifle Association advertisement, 1992.

24   The story described . . . Ed Magnuson, "Do Guns Save Lives," *Time,* August 21, 1989, 25–26.

24   The *American Rifleman* does not . . . Associated Press, "Woman Shot in Face With Gun Kept Under Pillow," *Los Angeles Times,* October 24, 1991.

24   A controversial Colt ad . . . Colt's Manufacturing Co. advertisement, July 1992.

25   Even Davis Industries . . . Davis Industries Inc. advertisement, May 1992; *Wall Street Journal,* February 28, 1992, 1.

25   A Smith & Wesson ad . . . Smith & Wesson advertisement, February 1993.

25   The company produced . . . Herschel C. Logan, "The Smith & Wesson Ladysmiths," *American Rifleman,* April 1954, 47–48.

25   "We're seeing . . ." Garen Wintemute, interview.

25   Joyce Mays-Rabbitt . . . Joyce Mays-Rabbitt, interview.

26   In fact, she was . . . Anne Pallie, interview.

26   "By getting over . . ." Paxton Quigley, interview.

27   One of Quigley's . . . Noelle Stettner, interview.

28   Her choice of . . . Paxton Quigley, interview.

29   "The first time . . ." Michelle Sullivan, interview.

31   "I didn't know . . ." Sean Smith, police tape.

32   "In other words . . ." Paxton Quigley, Armed & Female (New York: St. Martin's Press, 1990), 139.

32   A study of accidental . . . Garen J. Wintemute, et al., "When Children Shoot Children," JAMA 257:22 (June 12, 1987): 3107–9.

33   In fact, she told . . . Wayne King, "Target: The Gun Lobby," New York Times Magazine, December 9, 1990, 42.

33   A June 1993 . . . Louis Harris, "A Survey of the American People on Guns as a Children's Health Issue," (June 1993): 20.

33   Another study . . . Douglas S. Weil and David Hemenway, "Loaded Guns in the Home," JAMA 267:22 (June 10, 1992): 33–37.

34   Dr. Kellermann . . . Arthur L. Kellermann, interview.

34   A 1991 study by . . . "Accidental Shootings: Many Deaths and Injuries Caused by Firearms Could be Prevented," GAO, March 1991, 2.

34   The GAO began . . . Ibid., 3, 12, 28.

35   The GAO report . . . Ibid., 30–32.

35   "There's just so many . . ." Joanne Welsh, interview.

36   From 1980 through . . . FBI, FBI Law Enforcement Bulletin (May 1991): 2–5.

36   "The typical NRA . . ." Leonard Supenski, interview.

36   Police officers involved . . . Leonard Supenski, interview.

37   One of its members . . . Confidential source, interview.

39   Lisa Hilliard, the . . . Lisa Hilliard, interview.

39   "What people believe . . ." W. Eugene Hollon, Frontier Violence: Another Look (New York: Oxford University Press, 1974), 195.

40   For the average resident . . . Ibid., 197; Frank Richard Prassel, The Western Peace Officer (Norman, Okla.: University of Oklahoma Press, 1972), 20, 22.

40   People rarely locked . . . Hollon, Frontier Violence, 210, 211; Prassel, Western Peace Officer, 22.

40 Burglary was rare . . . Roger D. McGrath, *Gunfighters, Highwaymen and Vigilantes* (Berkeley, Calif.: University of California Press, 1984), 248, 249; Hollon, *Frontier Violence*, 203.

40 Frank Prassel, an . . . Prassel, *Western Peace Officer*, 20.

40 One of the great . . . Hollon, *Frontier Violence*, 165.

40 Moments before . . . *Abilene Chronicle*, January 5, 1871.

40 According to historian . . . McGrath, *Gunfighters*, 88, 184, 199, 255.

41 Nonetheless, the homicide rate . . . Ibid., 268; Hollon, *Frontier Violence*, 201; Prassel, *Western Peace Officer*, 47; Elliott West, "Wicked Dodge City," *American History Illustrated* (June 1982): 23–31.

41 On March 19, 1872 . . . *Missouri Republican*, March 19, 1872, 2.

41 Buffalo Bill Cody was . . . Joseph G. Rosa and Robin May, *Buffalo Bill and His Wild West* (Lawrence, Kans.: University Press of Kansas, 1989), 163.

42 The first book . . . Peter Lyon, *The Wild, Wild West* (New York: Funk and Wagnalls, 1969), 119.

42 After Jesse James . . . Robert Sherrill, *The Saturday Night Special* (New York: Charterhouse, 1973), 39.

42 After Jesse was murdered . . . Ibid., 39.

42 The *Gazette* described . . . Lyon, *The Wild*, 92.

43 Belle was a . . . Ibid., 89.

43 Billy the Kid, far . . . Ibid., 123.

43 In a rare act . . . Hollon, *Frontier Violence*, 189.

43 He was discharged . . . Deborah Berrier, "Clay Allison: Never Killed a Man Willingly," *American History Illustrated* (June 1982): 38–39.

43 Fabled gunfighter . . . Elliott West, "Wicked"; Ralph Brauer, *The Horse, the Gun and the Piece of Property* (Bowling Green, Ohio: Bowling Green University Popular Press, 1975), 200.

43 Contrary to popular . . . Prassel, *Western Peace Officer*, 110.

43 In Leadville . . . Ibid., 47.

43 The real marshal . . . Elliott West, "Wicked," 30.

44 In that mythic realm . . . Ibid., 27.

44 They were known . . . Lyon, *The Wild*, 15, 18, 21.

44   Morgan Earp, one . . . Ibid., 20.

44   A thief named . . . Ibid., 83.

44   The police officer . . . Brian McGinty, "John Wesley Hardin: Gentleman of Guns," *American History Illustrated* (June 1982): 32–36.

44   In one notorious . . . McGrath, *Gunfighters,* 90–91.

45   "Lawmen and . . ." Prassel, *Western Peace Officer,* 248.

45   The Colt Peacemaker . . . A. C. Gould, *Modern American Pistols and Revolvers* (Boston: Bradlee Whidden, 1894), 203. See also *Wall Street Journal,* June 24, 1993, 1.

45   On one journey . . . Glenda Riley, "The Specter of a Savage: Rumors and Alarmism on the Overland Trail," *Western History Quarterly* 15:4 (October 1984): 427–44.

45   In Bodie . . . McGrath, *Gunfighters,* 192.

45   Clay Allison shot . . . Berrier, "Clay Allison," 38.

45   Wild Bill Hickok . . . Hollon, *Frontier Violence,* 200.

45   On January 9, 1876 . . . Nyle H. Miller and Joseph W. Snell, *Great Gunfighters of the Texas Cowtowns, 1867–1886* (Lincoln, Nebr.: University of Nebraska, 1963), 83–84.

45   When Pat Garret . . . Prassel, *Western Peace Officer,* 104.

45   Jesse James's brother . . . Albert Castel, "The James Brothers," *American History Illustrated* (June 1982): 10–18.

45   Bill Tilghman . . . Prassel, *Western Peace Officer,* 247.

46   A former train robber . . . Jack Lewis, *The Gun Digest Book of Single-Action Revolvers* (Northbrook, Ill.: DBI Books Inc, 1982), 201; Richard Slotkin, *Gunfighter Nation* (New York: Atheneum, 1992), 236.

46   Cody's fame was . . . Slotkin, Ibid., 72–73.

46   As if to dispel . . . Ibid., 68.

46   Sitting Bull, the . . . Ibid., 74; Rosa and May, *Buffalo Bill,* 83.

47   Richard Slotkin, author . . . Slotkin, *Gunfighter Nation,* 87.

47   The proliferation of . . . Ibid., 77.

48   In 1903 . . . Ibid., 231; John G. Cawelti, *The Six-Gun Mystique* (Bowling Green, Ohio: Bowling Green University Popular Press, 1971), 3.

48   By 1925, William Hart . . . Lewis, *Gun Digest Book*, 199, 212, 214.

48   Fourteen feature-length . . . Slotkin, *Gunfighter Nation*, 347.

49   The underlying message . . . Ibid., 396.

49   In 1959, the networks . . . Brauer, *The Horse*, 54.

49   In 1959, eight . . . Cawelti, *Six-Gun*, 2.

50   An advertisement . . . American Sales & Manufacturing advertisement, July 1993.

50   In the "Wyatt Earp" . . . Lewis, *Gun Digest Book*, 27–28.

50   In 1982, Colt . . . Ibid., 31.

50   In 1992, Colt introduced . . . Colt's Manufacturing Co. advertisement, 1992.

50   The master . . . *Wall Street Journal*, June 24, 1993, 1.

50   In the autumn . . . Leighton Rockafellow, interview. Rockafellow represented the Nix family in a lawsuit against Sturm, Ruger. The family agreed to accept a settlement of $150,000.

51   Ruger continues . . . Sturm, Ruger & Co., catalog, 1993, 28.

51   A report in . . . Sturm, Ruger & Co., product liability log, entry dated March 14, 1980.

51   "It is quite . . ." Prassel, *Western Peace Officer*, 252.

51   ". . . Since the Western . . ." Slotkin, *Gunfighter Nation*, 352.

52   In 1970, historian . . . Richard Hofstadter, "Reflections on Violence in the United States," *American Violence* (New York: Knopf, 1970), 24.

52   Sturm, Ruger & Co. . . . *Wall Street Journal*, June 24, 1993, 1.

53   Why else . . . Frank W. James, "Snubnose Revolvers," *American Handgunner* (Combat Annual 1992): 29036. Photo: 34.

53   The company whose . . . ATF, Firearms Tracing Database Report, February 20, 1992.

53   By 1989 . . . "Handgun Production by U.S. Manufacturers, 1973–1989," *Shooting Industry*, 1991.

53   It fondly . . . Cox Newspapers, "Firepower: Assault Weapons in America," 1989, 2; Edward M. Owen, interview; Earl Taylor, interview.

54   "We've got technology . . ." Leonard Supenski, interview.

Chapter Four: Nicholas

55   "I didn't feel . . ." NES, 32.

55   "I was scared . . ." Ibid., 82.

55   "I was looking . . ." Ibid., 77, 80.

56   "I was scared . . ." Ibid., 81.

56   "I was kind of . . ." Ibid., 81–82.

56   "I was thinking . . ." Ibid., 82.

Chapter Five: The Gun

58   "I grew up . . ." Leonard Supenski, interview.

60   A 1989 study . . . Cox Newspapers, "Firepower: Assault Weapons in America," 1989, 2.

60   A study of all . . . ATF, "Project Detroit," April 19, 1992, 4–5.

60   The head of . . . Thomas W. Stokes, interview.

60   Shortly after nine . . . Homicide Report, Denver Police Department; George I. Ogura, Autopsy Report, County of Denver, June 19, 1984; Kevin Flynn and Gary Gerhardt, *The Silent Brotherhood* (New York: Signet, 1990), 244–250.

61   During a sweeping . . . U.S. vs. Pierce, et al., Second Superseding Indictment. CR85-001M, 43, 48, 64, 65, 78.

61   Later, on April 15 . . . Flynn and Gerhardt, *Silent Brotherhood*, 472.

61   "It slices . . ." Cox Newspapers, "Firepower," 12.

61   In March 1989 . . . Ibid., 8.

61   The same month . . . *St. Petersburg Times,* March 2, 1989, 12A.

62   Six months later . . . Det. Cheryl Jackman, interview.

62   "It's a terrible . . ." Cornelius J. Behan, tape of Maryland Handgun Roster Board Meeting, February 5, 1990.

62   The day before . . . Advertisement. *New York Times,* February 4, 1990; *Baltimore Sun,* February 6, 1990, 1A.

62   The third speaker . . . Elmer H. Tippet, tape of Maryland Handgun Roster Board Meeting, February 5, 1990.

62   The gun joined . . . Maryland Handgun Roster Board, Determination of Petition. Docket P-89085, February 13, 1990.

63   At about midnight . . . *Oakland Tribune,* October 11, 1990, A-11.

63   In May 1990 . . . *Vancouver Sun,* May 22, 1990, B1.

63   On October 20, 1991 . . . *Vancouver Sun,* March 7, 1992, A7.

63   The same month . . . *The Record* (Bergen County), October 11, 1991, A-1.

63   In 1991, New York . . . *The Record* (Bergen County), July 16, 1991, A-7.

63   The following year . . . *Denver Post,* October 1, 1992, 2-B.

64   A Baltimore rapper . . . *Baltimore Sun,* November 29, 1992, 1A.

64   At least two gangs . . . *Las Vegas Review-Journal,* May 17, 1992, 16; *Arkansas Gazette,* January 25, 1991, 4B.

64   Detailed renderings . . . *Baton Rouge State Times,* June 15, 1990, 1-A.

64   *Let me get* . . . *Indianapolis News,* June 25, 1992, A-1.

64   "I'll make it up . . ." *Boston Globe,* November 25, 1992, 19.

65   "When you look . . ." Leonard Supenski, interview.

65   The gun's direct lineage . . . Thomas R. Nelson and Daniel D. Musgrave, *The World's Machine Pistols and Submachine Guns,* vol IIA (Hong Kong: Chesa Limited, undated): 501, 504, 507.

66   Ingram saw . . . Ibid., 508.

66   The United States had . . . Ibid., 503–4.

66   The Army bought . . . Ibid., 508.

66   WerBell, who . . . Ibid., 509.

66   In 1969 Ingram . . . Ibid., 512.

66   To best capitalize . . . Ibid., 512.

67   From 1969 . . . Ibid., 512.

67   The investors . . . Ibid., 512.

67   It was *McQ* . . . Edward M. Owen, interview.

67   "Hey, Lon," the . . . *McQ,* Warner Brothers, 1974.

69   This enthusiastic bit . . . Nelson and Musgrave, *Machine Pistols,* 515, 517.

69   Under Wayne Daniel . . . Ibid., 521.

69   An operating manual . . . RPB Industries Inc., Ingram Submachine Gun Operating Manual, 1, 43.

69   One partner was . . . *Atlanta Journal-Constitution,* May 21, 1989, A-9.

69   Two others . . . US-PEG, 12, 13, 14.

69   Morgan was . . . Florida vs. Robert Morgan, Judgment and sentence, 20th Judicial Circuit of Florida. Case no. 79–86, June 2, 1980.

70   Leibolt, according to . . . US-PEG, 28.

70   "It became available . . ." Earl Taylor, interview.

71   At one point . . . Thomas W. Stokes, interview.

71   By the autumn . . . RPB Inc., minutes. "Special Meeting of Shareholders," December 28, 1981; RPB Inc., minutes. "Meeting of Stockholders," December 14, 1981; RPB Inc., minutes. "Special Meeting of Board of Directors," January 6, 1982.

72   Two weeks later . . . RPB Inc., minutes. "Special Meeting of Shareholders," December 28, 1981.

72   The minutes of . . . RPB Inc., minutes. "Special Meeting of Board of Directors," January 20, 1982.

72   ATF, meanwhile . . . Edward M. Owen, interview.

72   Any gun assembled . . . ATF, Ruling 82-8. Federal Firearms Regulations, 1988–89.

72   The threat . . . Earl Taylor, interview.

72   June proved . . . RPB Inc., Statement of income, six months ended June 30, 1982; Statement of income, seven months ended July 31, 1982.

73   They succeeded . . . Edward M. Owen, interview.

73   The company also . . . Edward M. Owen, interview; S.W. Daniel Inc., advertisement, "Beat the Heat."

73   The Daniels knew . . . Earl Taylor, interview.

74   Wayne Daniel may . . . ATF-CR1, 2.

74   Ledbetter and Motes . . . Peter Urrea, ATF affidavit in US-SWD.

75   Wayne Daniel went . . . ATF-CR1, 3.

75   Ledbetter and Motes founded . . . Ibid., 3–4.

75   Details of this . . . Peter Urrea, ATF affidavit in US-SWD; Keith W. Dunkel, ATF affidavit in US-SWD.

75   On April 27 . . . Keith W. Dunkel, ATF affidavit in US-SWD; Peter Urrea, affidavit in US-SWD.

76   On April 30 . . . Urrea, Ibid.

76   Urrea also . . . Ibid.

76   On July 19 . . . Keith W. Dunkel, ATF affidavit in US-SWD, 10–11.

77   The bureau used . . . ATF-CR2, 1.

77   In formal court . . . "SW Daniel Inc.'s Response to Government's Motion to Amend the Conditions of Release," US-SWD.

77   All in all . . . Keith Dunkel, testimony. US-SWD, February 10, 1986.

77   Only four buyers . . . "Government's Motion to Amend the Conditions of Release," US-SWD.

77   An ATF agent . . . ATF-CR2.

78   Agents also . . . Ibid., 8–9.

78   Another investigation . . . ATF-CR1, 4.

78   In Ohio . . . Ibid., 4–5; George Burton, statement to ATF. US-SWD, April 27, 1984.

78   The growing list . . . ATF-CR1, 6, 7, 14; Michael Molinari, ATF affidavit. US-SWD, May 17, 1985.

79   "There are literally . . ." Brian C. Leighton, "Government's Motion to Amend the Conditions of Release," US-SWD.

79   The Daniels pleaded . . . Wayne Daniel, affidavit. ET-SP.

79   On May 1 . . . Complaint, judgment. Exhibit A, ET-SP.

80   In a handwritten . . . Exhibit C, ET-SP.

80   "It wasn't . . ." Earl Taylor, interview.

80   They introduced . . . Northwest Distributing advertisement.

81   The company's latest . . . Maryland Handgun Roster Board, "Determination on Petition: Ladies' Home Companion," Docket 90148, July 16, 1991.

81   The trigger . . . Ibid., 1–2.

81   The board ruled . . . Ibid., 5.

81   An official . . . Confidential source, interview.

81   "Shit no . . ." Earl Taylor, interview.

82   "You put a gun . . ." Leonard Supenski, testimony. WF-SE.

83   "Well, I should say . . ." Leonard Supenski, interview.

Chapter Six: Nicholas

84   Nicholas did come . . . NES, 47–50, 70–72.

84   Nicholas, who . . . Samuel M. Marino, testimony. VA-NE, 7–8.

84   Marino said . . . Ibid., 8.

85   Just as Nicholas left . . . Ibid., 8.

85   "All of a sudden . . ." Ibid., 9.

85   "At first . . ." Ibid., 9

85   He saw Nicholas . . . Ibid., 40.

85   "In a situation . . ." Ibid., 39

86   "I've got something . . ." Ibid., 10–11.

86   Susan Allen, watching . . . Susan Allen, testimony. VA-NE, 50.

86   "What is it . . ." Samuel M. Marino, testimony. VA-NE, 31.

86   *"Give it to me . . ."* Susan Allen, testimony. VA-NE, 51.

86   "Here it is . . ." Ibid., 51.

86   Victims of . . . Det. Donald Adams, interview.

86   Marino held . . . Samuel M. Marino, testimony. VA-NE, 12.

Chapter Seven: The Purchase

88   Nonetheless, Guns Unlimited . . . Motion for judgment, WF-SE.

88   One peaceful weekend . . . Curtis Williams, testimony. US-CW.

89   "He wanted . . ." Ibid., 6.

90   "Man," he said . . . Ibid., 34.

90   "My husband . . ." Ibid., 9.

91   "After that . . ." Ibid., 10.

92   "They got in . . ." Ibid., 12–13.

92   Nicholas reached . . . Ibid., 14–15.

93   What Massengill . . . Tony D. Massengill, deposition. WF-SE, July 16, 1990, 38, 46–48, 116.

93   This clerk . . . Christopher Hartwig, testimony. WF-SE, January 15, 1992, 5, 14.

93   Williams testified . . . Curtis Williams, testimony. US-CW, 14.

93   Asked if anything . . . Ibid., 15.

93   (Raymond Rowley . . . Raymond Rowley, testimony. US-CW, 21.

94   "The only thing . . ." Curtis Williams, Testimony. US-CW, 17.

94   Massengill, in a . . . Tony D. Massengill, deposition. WF-SE, July 16, 1990, 16.

94   In an interview . . . Tony D. Massengill, interview.

94   Once outside . . . Curtis Williams, testimony. US-CW, 19.

95   "What would ever . . ." Robert W. Wiechering. US-CW, 42.

Chapter Eight: The Dealer

97   A Baltimore police . . . Confidential source, Baltimore Police Department, interview.

98   A thick printout . . . Printout of Virginia Federal Firearms Licensees. ATF, May 12, 1992.

98   One medical examiner . . . Allen M. Jones, et. al. "Suicidal Contact Gunshot Wounds to the Head with .38 Special Glaser Safety Slug Ammunition. *Journal of Forensic Sciences* 32:6 (November 1987): 1604–21.

98   The Dicks learned . . . J. Michael Dick, interview.

99   The domestic gun industry . . . *New York Times,* March 20, 1992, D1; *New York Times,* March 8, 1992, 1.

99   Financial statements filed . . . SNUG Enterprises, Bankruptcy File. U.S. Bankruptcy Court, Norfolk, Virginia, 91-22192-T.

100   At its peak . . . Ibid; See also photograph, *Virginian-Pilot,* December 19, 1988, A2.

100   In a deposition, Christopher . . . Christopher Hartwig, deposition. WF-SE, September 12, 1991, 38–40.

100   "Is that something . . ." Ibid., 39.

100   "I can't lie . . ." Ibid., 39–40.

101   "Guns Unlimited is . . ." J. Michael Dick, interview.

101   "Whatever you want . . ." Harry Boone, deposition. WF-SE, September 12, 1991, 16.

101   "It's good for nothing . . ." Christopher Hartwig, deposition. WF-SE, September 12, 1991, 32.

101   "Your blacks . . ." Ibid., 32.

102   "I hate to use . . ." J. Michael Dick, interview.

102   Just as Nicholas . . . *Norfolk Virginian-Pilot*, January 18, 1992, A1.

103   In August 1991 . . . "United States' Position on Defendant's Role in the Offense," US-AF, January 6, 1992.

103   All the dealer . . . Title 27, Code of Federal Regulations, Part 178: Commerce in Firearms and Ammunition, 178.126a; "Report of Multiple Sale or Other Disposition of Pistols and Revolvers," ATF form 3310.4; Jack Killorin, interview.

104   In 1992, ATF . . . *Atlanta Journal-Constitution*, February 14, 1993, H1.

104   Even Batman . . . Ibid., H4.

104   In the early 1970s . . . Ibid., H4.

104   Before it took effect . . . Ibid., H4.

105   At eight-forty . . . Criminal complaint. US-AF, September 8, 1991.

106   Requizo, the license . . . *Norfolk Virginian-Pilot,* January 18, 1992, A1.

106   Cooper said . . . John Cooper, sentencing hearing. US-AF, January 9, 1992.

106   Mike Dick was . . . J. Michael Dick, interview.

106   He made his first . . . Indictment. US-DA, January 14, 1991; *Wall Street Journal,* February 28, 1992, 1.

106   Moreover, she sold . . . J. Michael Dick, interview.

107   When ATF learned . . . John DePollo, testimony. US-DA, February 28, 1991.

107   A few days after . . . Criminal complaint/ATF affidavit. US-DA.

107   Again the form . . . John DePollo, testimony. US-DA, February 28, 1991.

107   A few days later . . . Ibid.

107 Four days later . . . Ibid.

107 Dick explained . . . J. Michael Dick, interview.

107 Federal law grants . . . ATF, "Federal Firearms Licensee Information," ATF P5300.15., January 1, 1989.

108 "Yes, they tell . . ." J. Michael Dick, interview.

108 "Well, actually . . ." Ibid.

108 On March 20, 1991 . . . J. Michael Dick, testimony. PA-JH, 963–97.

109 Yet from July . . . John W. Thompson, Jr., testimony. PA-JH, 1135–39.

110 Dick remembered . . . J. Michael Dick, interview.

110 He had never . . . J. Michael Dick, testimony. PA-JH, 997.

111 The executives . . . Judge O'Keefe, opinion. Court of Common Pleas, Philadelphia. PA-JH, January 21, 1993.

111 Robert Dowe hadn't . . . Robert Dowe, testimony. PA-JH, 1055–61.

111 Foy, who weighed . . . Dr. James Lewis, testimony. PA-JH, 1051.

112 Leonard Allen . . . Leonard Allen, testimony. PA-JH, 946.

112 "No. I did . . ." J. Michael Dick, interview.

114 "The object of . . ." Ibid.

115 "I would say . . ." Raymond Rowley, interview.

115 "That guy is . . ." Leonard Supenski, interview.

Chapter Nine: Nicholas

116 "Now you . . ." Susan Allen, testimony. VA-NE, February 28, 1989, 51.

116 At first . . . Ibid., 52.

117 "I hit . . ." Ibid., 52.

117 "It was not . . ." Det. Donald Adams, interview.

117 "My God . . ." Susan Allen, testimony. VA-NE, 52.

117 Two things . . . Samuel M. Marino, testimony. VA-NE, 43.

118 Nicholas knew . . . NES, 61–62.

118 "I saw Mr. Marino . . ." Maurice H. Matteson, testimony. VA-NE, 120.

119   "I saw Nicholas . . ." Ibid., 122.

119   Nicholas had seen . . . NES, 62.

119   "There were chairs . . ." (Billy Cutter), testimony. VA-NE, 173.

120   "Billy . . ." Ibid.

120   "I know . . ." NES, 87.

120   "Billy Cutter . . ." Maurice H. Matteson, testimony. VA-NE, 123.

Chapter Ten: The Enforcers

121   In a 1981 congressional . . . G. R. Dickerson, testimony. Dismantling of the Bureau of Alcohol, Tobacco and Firearms hearing, Subcommittee on Crime, Committee on the Judiciary, House of Representatives, April 30, 1981, 26.

122   "There's been . . ." Jack Killorin, interview.

122   "Illegal traffickers . . ." "A Study of Weapons Seized in Connection with Narcotics Investigations," ATF Detroit Division, 1992, 13.

122   "If it were not . . ." Ibid., 13.

123   It must police . . . Anthony Fleming, interview.

123   This ratio . . . Robert Sherrill, *The Saturday Night Special* (New York: Charterhouse, 1973), 143.

123   In 1990 . . . Firearms Program License Application Data, ATF.

124   Roughly half . . . Anthony Fleming, interview.

124   My ATF printout . . . Printout of Maryland Federal Firearms Licensees. ATF, May 12, 1992.

125   A *Los Angeles Times* . . . *Los Angeles Times,* May 18, 1992, A1.

126   Any consumer who . . . Title 27, Code of Federal Regulations, Part 178: Commerce in Firearms and Ammunition, Section 178.128 b and c.

127   ATF traces its . . . "Facts," ATF.

128   On January 16 . . . Robert T. Schoenberg, *Mr. Capone* (New York: William Morrow, 1992), 56–57.

128   What ATF neglects . . . Ibid., 58.

128   Eliot Ness urged . . . Ibid., 252.

129   Indeed, Schoenberg . . . Ibid., 297.

129   The real hero . . . Ibid., 298.

129   By the fall . . . Ibid., 139.

130   In 1969 . . . William J. Helmer, *The Gun That Made the Twenties Roar* (New York: Macmillan, 1969).

130   The Thompson . . . John Ellis, *The Social History of the Machine Gun* (Baltimore, Md.: Johns Hopkins University Press, 1975), 149–51.

130   In a 1922 magazine ad . . . Auto-Ordnance Corp., advertisement, 1922; Ellis, *Social History,* 151.

131   An article . . . Ellis, *Social History,* 77.

131   In 1923 . . . Ibid., 79.

131   The first recorded . . . Schoenberg, *Capone,* 139.

131   That day . . . Helmer, *Gun That Made,* 84.

131   Capone first . . . Ibid., 84–85.

132   One of the dead . . . Ibid., 85; Schoenberg, *Capone,* 150.

132   The attack triggered . . . Helmer, *Gun That Made,* 87.

133   The Thompson submachine . . . Ibid., 88.

133   On February 14 . . . Ibid., 88.

133   As other massacres . . . Ibid., 100.

134   *You've read* . . . Ibid., 111.

134   One result . . . Ellis, *Social History,* 160.

134   On October 14 . . . Schoenberg, *Capone,* 322.

134   A more significant . . . "Facts," BATF.; Sherrill, *Saturday Night,* 58; "BATF: Management Improvements Needed to Handle Increasing Responsibilities," GAO, March 1991, 10.

135   In 1938, Congress . . . GAO, Ibid., 10.

135   It boosted . . . Ibid., 11; Sherrill, *Saturday Night,* 295.

135   "When our law-enforcement . . ." Rex Davis, former director, BATF, interview.

136   In 1968 the NRA's . . . Osha Gray Davidson, *Under Fire: The NRA & The Battle for Gun Control* (New York: Henry Holt, 1993), 30.

137   Gradually, the hard-liners . . . Ibid., 31–41.

137   "To the NRA faithful . . ." Ibid., 31.

137   "That was a well-known . . ." Rex Davis, interview.

138   In March of 1978 . . . G. R. Dickerson, director, BATF, testimony. Firearms
        Enforcement Efforts of the Bureau of Alcohol, Tobacco and Firearms hear-
        ing, Subcommittee on Crime, Committee on the Judiciary, House of Repre-
        sentatives, July 2, 1980, 69.

138   "We didn't feel . . ." Rex Davis, interview.

138   It cited . . . G. R. Dickerson, director, BATF, testimony, Firearms hearing,
        70–71.

139   The NRA, however . . . Rex Davis, interview.

139   Davis, delighted . . . Rex Davis, interview.

140   The NRA went so far . . . Davidson, Under Fire, 50; Representative John D.
        Dingell, testimony. Proposed Dissolution of Bureau of Alcohol, Tobacco
        and Firearms special hearing, Subcommittee of the Committee on Appro-
        priations, U.S. Senate, February 23, 1982, 245–46.

140   "We often hear . . ." G. R. Dickerson, director, BATF, testimony, Firearms
        hearing, 72.

141   At the same hearing . . . Firearms Enforcement Efforts of the Bureau of Alco-
        hol, Tobacco and Firearms hearing, Subcommittee on Crime, Committee
        on the Judiciary, House of Representatives, July 2, 1980, 139–50.

141   That month . . . Davidson, Under Fire, 50.

141   At a February . . . Representative John D. Dingell, testimony, Dissolution
        hearing, 245–47, 249, 252.

142   The Gun Owners . . . Lawrence D. Pratt, testimony. Proposed Dissolution of
        Bureau of Alcohol, Tobacco and Firearms special hearing, Subcommittee of
        the Committee on Appropriations, U.S. Senate, February 22, 1982, 146.

142   Neal Knox, head . . . Neal Knox, testimony. Proposed Dissolution of Bureau
        of Alcohol, Tobacco and Firearms special hearing, Subcommittee of the
        Committee on Appropriations, U.S. Senate, March 8, 1982, 324.

142   The NRA's turnabout . . . Representative William J. Hughes, testimony. En-
        forcement Efforts of the Bureau of Alcohol, Tobacco and Firearms hearing,
        Subcommittee on Crime, Committee on the Judiciary, House of Representa-
        tives, May 4, 1982, 2.

142   "The NRA realized . . ." Davidson, Under Fire, 52.

142   "Some of the things . . ." Bernard La Forest, BATF, interview.

143   The bill banned . . . "Congress Relaxes Federal Gun Control Laws," *Congressional Quarterly Almanac* (1986): 82–85.

143   Before the act . . . Ibid., 84.

143   Representative Hughes said . . . Ibid., 84.

143   "I don't know . . ." Rex Davis, interview.

143   From 1988 . . . "Firearms and Explosives: Information and Observations on ATF Law Enforcement Operations," GAO, June 1993, 44–45.

144   "These are safe . . ." Rex Davis, interview.

144   From 1975 through . . . "Firearms Program License Application Data," BATF, 1975–1990.

144   In 1990, for example . . . "Firearms Program Inspection Activity," BATF, 1990.

144   But revocation can be . . . Al's Loan Office vs. U.S. Dept. of Treasury, 738 F.Supp. 221 (E.D.Mich. 1990), May 7, 1990.

146   In fiscal 1991 . . . "Cases in Select Categories: Firearms Enforcement," BATF, fiscal year 1991.

146   On July 1, 1989 . . . Special Agent Edward Wetterman, affidavit. U.S. vs. Carroll Landis Brown, U.S. District Court, Baltimore. Case: HM-91-0010, 2.

147   He advertised . . . Ibid., 5.

147   Beginning September 20 . . . Ibid., 4.

147   On November 16 . . . Ibid., 4.

148   On December 10 . . . Ibid., 6.

148   As of January 1991 . . . "Memorandum in Opposition to Defendant's 'Notice of Appeal.' " U.S. vs. Carroll Landis Brown, U.S. District Court, Baltimore. Case: HM-91-0010, 3–4.

148   Hunt and an associate . . . *Baltimore Sun,* December 29, 1991, 1D.

149   "Dear Judge . . ." Mykia Brown, letter (undated). U.S. vs. Carroll Landis Brown, U.S. District Court, Baltimore. Case: HM-91-0010.

149   Rev. James Ross . . . Rev. James Ross, letter, May 30, 1991. U.S. vs. Carroll Landis Brown, U.S. District Court, Baltimore. Case: HM-91-0010.

149   Soon after . . . M. Dion Thompson, "A Gun Dealer's Legacy."

149   Among the guns . . . List of distributors and guns. U.S. vs. Carroll Landis Brown. U.S. District Court, Baltimore. Case: HM-91-0010.

150   The remainder . . . Project Detroit, BATF, Detroit, April 19, 1991, 2.

150   In its report . . . Ibid., 7.

150   Yet of the five . . . Ibid., 12; Special Agent in Charge Bernard La Forest, interview.

151   Project Detroit also . . . Bernard La Forest, interview.

151   "We're not in . . ." Ken Jorgensen, interview.

152   "The wholesalers thought . . ." Bernard La Forest, interview.

152   "What would the results . . ." Project Detroit, BATF, Detroit, April 19, 1991, 7.

153   Early in 1989, two . . . Cox Newspapers, "Firepower: Assault Weapons in America," 1989.

153   ATF wasn't able . . . Gerald A. Nunziato, Special Agent in Charge, National Tracing Center, BATF, interview.

153   In fiscal 1990 . . . Los Angeles Times, May 20, 1992, A1.

154   "If they've got . . ." Bernard La Forest, interview.

154   Raymond Rowley, an agent . . . Special Agent Raymond Rowley, interview.

154   The ATF's Urgent trace . . . G. R. Dickerson, testimony. Dismantling of the Bureau of Alcohol, Tobacco and Firearms hearing, Subcommittee on Crime, Committee on the Judiciary, House of Representatives, April 30, 1981, 34.

155   But Stokes eventually . . . Thomas W. Stokes, interview.

155   "We're always looking for . . ." Raymond Rowley, interview.

155   "We don't make . . ." David Troy, interview.

Chapter Eleven: Nicholas

158   Forensic investigators . . . Det. Donald Adams, interview.

158   Cutter was splayed . . . (Billy Cutter), testimony. VA-NE, February 28, 1989, 94.

158   "It looked . . ." Ibid., 87.

159   "I was probably . . ." Maurice H. Matteson, testimony. VA-NE, February 28, 1989, 123.

159   "I don't have the gun . . ." Ibid., 124.

159   "What in the world . . ." Ibid., 131.

159   Rev. George Sweet . . . Rev. George Sweet, interview; George Sweet, testimony. WF-SE, January 14, 1992.

160   "He looked at me . . ." Ibid.

160   "I was like wondering . . ." Lora Sweet, testimony. WF-SE, January 14, 1992, 7.

Chapter Twelve: The Culture

161   He did not carry . . . Det. Donald Adams, interview; Det. Donald Adams, testimony. WF-SE, January 14, 1992.

161   "A gun enthusiast . . ." Det. Donald Adams, interview.

162   He carried hundreds . . . Ibid.; Det. Donald Adams, testimony. WF-SE, January 14, 1992.

162   "He could hold . . ." Det. Donald Adams, interview.

162   He filed a groove . . . Ibid.

162   The fact his mother . . . Ibid.

163   Hundreds "were . . ." Robert Sherrill, The Saturday Night Special (New York: Charterhouse, 1973), 165.

163   "I didn't sell . . ." James S. Dick, deposition. WF-SE, July 16, 1990, 43.

164   "I'm kind of flattered . . ." New York Times, March 10, 1992, 1.

164   Intratec was so . . . Los Angeles Times, July 7, 1993, 3.

164   "Everything was by . . ." Los Angeles Times, July 3, 1993, 1.

165   Only one of . . . Osha Gray Davidson, Under Fire, 171–72.

169   "The object of . . ." John Minnery, Kill Without Joy: The Complete How to Kill Book (Boulder, Colo.: Paladin Press, 1992), preface.

170   "I prefer to make . . ." Peder Lund, interview.

173   Once a week . . . Michael Hoy, interview.

175   Joseph Grubisic, commander . . . Joseph Grubisic, interview.

176   A few years ago . . . Confidential interview, BATF.

176   Some published recipes . . . Sgt. LeRoy Pereira, U.C. Berkeley Bomb Squad, interview; Lt. Walter Boser, commander, New York Police Bomb Squad, interview; Peder Lund, interview.

176   ("It's kind of like . . ." Charles Rose, interview.

176   "They're wrong . . ." Peder Lund, interview.

176   Most of his customers . . . Billy Blann, interview.

177   In August 1992 . . . Jack Killorin, spokesman, BATF, interview; Charles T. Ziegler, police chief, Athens, Tennessee, interview; Ptl. Don Long, Athens police, interview.

177   In San Juan Capistrano . . . Sgt. Charles Stumph, Orange County Sheriff's Bomb Squad, interview.

177   In 1983 he set . . . Park Elliott Dietz, interview.

178   His work brought . . . Park Elliott Dietz, interview; Dietz, "Dangerous Information: Product Tampering and Poisoning Advice in Revenge and Murder Manuals," *Journal of Forensic Sciences* 33:5 (September 1988): 1215.

178   In an article . . . Dietz, "Dangerous Information," 1208–9.

178   In 1973, Dr. Dietz's . . . Ibid., 1212–13.

180   "The general rule . . ." Bruce Ennis, interview.

180   "These are difficult . . ." Floyd Abrams, interview.

180   "You can't say . . ." Joseph Grubisic, interview.

180   No problem would exist . . . Sgt. Charles Stumph, interview.

180   That Paladin can . . . Jack Thompson, interview.

182   In July 1989 . . . *Washington Post*, August 15, 1989, a10.

182   *Shotgun News* also . . . *Atlanta Journal-Constitution*, March 12, 1993, G3.

182   "There's no difference . . ." David Uhrig, interview.

183   Private buyers . . . *Wall Street Journal*, October 23, 1992, 1.

183   Once notorious . . . *New York Times*, March 30, 1992, D8.

183   It now includes . . . See *Shotgun News*, July 1, 1992, 3.

183   Nonetheless, my April . . . *Shotgun News*, April 1, 1993, 5, 25.

183   During a reporting journey . . . *Wall Street Journal*, March 12, 1993, 1.

184   "It's called . . ." Jim Moore, interview.

185   "My friend . . ." John G. Mitchell, " 'God Guns & Guts Made America Free,' " *American Heritage* (February/March 1978): 9.

186   At times . . . Ibid., 8.

187   The NRA was founded . . . Certificate of Incorporation, New New York, November 17, 1871; Osha Gray Davidson, *Under Fire*, 20–22.

187   It remained a small . . . Davidson, Ibid., 27.

187   The association began . . . Mitchell, " 'God Guns & Guts,' " 9.

187   As originally proposed . . . Robert Sherrill, *The Saturday Night Special* (New York: Charterhouse, 1973), 58.

187   By 1946 . . . Mitchell, " 'God Guns,' " 9.

187   In 1956, the NRA . . . Certificate of Extension of Purpose, New York Department of State, March 22, 1956.

188   . . . Lee Harvey Oswald . . . Henry S. Bloomgarden, *The Gun* (New York: Grossman, 1975), 92.

188   For Carter was . . . Davidson, *Under Fire*, 31–33.

188   It shifted emphasis . . . Certificate of Amendment of the Certificate of Incorporation, New York Department of State, September 23, 1977.

188   A study conducted . . . Mitchell, " 'God Guns,' " 10.

189   Nonetheless, by 1978 . . . Ibid., 2.

189   By 1983, its . . . Davidson, *Under Fire,* 39.

189   One of those attacked . . . Joseph McNamara, interview.

190   From 1989 to 1991 . . . Davidson, *Under Fire*, 157; Bradley O'Leary, PM Consulting Inc, interview, membership data.

190   The historic site . . . Davidson, *Under Fire*, 161.

190   Its political action . . . Center for Responsive Politics, Washington, D.C.

190   Between the 1990 . . . Center for Responsive Politics, "PACs in Profile," June 1993, 8.

190   The NRA also stepped . . . Peter Stone, "Under the Gun," *National Journal* (June 5, 1993): 1335.

190   In 1992 alone . . . Bradley O'Leary, interview.

191   The drive worked. . . . O'Leary, interview.

191   The NRA was indeed bigger . . . "1992 Report to Members," NRA, 1992.

191   In 1993 . . . Peter Stone, "Under the Gun," 1337.

191   One New York assemblywoman . . . Naomi Matusow, interview.

191   In 1993, a hard-right . . . Osha Gray Davidson, interview.

192   A survey by . . . Louis Harris, "A Survey of the American People on Guns as a Children's Health Issue," LH Research Inc. (June 1993): 6, 15.

192   In the 1992 membership . . . Bradley O'Leary, interview.

193   At the NRA's 1993 . . . Wayne LaPierre, "This is a Fight for Freedom!" *American Rifleman,* July 1993, 31.

193   During the same . . . "The 'Duke' Takes His Stand in Nashville," *American Rifleman,* June 1993, 79.

194   In his Nashville speech . . . Wayne LaPierre, "This is a Fight," 31.

194   In a column . . . "The President's Column," *American Rifleman,* June 1993, 60.

194   In 1993 . . . Susan Lamson, "TV Violence: Does it Cause Real-Life Mayhem?" *American Rifleman,* June 1993, 31–33.

195   In its "Combat Annual" . . . Mark Moritz, "Volkspistol," *American Handgunner* (Combat Annual 1992): 46–48.

196   A writer for . . . Jim Benson. "Ladies' Home Companion," *American Survival Guide* (July 1990): 24–25, 66.

196   The author described . . . "Return of the Ingram," *Gun Digest Book of Assault Weapons,* 66–71.

196   Dr. Park Dietz . . . Cox Newspapers, "Firepower: Assault Weapons in America," 1989, 12–13.

197   Dr. Dietz told . . . Park Elliott Dietz, interview.

197   Add to this . . . Harry F. Waters, et al., "Networks Under the Gun," *Time,* July 12, 1993, 64–66.

Chapter Thirteen: Nicholas

200   Two different . . . Lora Farley, testimony. WF-SE, January 14, 1992, 8.

201   Sweet was at . . . George Sweet, testimony. WF-SE, January 14, 1992.

201   "She did say something . . ." NES, 64.

201   "I know I went . . ." Ibid., 76.

201   Bill Farley learned . . . William Farley, interview.

201 The Virginia Beach . . . Det. Donald Adams, interview.

202 "It was unbelievable . . ." William Farley, interview.

202 The formal cause . . . Det. Donald Adams, testimony. WF-SE, 211.

202 "It's the only . . ." Det. Donald Adams, interview.

202 The next night . . . Beverly Cook, testimony. WF-SE.

202 Months later . . . William Farley, testimony. WF-SE.

202 "I just try . . ." William Farley, interview.

203 Three months later . . . EE-ASC.

203 On October 31 . . . Norfolk Virginian-Pilot, December 13, 1989, 1.

203 Nicholas sat . . . Norfolk Virginian-Pilot, November 1, 1989, 1.

203 On December 12 . . . Jimmy Edney, testimony. VA-NE, December 12, 1989, 3.

204 "These were offenses . . ." Norfolk Virginian-Pilot, December 13, 1989.

204 "Number one . . ." William Farley, interview.

205 "One thing . . ." Randy Singer, interview.

206 "This is not . . ." Randy Singer, opening statement. WF-SE, January 14, 1992.

206 Bill Farley lost . . . William Farley, interview.

207 In an order . . . John K. Moore, letter, response to defendants' demurrer. WF-SE, October 4, 1990.

207 "Unfortunately," Judge Moore . . . Ibid., 2.

Chapter Fourteen: The New Tyranny

211 Strict gun controls . . . Daniel Abrams. "Ending the Other Arms Race." Yale Law and Policy Review 10:2 (1992): 515–16.

212 On December 14 . . . New York Times, December 28, 1992, 1.

213 In his book . . . David B. Kopel, The Samurai, the Mountie, and the Cowboy (Buffalo, N.Y.: Prometheus Books/The Cato Institute, 1992), 319–20.

215 A 1993 survey . . . Louis Harris. "A Survey of Experiences, Perceptions and Apprehensions About Guns Among Young People in America," LH Research Inc. (July 1993): ix.

215   Fifty-five percent . . . Ibid., x.

215   In a related . . . Louis Harris, "A Survey of the American People on Guns as a Children's Health Issue," LH Research Inc. (June 1993): 6, 9.

216   I read with . . . Mick Luckovich, "Remember, Carry a Map . . . ," *Newsweek*, July 12, 1993, 15.

216   In 1975 . . . Josh Sugarmann, *National Rifle Association: Money, Firepower/& Fear* (Bethesda, Md.: National Press Books, 1992), 45.

224   The 1993 Harris survey . . . Harris, "Survey of the American People," viii.

224   Robert Sherrill . . . Robert Sherrill, *The Saturday Night Special* (New York: Charterhouse, 1973), 322.

226   A Sandston, Virginia . . . *Baltimore Sun*, July 20, 1993, 9A.

229   "Maybe that's the answer . . ." David Troy, interview.

Coda

231   The site Dick chose . . . J. Michael Dick, interview.

ACKNOWLEDGMENTS

ANY WORK OF JOURNALISM REQUIRES THE assistance of a large array of sources; any journalistic work on the subject of guns seems to require that many of these sources retain some degree of anonymity. To all those men and women who spoke with me on condition I would not reveal your names and professions, thank you. I recognize that trusting your privacy, livelihood, and perhaps even your personal safety is not an easy thing. I'd also like to thank the many honest, clear-eyed gun owners of America who told me, in correspondence and over the telephone, of their love of guns and the kinship that guns afford, and in a few cases of their real and pressing need to possess a weapon for self-defense. You provided me, often with a good deal of heat and enthusiasm, a much-needed perspective.

I owe an especially great debt to Bill Farley, Randy Singer, Dennis Henigan, Col. Leonard Supenski, Earl Taylor, Rex Davis, Jack "Ganja" Killorin, Thomas Stokes, Bernard La Forest, David Troy, Edward M. Owen, Donald Adams, Paxton Quigley, and Peder Lund. A special thanks goes to J. Michael Dick, for having the courage to talk on the record about matters that are too often buried beyond public view.

Betty Prashker, Michelle Sidrane, Kim Reilly, Andrew Martin,

Joan DeMayo, and Penny Simon made me feel extraordinarily welcome at Crown Publishers, and convinced me from the start that there is still a taste among American publishers for confronting the most troubling issues of the day. Denise Shannon got the ball rolling. Court TV, in New York, graciously allowed me to watch a video of the entire Farley vs. Guns Unlimited trial. Mike Curtis, Cullen Murphy, and William Whitworth of *The Atlantic Monthly* demonstrated an exceptional tolerance for lengthy prose; Sue Parilla, queen of the *Atlantic*'s fact-checking squad, taught me the meaning of pain.

The award for patience goes to my wife, Christine Gleason, and my children, Kristen and Lauren, for not ejecting me from the house as my deadline neared and my mood decayed. Jane Berentson, my boss at the *Wall Street Journal,* cheerfully engineered a much-needed month of leave, which her bosses, John Brecher and Paul Steiger, magnanimously granted.

Last, I'd like to acknowledge a debt to the occupants of that white Cadillac with Virginia plates who paid my neighborhood a visit—who fired a paint ball gun four times at my home at 3:30 one Sunday morning. If I ever needed reassurance that I was on the right track, you gave it to me in as vivid and convincing a manner as any I could imagine.

INDEX